*Jeanne Guyon's Mystical Perfection
through Eucharistic Suffering*

Jeanne Guyon's Mystical Perfection through Eucharistic Suffering

Her Biblical Commentary on Saint John's Gospel

Jeanne de la Mothe Guyon

Introduction and Translation from the Original French by
Nancy Carol James, Ph.D.

Foreword by
The Rev. William Bradley Roberts, D.M.A.

◆PICKWICK *Publications* · Eugene, Oregon

JEANNE GUYON'S MYSTICAL PERFECTION THROUGH EUCHARISTIC SUFFERING
Her Biblical Commentary on Saint John's Gospel

Copyright © 2020 Nancy Carol James. All rights reserved. Except for brief quotations in critical publications or reviews, no part of this book may be reproduced in any manner without prior written permission from the publisher. Write: Permissions, Wipf and Stock Publishers, 199 W. 8th Ave., Suite 3, Eugene, OR 97401.

Pickwick Publications
An Imprint of Wipf and Stock Publishers
199 W. 8th Ave., Suite 3
Eugene, OR 97401

www.wipfandstock.com

PAPERBACK ISBN: 978-1-5326-8422-7
HARDCOVER ISBN: 978-1-5326-8423-4
EBOOK ISBN: 978-1-5326-8424-1

Cataloguing-in-Publication data:

Names: Guyon, Jeanne Marie Bouvier de La Motte, 1648–1717, author. | James, Nancy Carol, translator | Roberts, William Bradley, foreword writer.

Title: Jeanne Guyon's mystical perfection through eucharistic suffering : her biblical commentary on Saint John's Gospel / Jeanne de la Mothe Guyon; translated by Nancy Carol James; with a foreword by William Bradley Roberts.

Description: Eugene, OR: Pickwick Publications, 2020 | Includes bibliographical references and index.

Identifiers: ISBN 978-1-5326-8422-7 (paperback) | ISBN 978-1-5326-8423-4 (hardcover) | ISBN 978-1-5326-8424-1 (ebook)

Subjects: LCSH: Guyon, Jeanne Marie Bouvier de La Motte, 1648–1717 | Bible—John—Commentaries | Spiritual life—Catholic Church

Classification: BX4705.G8 G89 2020 (print) | BX4705.G8 (ebook)

Manufactured in the U.S.A.   SEPTEMBER 10, 2020

Dedicated to Hannah and Melora

Table of Contents

Foreword by The Rev. William Bradley Roberts, D.M.A. ix
Preface xv
Acknowledgements xvii

Introduction 1
Guyon's Commentary on John 11

Bibliography 273

Foreword

The Rev. William Bradley Roberts, D.M.A.

> 'Tis folly all—let me no more be told
> Of Parian[1] porticos, and roofs of gold;
> Delightful views of nature, dressed by art,
> Enchant no longer this indifferent heart;
> The Lord of all things, in his humble birth,
> Makes mean the proud magnificence of earth;
> The straw, the manger, and the mouldering wall,
> Eclipse its lustre; and I scorn it all.
>
> (Madame Jeanne Guyon, trans. William Cowper, English, 1731–1800)

Above is the first verse of the English translation of an extended poem by Guyon. The translator William Cowper (pronounced "Cooper") was the foremost English poet of the generation between Alexander Pope and William Wordsworth.[2] With precision and yet with tender care, he translates Guyon's poem into English verse that has its own integrity, while still reflecting the mystical piety and devotion of the original.

Such personal piety is emblematic of the writings of Madame Jeanne Guyon. She portrays a humble Jesus, whom she greatly prefers to the opulence of either natural beauty or beauty created by humans. In this poem, as well as in her commentary on the book of John, she places a relationship with Jesus above everything else. ("I scorn it all.")

Though Guyon didn't greatly concern herself with issues of authorship, provenance, or textual analysis, it is interesting to discover what modern scholarship uncovers in the fourth Gospel, which stands in

---

1. White marble typical of the Greek island of Paros.
2. Website of The Poetry Foundation.

contradistinction to the Synoptic ("seeing with the same eye") Gospels of Matthew, Mark, and Luke, which are similar in content, form, and statement. Despite Guyon's apparent lack of interest in such scholarly investigation, she would surely not have disapproved of those scholars and contemporary readers who are drawn to scholarly analysis.

Scholars disagree about the authorship of the Gospel of John, arguing persuasively for this theory or that. Perhaps Bruce Vawter CM (1921–86), writing in *The Jerome Biblical Commentary*, is most certain of his position. He holds out the alluring possibility that the earliest witness to authorship is Irenaeus, Bishop of Lyons, (A.D. 120/124–200/203), who studied with Polycarp of Smyrna (A.D. 69–155), who knew John personally! Both these bishops were persuaded that John was the anonymous "disciple whom Jesus loved," who "reclined on his breast at the Last Supper" and the author of the fourth Gospel.[3]

Fr. Vawter goes on to support Johannine authorship by pointing out that John was a Jew who was familiar with Palestinian culture and geography. The fourth Gospel mentions places that don't appear in the Synoptic Gospels (Matthew, Mark, and Luke), such as the Pool of Bethesda and Lithostrotos (*Gabbatha* in Aramaic). He further states that the language in John is that of a Palestinian Jew. Additionally, the persistence of detail in the text strongly suggests a firsthand witness. Though the Gospel writer's Greek is not the best in the New Testament, it correctly reproduces the common language of the time. Fr. Vawter finds evidence that John employed a disciple-scribe whose Greek was superior to his own. He goes on to say that the Gospel of John presupposes the Synoptic Gospels, and that John, in some respects, would be difficult to understand, were we not already familiar with the story as found in the Synoptic Gospels.[4]

Jerome H. Neyrey SJ cites contemporary scholarship that distinguishes between a "writer" of this Gospel and an "author." A writer might merely take dictation, but an author imagines and organizes the project and establishes an editorial point of view. Unlike Vawter, Neyrey believes that we are still uncertain who the author is or where and when the document was written and revised. (Its provenance is debated, but

---

3. Bruce Vawter CM, "Introduction to John," in *The Jerome Biblical Commentary*, edited by Raymond E. Brown SS, Joseph A. Fitzmyer SJ, Roland E. Murphy OCD (Englewood Cliffs, N.J.: Prentice-Hall, 1968), 414–21.

4. Vawter, "Introduction to John."

traditionally assumed to be Ephesus.) Neyrey takes the position that we may learn a lot about the author by asking "what does he know."[5]

Neyrey finds, for example, like Vawter, that the author of the Gospel has intimate knowledge of the geography attested in the writing. In fact, this Gospel writer displays a unique knowledge, superior to that of the Synoptic writers. Likewise, he has keen insight into practices of Temple Feasts and Sabbath. The Synoptics know, for instance, of only one Passover in the career of Jesus, whereas this author knows of three.[6]

As Neyrey continues to investigate the relationship between John and Synoptics, he posits that, even though no proof exists that John drew upon the Synoptics, most scholars believe that the author frequently draws on traditions shared with the Synoptics. Setting aside the question of dependency on the Synoptics, perhaps it is more important that the author knows a great deal about the Jesus tradition.[7]

Scholar Johannes Beutler SJ says that when readers read John they enter a new world, hear a new language. The Divine Logos (Word) brings "light" (mentioned in sixteen verses) and "life" (in thirty-eight verses). Even when standing before Pilate, Jesus claims to be the king who came to "bear witness to the truth." The tone of this Gospel is not heard in the Synoptics.[8]

Whereas in the Synoptics dualistic language is temporal, in John it is spatial. Jesus comes "from above," his opponents "from below." While they are "of this world," he is "not of this world." Interestingly, the sequence of events in Jesus' life do not always correspond to that of the Synoptics. The Gospel of Mark is selective in the miracles included, and so is John. In the fourth Gospel there is no exorcism or healing of a leper, and the number of Jesus' miracles is considerably smaller. On the other hand, the account of the miracle at the wedding in Cana, changing water into wine, appears only in John. The Parables of the Kingdom, characteristic of the Synoptics, are missing from John. A striking feature of the fourth Gospel is its language about Jesus' identity, the so-called "I Am Sayings:" "I am the bread of life." (6:35) "I am the light of the world." (8:12), as well

---

5. Jermon H. Neyrey SJ, "The Gospel of John" (Cambridge: Cambridge University Press, 2007).

6. Neyrey SJ, "The Gospel of John.".

7. Neyrey SJ, "The Gospel of John.".

8. Johannes Beutler SJ, "A Commentary on the Gospel of John," trans. Michael Tait (Grand Rapids: Eerdmans, 2017), 1–29.

as extended metaphors of his identity: the Good Shepherd (10:1–5) and the True Vine (15:1–8).[9]

Strikingly, John has no account of the birth and infancy of Jesus, but begins instead with Jesus' identity as the eternally existent Divine Logos (Word). John's Gospel intends to lead to faith in Jesus, the Messiah and Son of God, and to strengthen the faith of those who already believe. Some scholars (especially German ones) find this to be its *only* aim. John is concerned with *following* Jesus.[10]

Small wonder, then, that Madame Guyon, the deeply devoted mystic, was drawn to write a commentary on John. She would have naturally been attracted to the message of faith, belief, and, above all, the call to follow Jesus.

Unlike scholarly theological works, Guyon's commentary is intentionally devotional. Theologian Katherine Sonderegger in her recent book *The Doctrine of God*, speaks with a similar devotion that one of her students describes as, "a love letter to God."[11] Guyon possessed a love for Jesus that, from our vantage, seems a consuming passion, redolent of modern-day evangelicals. In fact, however, she was a committed Roman Catholic (see Preface), one who unashamedly spoke of her "Master Jesus Christ" in language that at times sounded unapologetically romantic.

As insightful as Guyon's commentary is in some respects, what we may gain from it is not so much a scholarly understanding as a portrait of Jesus, drawn tenderly by someone who loved him with her whole heart. Elsewhere among Nancy Carol James' prolific writings on Guyon, we may discover this mystic's struggles with the Church, despite her love for it. Nevertheless, she persisted and declared her commitment to the Roman Catholic Church throughout her life.

Nancy Carol James, PhD, has devoted years of study to Guyon. Prior to this translation of Guyon's commentary on the Gospel of John, James had published fourteen books about the Catholic mystic. Her rich history of research into Guyon's life and work allows James to speak with wise and eloquent insight. James is able to give voice to Guyon's inner-most thoughts and prayers. Indeed she can describe the very faith of Guyon.

What we may say with a certainty about Madame Guyon is that her deep faith was authentic. When she shared her faith with others in her

---

9. Beutler, "A Commentary on the Gospel of John,".

10. Beutler, "A Commentary on the Gospel of John,".

11. Jason Byassee, "How Katherine Sonderegger Finds Delight in a Humble God." *The Christian Century*, January 7, 2020.

writing, she showed marks of a true Catholic, allowing the Holy Spirit to bring people to faith in Jesus. The witness of her life and her writing are compelling—so compelling in fact that the reader's interest is piqued, a new curiosity aroused, and one is motivated to learn more about the faith she professed. Her unwavering faith in Jesus, her deep desire to follow him, are everywhere in evidence in this volume. Encountering her, the reader is strengthened in the faith.

> The Rev. William Bradley Roberts, D.M.A.
> Professor Emeritus of Church Music
> Virginia Theological Seminary (Episcopal)
> Alexandria, Va.

Preface

NANCY CAROL JAMES

THROUGHOUT HISTORY, THE WRITINGS of Jeanne Guyon have attracted some of the greatest thinkers and faithful ministers of the Christian gospel. Among those who admire her Christian testimony include Archbishop Fénelon, William Cowper, Sir Isaac Newton, John Wesley, and John Newton, author of the hymn "Amazing Grace." The list continues to grow, revealing how her quiet but powerful voice continues to influence the Christian faith.

After years of research and translating Jeanne Guyon, I have found her commentary on the Gospel of John to be her most powerful document declaring her profound Christian beliefs. In this commentary, Jeanne Guyon reveals her deepest devotion and thought about the Christian faith. She describes her love and commitment to the Roman Catholic Church, her lifelong church. We read of her devotion to Mary. Guyon writes, "Although there is one mediator between God and human beings, Mary is a mediator between sinners and her son. O Mary, full of pain and love! Who is the sinner who will not hope from your protection given by your Son?" Guyon describes her fervent belief in Transubstantiation; in the Eucharist, she says, the believer receives the very Body and Blood of Jesus Christ. She affirms that we receive mystical perfection, called theosis, as we participate in the holy sacrament of the Eucharist.

Jeanne Guyon's faith and testimony, filled with joy and praise, continue to help guide human souls to the one she knew as Master Lord Jesus Christ. Her commentary on St. John's Gospel, so filled with joy and ecstasy, offers wisdom and heart-felt love to all those seeking to imitate the life and faith of Jesus Christ.

Nancy Carol James

Acknowledgements

MANY PEOPLE HAVE CONTRIBUTED to this volume. I am grateful for the support of Dr. Carlos Eire during my dissertation work on Jeanne Guyon. I thank the Rev. William Roberts for his understanding of Jeanne Guyon's theology and his foreword which makes a substantial contribution to this book.

I want to thank the parishioners of St. John's, Lafayette Square, Washington, DC for their dialogue about Jeanne Guyon and her rich theology. I thank the Diocese of Alaska for their many events and their warm welcome of Jeanne Guyon's Christian witness.

Many thanks go to those who share my passion for the work of Jeanne Guyon. Hannah and Melora have read, explored, and researched Jeanne Guyon along with me. I am grateful that we share this love.

Above all, I think my readers who share a love for Jeanne Guyon and her ideas about interior faith. Guyon's books have been kept alive by those who continue to seek a profound interior life where Jesus Christ lives and moves and has his being. I hope that Jeanne Guyon's Christian interior faith lives for centuries yet to come.

Introduction

Nancy Carol James, PhD

SINCE THE SEVENTEENTH CENTURY, the writing of Jeanne Guyon (1648–1717) has spread throughout the globe, encouraging those in spiritual need and providing enthusiastic nourishment for those living the Christian faith. Because Madame Guyon was accused of heresy by the Inquisition of the Roman Catholic Church instigated by Bishop Bossuet, a powerful archbishop well connected with the King of France and the Vatican Hierarchy, she bears heroic witness to her Catholic Faith. Guyon spoke continually words of love for her church despite her incarceration for nearly ten years, including nearly five years in the Bastille. In her heroic witness, she lived spiritually free for she knew in her mystical relationship with Jesus Christ, that he, and he alone, sets us free. The paradox of Jeanne Guyon's life is that she had every right to condemn and even hate her Catholic faith and those clergy representing clerical abuse, yet her kind voice of love and mercy spoke words telling others of a living, loving, and forgiving Christian way. In the image of Jesus Christ, she portrayed a true Christian witness praying for and instructing her persecutors. Jeanne Guyon testifies to the way, the truth, and the life of Jesus Christ in her suffering and in her prayers and so her testimony continues to be received and revered as a Christian martyr to the scandals and abuses we constantly experience throughout history, either from within the church in her case, or from outside the church in other cases.

A brief summary of Jeanne Guyon's life shows the dramatic and still-debated arrest, incarceration and release of Jeanne Guyon. (For a more detailed account of her life, please read my introduction in *The Complete Madame Guyon*.)

From an early age, Jeanne Guyon lived a life of suffering. Born into an aristocratic family in 1648, when she was fifteen, her parents forced her into an arranged marriage with a man she had not met, the thirty-eight-year-old Philippe Guyon. This unhappy marriage led to the nineteen-year-old Jeanne's serious crisis about how to endure such desolation and following this, her profound spiritual conversion. She committed herself to Jesus Christ, saying she loved him as Mary Magdalen had loved him. Soon Jeanne became actively and passionately involved with caring for the peasants, founding hospitals, and raising her five children, two of whom died of smallpox. In her late twenties, her husband also died, leaving Jeanne as a young, attractive, wealthy widow who was widely sought after.

With the recognition of her spiritual gifts, Jeanne was welcomed at King Louis XIV's royal court at Versailles. She joined a prayer group with Madame de Maintenon, the third wife of Louis XIV, and Archbishop Francois Fénelon, the royal tutor to the son expected to become king. Sadly, later Madame de Maintenon withdrew her support of Jeanne, which led to the Roman Catholic Inquisition led by Bishop Bossuet arresting Jeanne and keeping her incarcerated for a total of nearly ten years, while the church hierarchy searched for ways to remove her influence over Archbishop Fénelon. Guyon was imprisoned, suffered psychological and physical abuse, and threatened with death by burning, as the French hierarchy had done with St Joan of Arc.

Throughout this time, however, Archbishop Fénelon defended Jeanne continually and passionately, which led to King Louis XIV banishing him from Versailles and sending him to the front-lines in the War of Spanish Succession. Years of debate ensued at the Vatican by the cardinals and the pope, leading to a papal censure of some points of Fénelon's book, *The Maxims of the Saints*, which he wrote to defend Guyon. Eventually Guyon was exonerated and lived in a cottage near her daughter. Fénelon and Guyon remained in close correspondence for the rest of their lives, including personal visits with one another. Jeanne Guyon's works are still revered by Christians internationally.

In this controversy over Jeanne Guyon's life and works, she was considered a semi-quietist: a heresy that denied the need for the development of personal virtues and relied solely on God's grace being annihilated by divine love. Her works, though, are still revered by Christians and non-Christians internationally. She is considered by many as a mystic who influenced others with her charm and charisma being a warm and enthusiastic woman who brought joy to others with her vibrant spirit.

One of the great joys of being a Jeanne Guyon scholar is talking with others who share my respect and passion for her mystical theology. A natural and profound intimacy exists between those who desire mystical perfection and those how have read and benefitted from her ideas and interpretation of the Christian faith. Guyon's thought creates a heart-felt commitment to our relationship with our Master Jesus Christ, as she called him. We share the belief that abandonment to Jesus Christ and imitating him with our very lives begins the beautiful process of being transformed by grace and being united with God through divine love. This transformation is known as theosis, an early Christian teaching of the Eastern Patristic Fathers. We love Jesus Christ, who in his great mercy to us, offers us his perfection and carries us into the heart of God the Father.

Lost in the infinite beauty of God, we praise God, Father, Son, and Holy Spirit, in expressible words of adoration and love that echo the beauty, majesty, and glory of his transforming love dwelling in our souls. We devotees of mysticism not only share Guyon's insights with others, but, in reality we share Christ with others who is the source of these insights.

This book, the first English translation of Guyon's Commentary on the Gospel of John, came out of a conversation I had with another who also treasures Jeanne Guyon. I still remember when he said to me, "We need a translation of Jeanne Guyon's Commentary on the Gospel of John." I had recently finished translations of Guyon's commentaries on Ephesians, Colossians, Galatians, Luke, and Revelation, but still I knew I had missed something valuable. His words poured in my heart and within a week, I began translating the Guyon commentary on John.

I have found in Guyon's Commentary of John a pearl of great price and the resolution of many problems still existing in Guyon scholarship. One of the great debates about Guyon has been and still is whether she was an orthodox, faithful Catholic believer or whether she secretly harbored Protestant ideas and sensibilities. From the historical perspective, Guyon as a secret Protestant might appear a reasonable conclusion because of the strong support she early on received from Anglicans and Protestants in Europe, the United Kingdom, and the New World.

Yet, her greatest supporter and advocate was the powerful and mysterious Roman Catholic Archbishop Francois Fénelon, who wrote a book about her theology called *The Maxims of the Saints*. He saw her as a faithful Catholic woman, in love with Jesus Christ, and defended her even though his support of her and her writing led to the destruction of his powerful ministry both in France and at the Vatican.

Was Jeanne Guyon a faithful Catholic? I can say definitively after translating her commentary on John's Gospel that indeed she sought to be a good Catholic, spending her very life-force to purify and expand the Catholic faith. She speaks words of wonder and love about her faith, but also ones of challenge and correction. She remained committed to the Roman Catholic Church, which had incarcerated her—its reasons for doing so are many and the decision may have been influenced by her wealth, beauty, and charisma rather than any actual unorthodoxy.

In her writings, Madame Guyon describes her intense and brutal sufferings not in terms of the physical and emotional anguish that anyone feels being locked up in prison. We know her sufferings were real, but she describes her greatest suffering in terms of the spiritual loss. She could not participate in the Roman Catholic Church's most sacred Liturgy, commonly called today the Mass, and receive the Eucharist daily.

Even after her exoneration and return to life on the Loire River, she wrote no angry or critical words to or about the Roman Catholic hierarchy who had interrogated and incarcerated her. Instead, continually and frequently, Jeanne Guyon professed the Christian faith as believed and practiced by the Roman Catholic Church. In her commentary on John, Guyon's love for the Roman Catholic Church shines clearly.

Jeanne Guyon's Roman Catholic Beliefs

Jeanne Guyon testified to the truth of the Roman Catholic Church in this commentary on John. She explains and defends the real presence of Jesus Christ in the Eucharist, the most sublime of the seven sacraments of the Catholic Faith and defends the other six sacraments of the church.

Not only did she believe in the sacramental life of the church, she also believe in the Catholic Church's ecclesiology, which upholds and promotes the communion of the saints. The Catholic Church believes that the saints are in heaven and are examples of holiness and intercessors for us, still seeking that transforming grace to become perfect as our heavenly Father is perfect. She developed a deep and profound devotion to two saints, Francis de Sales and Teresa of Avila, who were influential in her life, for both of them suffered much in their earthly lives.

Through many pages in this commentary, Jeanne Guyon makes a passionate defense of transubstantiation: the real presence of the body and blood (soul and divinity) of Jesus Christ in the Eucharist as a living and everlasting offering. She writes, "St. John testifies to the truth of the Eucharist, regarding Jesus Christ being immolated not only on the cross, but again on the altar until the end of the centuries. O divine Lamb, you take away the sins of the world!" (19–20) Guyon states that Jesus Christ will be present in the world through his presence on Roman Catholic altars, writing, "Jesus Christ also dwells on the earth until the consummation of the centuries through means of the Holy Eucharist. He cannot remain in another way. His glory will never end and never be consummated." (178)

Guyon describes her Roman Catholic belief in the Eucharist through which Jesus Christ joins himself with the faithful. She writes the following.

> The institution of the Sacrament . . . perpetuates his glorious sacrifice to his Father and his ministry to human beings. As he was made man to give himself entirely to human beings and God, so he finds a way of giving himself in the most particular way possible. No union equals that of food, which becomes the substance and sustenance of the person who takes it. And what better way to make human beings God than to have them live as God? All human beings could not have hypostatic union, so he married human nature by his same union. To do this he made a real and sacramental union, so that each human being may be united with him in a way which closely approaches hypostatic union. (197)

Guyon gives strong warnings to those who did not believe in his real presence in the Eucharist. She writes,

> Jesus Christ tells us, *My flesh will be given for you.* He clearly promised this without any intention to deceive. To say that he could not do this is clearly blasphemy since he is God and all-powerful. To doubt his power is to doubt his divinity. Does he not say that all power on heaven and earth has been given to him? If all power has been given to him, he is able. Not willing to deceive us, he acts in good faith and did this for us. If he gives his own flesh to death, I must conclude that he gives his own flesh to eat. When he says he gives his flesh to eat, this is not a figure of speech. (99–100)

Guyon also emphasizes the need for the confession of sins in the Sacrament of Reconciliation. Catholics believe that Jesus gave power not only to the apostles in the upper room when he reveals to them his resurrected body, but also empowers them with the Holy Spirit to forgive sins. Catholics believe that this power was not given solely to the apostles, but was given to their office, that is the priesthood itself and the successors to the apostles (apostolic succession) receive this grace to forgive sins, as did the eleven in the upper room. Guyon quotes John 20:23, "If you forgive the sins of any, they are forgiven them; if you retain the sins of any, they are retained." Guyon interprets this, writing, "Jesus Christ gives them the Holy Spirit and the apostolic mission with the power to deliver *from sins*. This passage supports the priest hearing confession." (263)

Guyon supports the Roman Catholic Church's teaching on sacraments throughout her commentary on the Gospel of John, the Evangelist.

John's Gospel uses seven signs as a format (paradigm) for his Gospel that some modern authors, such as John Bergsma, would claim are the teachings concerning the seven sacraments.[1] For example, Jesus' first miracle, The Wedding Feast of Cana, is obviously about the sacrament of marriage. Guyon fervently supports these sacraments throughout this commentary.

She does all of this in her most passionate way of writing with cries of love and even ecstasy. In other documents, Guyon at times has defended Catholic theology in prosaic terms in awkward sentences, as if written for the inquisitors, or even by the inquisitors, who were interrogating her. Her terminology and almost tormented writing style raised questions about the authenticity of her words. Yet, when Guyon speaks of words of truth, her sentences flow with joy and she uses more and more exclamation points and cries of "Oh!" That is one reason Guyon fans adore her intimate and mystical insights and ideas. We do not need to interpret and suck meaning out of her theology through a narrow straw of thinking. Instead, she pours her meaning into us with ecstatic joy. In this commentary on John, Guyon articulates her impassioned and beautiful love for her Roman Catholic Church and her mystical love for Jesus in a way not present in other writings.

---

1. Bergsman, "John: Signs and Sacraments."

Jeanne Guyon's Christian Mysticism

So why did Bishop Bossuet and others in the Roman Catholic hierarchy raise doubts about Jeanne Guyon's faithfulness and orthodoxy? Jeanne Guyon was a Christian mystic who believed that Jesus Christ still desires intimacy and seeks to join spiritually with those who follow him. Her written words are not detailed and deliberate, as a scholar and theologian's words, but ones of passionate love and intimacy, describing her growing union with Jesus Christ. As she says repeatedly, she had no theological training but felt that the Holy Spirit inspired her reflections on the scriptures. Ironically, in some of her responses to her inquisitors, she shows more theological understanding and insight than they did.

In this commentary, Jeanne Guyon discusses the intimacy present between Jesus Christ and Mary. She says that Mary had knit together Jesus Christ's body in her womb and shared complete intimacy with him in her life. Yet at the wedding in Cana, there seemed to be a change between them.

Guyon writes about the wedding described in John 2:3-4.

> The words of Jesus Christ to his holy mother appear to be rebukes but they are very mysterious. First, if we look at the natural miracle, Jesus Christ says, *Woman, what concern is that to you and to me*? The union between us is so close, do not you have all you want? You can do everything through me. (25)

Guyon continues,

> In the mystical sense, Jesus Christ says to his mother, I have made a union with you so close that I cannot do the same with any other. *What concern is that to you and to me*? Is not my body formed in your blood? In you I was married with human nature in a hypostatic union that will never happen in any other creature. (26)

Guyon emphasizes the holy and exalted role of Mary, a core belief that continues to be held strong still in the Roman Catholic Church though it is also a point of great discussion. As another French saint, St Louis Marie de Montfort, would later write, Jesus came to us through Mary, we go to Jesus through Mary. In the context of intimacy and a wondrous closeness between Jesus and Mary, Guyon invites us, the faithful, to share in the great wedding feast of Jesus Christ intimate and present with his church, in a way similar to that of Jesus Christ and Mary. Guyon calls this the mystical incarnation.

In this commentary, Guyon describes clearly how Jesus Christ himself unites with the follower in a mystical incarnation. Guyon describes this in the following way. When a person through the actions of the Holy Spirit repents and accepts the motion of grace, the believer lives the faith imitating the life of Jesus Christ. In this imitation of his life, the believer also experiences within his or her interior life the same or similar heartfelt feelings, ideas, and convictions that Jesus Christ experienced in his suffering and sacrifice, his joy and faith. Guyon called this bearing the states of being of Jesus Christ. Guyon reveals that mystical perfection comes from suffering as Jesus did when he instituted the sacrament of the Eucharist in three parts: Holy Thursday, the institution of the Eucharistic ritual; Good Friday, his suffering and death on the cross; and Easter Sunday, his risen presence revealed to his disciples. Out of this imitation, the believer will also have some form of spiritual, emotional, social, or physical crucifixion. Through this, Jesus Christ enters the believer's heart and becomes formed within the heart. When this formation is strong, Jesus Christ gently leads the follower out of the human heart and guides the soul into the very heart and bosom of God the Father. There the soul lives intimately with Jesus Christ lost in the infinite beauty and majesty of God the Father.

Guyon's clearest exposition of this comes in the following passage, based on John 14:3. Jesus said, "And if I go and prepare a place for you, I will come again and will take you to myself, so that where I am, there you may be also." Guyon writes the following about John 14:3.

> I am leaving, Jesus Christ said, to prepare the place and to open the entrance to my Father's bosom. Then *I will come again and take you to myself.* Oh, what admirable words! Will Jesus Christ be incarnated once again and have we seen him come to seek his apostles? However, these words are true! It is true that Jesus Christ goes first as an example and model to prepare the place. We need to follow Jesus Christ and bear his states until we are crucified with him. O then he truly becomes incarnate in the soul in a mystical way. Then he takes the soul into himself. After hiding the soul within him, he is formed within her, born there, and believes until to the perfect day of eternal glory. Then he then leads her to himself and she remains with him eternally where he is himself and not in another place. (200–201)

According to her understanding of the Bread of Life discourse in John's famous passage (John 6), she along with all believing Christians see Jesus Christ's unconditional love displayed perfectly, though mystically upon the cross. In Guyon's commentary, we see she believed in transubstantiation, that is the bread and wine become the body and blood of Jesus and when she received this Eucharist, she is in him and he is in her: the mystical perfection that so many seek.

In her sufferings, which echoed Jesus Christ's sufferings, she sensed his real presence and her need for his divine provision. She expressed our human yearning for a real union with the physical Jesus providing us with a transformative union in his divine love. This unconditional love is solidified by his promise to give us the Advocate, who becomes ours through our adoration and reception of the Eucharist. Jesus Christ promised the Holy Spirit later in the Passover Discourse, and if we hold fast to our crucifixion, we too receive Jesus Christ's pure Spirit through his sacrificial love as did his followers and anyone who still seeks him.

I offer this first English translation of Jeanne Guyon's commentary on John in a spirit of thanksgiving that her voice was not successfully silenced by the powers of the Inquisition. The aggressive and antagonistic tactics of the Inquisition were more humanistic rather Christocentric, which led to many abuses and scandals. Guyon in her response to the Inquisition reveals a spiritual maturity that, despite her lack of theological training, reveals a deep spiritual theology, even a mystical love and understanding of her Lord Jesus. Her meditation on John displays a mystical perfection through her Eucharistic sufferings, though obviously too exuberant for the Catholic hierarchy at that time.

As the Inquisition tried to squash her more exuberant and emotional expression of the Catholic faith, due to their more objective and orthodox/stoic demands to keep Catholicism free from theological error, a Catholic proverb of the twentieth century may shed light on silenced the French mindset of the seventeenth century: *Charity without orthodoxy is heterodox; Orthodoxy without charity is heterodox too.*

The greatest lesson we learn from Guyon may not be her exuberant and even ecstatic expressions of her mystical love for Jesus, but her virtuous embrace of her sufferings caused by those whose sole focus was orthodoxy without true charity. As her divine Master did the will of the Father in silence, like a lamb led to the slaughter, so too Guyon was silent about her sufferings despite her many poems, commentaries, and letters.

The accusations riled against her by the inquisitors for being interiorly passive and seeking annihilation of the self and not demanding an active and positive response through virtue and moral integrity to the demands of the Christian life, may be false, for perhaps, she just lived a virtuous and moral life inspired by her deep love of Jesus: the work of her spiritual writings displayed her interior faith.

In this light, recalling the other great French mystic of the thirteenth century, St Joan of Arc, who also was condemned as a false prophet, history may ultimately reveal that Guyon was a true mystic, whereas, heaven already knows.

And so to those who read Jeanne Guyon's commentaries, I say thank you. This is one of her crucial documents for by her words, she intimately, passionately, and mystically shares with us her love of Jesus Christ. Once again, in Jeanne Guyon's words on the Gospel of John, we experience the anointing of the Holy Spirit and intimacy with the one Jeanne Guyon called Master, the Lord Jesus Christ.

Nancy Carol James
March 3, 2020

The Holy Gospel of Jesus Christ according to John

Translated by Nancy Carol James, PhD

> In the beginning was the Word, and the Word was with God, and the Word was God. 2 He was in the beginning with God. (John 1:1–2)

St. John writes about both the beginning of eternity and the beginning of the world.

The generation of the Word has been throughout all eternity. The *Word* is always the beginning, as God is where the Word is. The Father produces the Word, but they are co-equal and the Father was not before him. *The Word is in God*, since it is continually in the same God, therefore it emanates in unity of principle. *The Word* distinct as a person *is God* in perfect union without division. The fact that there is the distinction of persons does not divide the essence. *He was in the beginning with God* and equal to him, the Father being in the Son, as the Son is in the Father.

The Word was also with him in the *beginning* of creation of the world for though this creation is attributed to the Father, the Son was of one essence with the Father and the Holy Spirit. When God created the world, he communicated the spirit of his Word to all beings who were ready to receive it.

> All things came into being through him, and without him not one thing came into being. (John 1:3)

O God! I have no way to express these wonderful things. Our Evangelist writes well about inexpressible ideas. I am silent out of love and respect and express more by my silence than all my words. O incarnate love! O Word of God! I see that you are so grand, nothing can be said about you! Your lights dazzle with strength. We are ravished and can say nothing. You give us a most certain testimony. O being of beings, in which all beings participate! *All things came into being through him* and you are the arm of the All-Powerful. *Without him not one thing came into being.* The arms of the Word always hold to your Father in interior communication. The Father sends him out in exterior operations, as was done in the incarnation, according to the knowledge given to divine Mary, when she said, *He has shown strength with his arm* (Luke 1:51).

O sovereign power, by whom everything was made! This is understood in two ways. The concomitance and unity of God shows that the divine persons are necessarily matching and are all together. They have one indivisible essence; one does nothing that is not done by the other.

This means that all spiritual beings have the life of the Word and he communicates this life to all human beings and to all the angels. That is what makes all living things alive in him. Nothing is done without him.

Also, nothing can be done in a particular human being except by the Word.

Therefore, everything consists in giving a place to his Spirit to work in us. The demon opposes this and begins thousands of persecutions against those who are interior souls. The demon wants to extinguish the spirit of the Word in creation. Sin blocked all the avenues to the Word and disfigured in the human being the beautiful image of God. Only the interior life reestablishes the beautiful image.

> In him was life, and the life was the light of all people. (John 1:4)

O great and wonderful words! The Word has essential life communicated from the Father who lives in him and who has life in him. We receive our life from the Father. The life of the Word is the true life of human beings. All the light we have is communicated from the Word. The light of study and reasoning are not the true light. Shadows and darkness are not the true light. We may only have the light of the Word through the loss of our self-life. We must die to ourselves to have the light of God. When we die and our life is hidden with Jesus Christ in God, then we may say with Jesus Christ that we no longer live, but Jesus Christ lives within us. In vivifying, he enlightens and in enlightening he brings life. But he alone may introduce us to union with him, and we receive this only from him. He is the Way.

> The light shines in the darkness, and the darkness did not overcome it. (John 1:5)

The light of Jesus Christ is the holy darkness of faith. The soul is penetrated by truth but does not distinguish this. This holy darkness is full of light but we cannot comprehend the light because it surpasses all darkness and is greater than we ourselves. We do absorb it in the same way that we absorb the sun, but like the sun, it blinds our eyes, putting us in darkness and placing all other lights in darkness. O the sacred darkness of faith! We do not understand it, so we think we are always in darkness. It is wonderful that the souls of faith have light surpassing all other lights, yet this light is not distinct and small.

> There was a man sent from God, whose name was John. 7 He came as a witness to testify to the light, so that all might believe through him. 8 He himself was not the light, but he came to testify to the light. (John 1:6)

As has been said in the gospel of Matthew, John came as a sign of repentance. He was not the light, but he came to announce and give testimony to the light. Repentance precedes the way of faith. Jesus Christ as the way leads a soul and shines with the light. Through repentance, we begin to believe, and we confess to Jesus Christ. O divine Word! Enlighten us yourself with the divine light! Come to us, Word of God, and we will have true light. This is the point of repentance and conversion that brings light and the state of truth. We cannot discover this light without the revelation of Jesus Christ. However, many that understand the advantage and truth of this first degree, want to stay there, and not pass into Jesus Christ. John says, "I am not the light. Behold, the Lamb of God who takes away the sins of the world." We must go to Jesus Christ to be delivered. Repentance introduces faith, but then we must pass out of it and into faith. We must ourselves be led by Jesus Christ and let him put his light into our interior.

> The true light, which enlightens everyone, was coming into the world. (John 1:9)

The divine Word which was *coming into the world* enlightens everyone. We should therefore have no other light but him. This is the divine light that was infused into Adam at the moment of creation. This Spirit of the Word communicated this light to *all human beings*. His blood given to them through baptism gave them faith, which is the true light. There are many false lights which pass for true and good, yet Jesus Christ is the only true light and truth. Therefore, we must abandon ourselves entirely to him without reservation, so he can lead us in the way of truth. We try to inspire everyone to be imprinted and possessed by the truth. As we are exposed to the light, we are enlightened.

> He was in the world, and though the world was made through him, the world did not recognize him. (John 1:10)

This is a strange thing that this divine light is in all people, and almost all people do not know this. *He was in the world* and the world condemns this. *The world was made through Jesus Christ. Through him all things were made; without him nothing was made that has been made.* Yet we fear letting ourselves be led by him. What! To fear letting the one who has made us govern us? Ignoring the Spirit of the Word that is in us causes all the evils. O human being, you presume when you lead yourself! O abandon yourself to the one who made you. He keeps you and brings glory to God. O blind human beings, who ignore their Creator, you imagine that you know how to lead yourself! They mistrust because they do not want to be imprinted by the Word and image of God.

> He came to what was his own, and his own people did not accept him. (John 1:11)

We are all the *home of God* (Hebrews 3:6). *He came* to dwell and *live in us. I will come to them*, he said, *and make my home with them* (John 14:23). Therefore, he comes into the heart of a human being as in a house where he desires to make a home. He does this because he *delights in the human race* (Proverbs 8:31). Yes, unfaithful human beings *did not accept him* because they did not want to enjoy his kind presence. Always at the door of the heart, he says, as to a spouse, *Open to me, my sister, my love, my dove, my perfect one; for my head is wet with dew, my locks with the drops of the night* (Song of Songs 5:2-3). "I am fatigued by my search for you. I have poured my blood on you, and yet you do not open to me." And why, ungrateful one? She does not leave her own corrupting pleasures to open up to her spouse. O blind fright! Jesus Christ was born in a manger because *there was no place for them in an inn* then and now (Luke 2:7). He is refused by most of humanity and finds no place in their hearts. If these were not his people, it would be excusable. But that his *own people* refuse him, O! this is intolerable.

> But to all who received him, who believed in his name, he gave power to become children of God. (John 1:12)

If the state of sinners who do not receive Jesus Christ is worthy of horror, those who *receive* Jesus Christ in them are worthy of envy. We receive Jesus Christ in the heart and submit to his kingdom. When we are led by him, we have a home in his company and are possessed by him. O, what an inconceivable happiness! Those who are given this advantage *become children of God*, because they participate in him only, and as Paul says, they are his adopted children. As they *become one spirit with him* (1 Corinthians 6:17), they are *transformed into his image*. But how is this power given to become children of God? According to Paul, *For all who are led by the Spirit of God are children of God* (Romans 8:14). Receiving Jesus Christ is no other thing than being led and moved by his Spirit. Therefore, to be his disciple, we invite our Master Jesus Christ to lead, possess, move, and act upon us by his Spirit. A Spirit of servitude holds us captive, and yet we submit to this Spirit who gives us liberty. *This Spirit, who leads and possesses our heart, bears witness through this freedom that we are children of God* (Romans 8:16).

John adds, *To all those who believe in his name*, after trusting him, we leave our concerns with him. His name is like a spreading oil that penetrates our soul and spreads throughout us.

> Who were born, not of blood or of the will of the flesh or of the will of man, but of God. (John 1:13)

Here John speaks of the spiritual birth and its production in the soul. Our interior state must be conformed to the divine Son. Those born of the *flesh* do not understand the things of the Spirit. *Blood* and *flesh* and the *will of human beings* do not make true children of God. Although they might be good, they do not have the qualities of children of God. But to his faithful servants, he says, Good and faithful servant. They must participate in God who operates himself by placing the principle of all his actions in their interior. Because his children are his productions, what we produce also belongs to God by the right of filiation. All the actions that come from the principle of flesh are entirely carnal. Those that come from a human principle are entirely human. Those that come from the principles of virtues are virtuous and participate in the good will of a human aided by grace. Therefore, those that have the principle of God are divine. Therefore, to be *born in God*, we must be a new creation in Jesus Christ. All that came before as productions of flesh, blood, and the will of human beings has *passed away*. It is necessary that our actions participate in the principle of God.

> And the Word became flesh and lived among us, and we have seen his glory, the glory as of a father's only son, full of grace and truth. (John 1:14)

But so that such great things would not seem impossible, things which should animate and vivify us, we participate in the divine sonship. The Word *became flesh* so that we are no longer carnal. He was made man, so that we are made Gods. Oh, ineffable goodness, that he is made flesh to make us animated by his Spirit! And as the human in Jesus Christ was entirely led by the Word without any additional support, he wants us to be the same with this difference. We always have a spiritual and intimate or mystical union with his hypostatic union. He wants us to have no life, support, sustenance, or action except through him. And so that we could all claim so much good, he became human for all of us. Not only did he become *flesh* but he *lived* and truly *lived among us*. He wants to make his home in us and always communicate to us more and more of his life. St John assures us that *he has seen his glory* but he did not see it alone because all the souls with whom he is truly united and operates *within* have truly seen his glory by the impression they are given. But what glory do they see? They know that he is the *only Son of the Father*. The filiation of the others is only the filiation of adoption and no one can be adopted except by the only Son who is in himself *full of grace and truth*. This may only be communicated to human beings through him.

> (John testified to him and cried out, "This was he of whom I said, 'He who comes after me ranks ahead of me because he was before me.'") (John 1:15)

As has been said, St John gives testimony to Jesus Christ, saying that the way of penance that reverberates in the interior life, which consists in being led by Jesus Christ, is *preferable* to his. To be led by Jesus Christ is the greatest, most elevated and also the most ancient of ways since it was the way in innocent Adam, who was led by the Spirit of the Word before his fall. Penance only occurs since sin entered and the divine motion preceded sin. In the law of grace and the reparation, the divine motion was first, but is stopped by sin. Penance prepares the way our of sin as it had prepared from the beginning of the centuries. But as soon as the way is prepared, the sinner must let Jesus Christ take his place, because to be led by Jesus Christ is the greatest and most ancient of all penance.

> From his fullness we have all received, grace upon grace. (John 1:16)

We have all received his superabundance and *fullness* because he is full of grace. This grace is spread over our penitence, as it says, *grace upon grace*. It is necessary to receive a small grace first before receiving a fuller and more complete grace.

> The law indeed was given through Moses; grace and truth came through Jesus Christ. (John 1:17)

And to confirm what has been said, the Evangelist assures that *Moses* had *given the law*, the law of rigor and penitence. Jesus Christ in his mercy brought abundant *grace* and *truth*. We may have no other grace and truth except through him. The practice of the law without the interior Spirit which is the Spirit of Jesus Christ may bring some grace but it can never bring the fullness of grace or truth. Only Jesus Christ brings grace and truth to the soul where he lives and who receives this.

> No one has ever seen God. It is God the only Son, who is close to the Father's heart, who has made him known. (John 1:18)

And finally, so that we let ourselves be led and animated by Jesus Christ, the Evangelist warns us that we do not know God through reason or natural understanding or light. All the lights of human beings have only shown their error, bewilderment, and their ignorance. *No one has ever seen God*. It is therefore futile to believe that we can give a just idea of God. The *only Son of God who is close to the Father's heart*, and who has come from God's heart to be manifested to human beings, he *has given a* true *knowledge of the Father*. Because being the perfect image of the Father, the *one who sees him sees also the Father*. Jesus Christ said this to St Philip, *Whoever has seen me has seen the Father* (John 14:9). We only know God through Jesus Christ; therefore, he alone gives true knowledge of the Father. Since Jesus Christ knows the Father, we let Jesus Christ act in us and imprint his image on us, so that we know the Father. Moreover, Jesus Christ hides us with him in the heart of the Father. It is there that we have the knowledge that no one else may give.

> This is the testimony given by John when the Jews sent priests and Levites from Jerusalem to ask him, "Who are you?" 20 He

> confessed and did not deny it, but confessed, "I am not the Messiah." (John 1:19–20)

John gives a testimony to all the *priests and Levites,* to those who charge of souls. *He confessed* truly that *he was not the Christ.* The ways of penance lead to the states of Jesus Christ. However, we do not want to believe this. If we do not believe by St John, how will we believe? Penitence is necessary, holy, and salutary but it only serves to lead us to Jesus Christ. This is the way but it is not an end in itself. We must make the interior our principal occupation, regarding others as accessories as a help and way but not the goal.

> And they asked him, "What then? Are you Elijah?" He said, "I am not." "Are you the prophet?" He answered, "No." 22 Then they said to him, "Who are you? Let us have an answer for those who sent us. What do you say about yourself?" 23 He said,
> "I am the voice of one crying out in the wilderness,
> 'Make straight the way of the Lord,'
> as the prophet Isaiah said." (John 1:21–23)

The humility of St John is admirable. He says nothing about himself because he is annihilated. He speaks of himself only by negation. As soon as someone says he is someone, he says, *No,* and that he is none of this. This humility in St John was not contrary to the truth because an annihilated soul may say nothing about himself. He knows well what he is not and he ignores what he is. St John, as a figure of penance, responds affirmatively to the interrogations, *I am the voice of one crying out* to prepare the *way of the Lord.* But what preparation? To *make straight,* that is to say, one converts, turns, and remains exposed to the eyes of the God. When we turn directly toward him, and completely abandons one's self to him, God passes into and entirely penetrates the soul. If we want the sun to penetrate a room, we must prepare the way and passage to expose the room to the sun in a way that there are openings to let light in. We must first expose ourselves to God, to turn directly to Jesus Christ by a perfect conversion both exterior and interior. Because after the soul is exposed in the same way to the eyes of God, our heart must be opened by God's love and affection. When the beautiful sun penetrates and enters the soul. This is how penance operates in the soul. It *cries* to the soul, Go into the interior; *Make straight the way of the Lord.* Give God passage. This is why penance is both useful and necessary.

> Now they had been sent from the Pharisees. 25 They asked him, "Why then are you baptizing if you are neither the Messiah, nor Elijah, nor the prophet?" 26 John answered them, "I baptize with water. Among you stands one whom you do not know, 27 the one who is coming after me; I am not worthy to untie the thong of his sandal." (John 1:24-27)

The Pharisees who were only concerned with the exterior of penance and what was extraordinary, made further questions to St John who makes admirable responses. *For me*, says the great saint, as figure of penitence and forerunner to the Messiah, *I baptize with water, I only serve to purify the outside. Among you stands one whom you do not know*, and you are not attached to him. He is in the middle since he is in your heart in your most profound part of you, and *you do not know him*. Is it not a strange thing, having such a great good within us, that we do not know this? St John says, because you do not know him, your ignorance leads you to ask me the questions that you do. Oh, if you knew him and were attached to him you would be blessed! He was before me because he lived in souls at the moment so their creation. This is why St John says, he was in the beginning. He merited to be preferred to me. Although I may purify the exterior, I am so little compared to him, *I do not merit to untie his shoes*, that is to say, letting him to enter into my soul, if he did not make my value and merit, I would be very little. In myself I have no value and merit, except what I borrow from him

> The next day he saw Jesus coming toward him and declared, "Here is the Lamb of God who takes away the sin of the world! 30 This is he of whom I said, 'After me comes a man who ranks ahead of me because he was before me.'" (John 1:29-30)

St. John is not content with what he has said, but also confirms this, leaving no doubt, when he says, *Here is the Lamb of God*, because he is always immolated before his Father like a lamb and will be immolated until the end of the centuries for the sins of his people. *This is he who takes away the sin of the world*. John the Baptist says, This is he and not me. You have to trust in him. I can give you knowledge but I cannot take away sins. You need to go to him. *This is he of whom I speak*. Therefore, follow him. Let me lead you to him. He ranks *ahead of me* and *was before me*. It is in vain that you rise early in the day. The beautiful sun is always risen to enlighten you with its life. Follow him! The office of penance teaches you about Jesus Christ and gives you knowledge. St John testifies to the truth of the Eucharist, regarding Jesus Christ being immolated not only on the cross, but again on the altar until the end of the centuries. O divine Lamb, you take away the sins of the world! And how do you take them away? By putting them on yourself. When the soul addresses Jesus Christ and, abandoning herself to him without reserve, he carries himself the languor and wounds. O the advantage to be led by the divine Lamb, who is both Lamb and Shepherd, and gives his life for the sheep.

> "I myself did not know him; but I came baptizing with water for this reason, that he might be revealed to Israel." (John 1:31)

For myself, says St John, as a figure of penance, *I myself did not know him* for myself, and I would not have known him but he manifested himself to me. *I am* however *come baptizing with water*, washing what was dirty and bringing penance, so *that he might be revealed to Israel*, that is to say, interior and abandoned souls.

> And John testified, "I saw the Spirit descending from heaven like a dove, and it remained on him. 33 I myself did not know him, but the one who sent me to baptize with water said to me, 'He on whom you see the Spirit descend and remain is the one who baptizes with the Holy Spirit.'" (John 1:32–33)

We *know the Spirit* of the Lord, when he lives on a soul with simplicity but this Spirit only reposes and *remains on Jesus Christ*. We must become Jesus Christ as we participate in his states, before having this permanent dwelling of the Holy Spirit. The Spirit reposes on just souls. But finally, to make his home there, we must become another Jesus Christ. With the simplicity of the exterior and the transformation of the interior in Jesus Christ, the Spirit remains in the soul.

St. John says again, that he did not know who he was, though he was certain of the truth that he was in the world. *I myself did not know him* by sight. Penance has faith who Jesus Christ is, and he is in the soul. But it does not have the true experience of who he is, until the one was sent before him to prepare the way, manifested this to him. When he was manifested, he was ravished with joy.

He was told, that *He on whom you see the Spirit descend and remain is the one who baptizes with the Holy Spirit*. Jesus Christ is truly the only one on whom the Holy Spirit reposes, not only because of the concomitance there is between the divine persons, which makes the Word always accompany the Holy Spirit, but also because he always reposes in the incarnation. Mary only conceived the Word because he covered her with his shadow. The Holy Spirit reposed again at the baptism of Jesus Christ to show that Jesus Christ at his baptism merited for human beings the communication of the grace of the Holy Spirit which rested on these waters making them fertile so that they may operate the merited grace of Jesus Christ. But John's baptism was only a figure of Jesus Christ's baptism, as exterior penance is only a figure of the interior. John's baptism and exterior penance has only the value it borrows from Jesus Christ, who operates in the soul in a way most perfect.

> "And I myself have seen and have testified that this is the Son of God." (John 1:34)

As soon as the penitent soul discovers Jesus Christ within her, she sees a great difference with what she feels than she had before. She *testifies that this is the Son of God*. She says, Oh, it is now that God works in me! And this penitent interior, that comes to her is different than the one I make with my own efforts. Oh, the true God operates in my soul! I do not doubt that this is God and I give my testimony, that he is the Son of God. We see here how necessary it is to have penance for us to know Jesus Christ. But once we know him, we must follow him.

> The next day John again was standing with two of his disciples, 36 and as he watched Jesus walk by, he exclaimed, "Look, here is the Lamb of God!" 37 The two disciples heard him say this, and they followed Jesus. (John 1:35-37)

St. John is the model of the perfect disinterested spiritual director. He leads the soul to the truth but he only leads him to give him the knowledge of Jesus Christ. But he does not stop there, but he teaches her to follow Jesus Christ. *The two disciples* are the figure of the docile soul, who does not stop and is attached to nothing, and who is always ready to leave its practices to follow Jesus Christ. And would it not have been a fault to attach themselves to St John after knowing Jesus Christ and yet not following Jesus Christ?

> When Jesus turned and saw them following, he said to them, "What are you looking for?" They said to him, "Rabbi" (which translated means Teacher), "where are you staying?" 39 He said to them, "Come and see." They came and saw where he was staying, and they remained with him that day. It was about four o'clock in the afternoon. (John 1:38-39)

Jesus turned and saw them. O Love! If we do not follow you at the first signal that you make, that you turn yourself. The soul is not yet converted to you and turned toward you, you turn toward her, according to the assurance given by your prophet, *Return to me, says the Lord of hosts, and I will return to you, says the Lord of hosts* (Zechariah 1:3). The soul is not yet returned to his God, when God turns toward him and asks him, *What are you looking for?* He asks, What do you desire, in order to give it to him. O, divine Lover! He looks for you. It is you for whom he searches. As soon as we know you, we abandon everything else to follow you. You alone satisfy. They ask you, *Where are you staying?* He does not respond to this soul's question, but you are content to make another. Where do you live, they say, so that I can remain with you? Oh, soul lovers! What do you ask? You ask already to remain with Jesus Christ! Do you not know that he remains in his Father's heart? Alas! You say, This is also the place where I desire to go, and this is where I want you to lead me because I may not go to my Father except through him.

Jesus Christ shows them the place where he lives, that is to say, he gives some knowledge to this soul of his divine life. He shows them a temporary union, as if to show them what he will give them one day in his favor. Everything happens in knowledge and distinct light.

> One of the two who heard John speak and followed him was Andrew, Simon Peter's brother. 41 He first found his brother Simon and said to him, "We have found the Messiah" (which is translated Anointed). 42 He brought Simon to Jesus, who looked at him and said, "You are Simon son of John. You are to be called Cephas" (which is translated Peter). (John 1:40–42)

The soul who knows Jesus Christ through the way of penance and tastes his sweet presence, wants to share this with everyone. In her ardor and joy with this new revelation, we want to announce this to the world and convince others to participate in such a great good. God often uses these beginning souls in service to their love to win others.

St. Peter had just arrived at Jesus Christ when he changed Peter's name, choosing him as the *foundation rock of its building*.[2] According to human reason, St Andrew who was the brother of St Peter and the

---

2 Guyon adds the following. The apostles are the foundation rocks of the church and the New Jerusalem (Revelation 21:14). St Peter was the first among the apostles. We do not need to find this strange that Jesus Christ called Peter as the rock of the church and the one upon whom it is based. See St Cyprian in his Epistles 59. 70, 71, and 73 and *De Unitate Ecclesias*.

first of the apostles, had won St Peter for Jesus Christ. Andrew always persevered with failing as St Peter did. So why was St Peter the foundation rock? O God! You do not judge by things as humans judge and your conduct is different from ours.

> The next day Jesus decided to go to Galilee. He found Philip and said to him, "Follow me." 44 Now Philip was from Bethsaida, the city of Andrew and Peter. (John 1:43–44)

Jesus begins his apostolate by attracting souls to him and making disciples who can support his doctrine. One simple call from Jesus Christ suffices all the others. The Pharisees were not won by a great number of sermons and miracles that Jesus Christ made in their favor, but the apostles were won by a single appeal. We must note that there are an infinite number of souls who follow Jesus Christ. One single call attracted them. One secret virtue raised them up and makes them follow him into deserts, without thought of nourishment, and with a total forgetfulness of all that concerns them. To follow Jesus Christ as the way, truth, and life, there must first be an interior attraction and there is no need for a particular vocation. But when it is a question of making apostles, they are called in a particular way. To be in the apostolate, they must be called singularly and no one may be placed into it without a particular vocation. However, we do the contrary and put ourselves into the apostolate and this is why we have so little fruit. Everyone wants to teach, govern, and lead others; they do not wait for a particular call. But when it comes to following Jesus Christ, and letting ourselves be led by his attraction, we want to examine the vocations and see if the call is good. Then we do not fear to go.

> Philip found Nathaniel and said to him, "We have found him about whom Moses in the law and also the prophets wrote, Jesus son of Joseph from Nazareth." 46 Nathaniel said to him, "Can anything good come out of Nazareth?" Philip said to him, "Come and see." (John 1:45–46)

Nathaniel asks whether good can come out of Nazareth because he does not want to make a mistake. He is assessing the situation and does not to mistakenly believe Philip. This is why Philip says to Nathaniel, *Come and see* and judge for yourself about Jesus Christ, before he declares himself against Jesus Christ.

> When Jesus saw Nathaniel coming toward him, he said of him, "Here is truly an Israelite in whom there is no deceit!" (John 1:47)

Some people surprise us by their simplicity, while others surprise by their malicious judgment and condemnation. Jesus Christ tells us here the true character of an interior and abandoned soul, called by the term *Israelite*, which is simplicity, candor, and lack of deceit. The character of a soul in multiplicity is artifice, detours, and disguise. The one who walks in righteousness with God walks in righteousness with his neighbor. Disguise only comes from a reflection of self-love and prevents speaking openly. Then we try to persuade others what is not only because we want to hide what is.

> Nathaniel asked him, "Where did you get to know me?" Jesus answered, "I saw you under the fig tree before Philip called you." 49 Nathaniel replied, "Rabbi, you are the Son of God! You are the King of Israel!" (John 1:48–49)

Jesus Christ *sees* and knows us before calling us. In the first call of Jesus Christ, he looks at the soul and by his regard attracts us sweetly with strength. After he disposes the soul by his attraction, Jesus Christ sends somebody by providence to teach him. As much as possible, Jesus Christ uses ordinary ways to do this and not extraordinary ones. He calls interior souls by his look, but he sends apostolic people to communicate his Spirit, who serve as a guide to introduce them to Jesus Christ. These apostolic people say one thing: *Come and see* and judge by your experience. All that can be said does not equal what is. We follow the interior attraction and this carries us to Jesus Christ. In him we find what is uniquely and truly extraordinary. In approaching Jesus Christ, we hear him speak and we are truly taken. Then we cry out in joy for this great good. O divine Master, who speaks to me and pulls everything together, whom I want to obey without reservation, *You are the Son of God! You are the King of Israel!* You are God and King. Our God attracts and merits our worship and our King must reign absolutely within us and to whom we submit without reservation.

> Jesus answered, "Do you believe because I told you that I saw you under the fig tree? You will see greater things than these." 51 And he said to him, "Very truly, I tell you, you will see heaven opened and the angels of God ascending and descending upon the Son of Man." (John 1:50–51)

Jesus Christ promises Nathaniel even greater things. Nathaniel speaks out of a state of light that always accompanies the beginning soul. Jesus Christ says to him, My love for you has won you and by what I have given you, you pass into me. As seen in Nathaniel, visions are only the first degree in the illuminative life, where the soul is entirely applied to the holy humanity of Jesus Christ through the union of love. These are favors that raise the soul suddenly. God gives these visions to win the soul totally.

> On the third day there was a wedding in Cana of Galilee, and the mother of Jesus was there. 2 Jesus and his disciples had also been invited to the wedding. (John 14:1–2)

We wish that all *weddings* invited Jesus Christ, his mother, and his disciples because then all weddings would be holy. The world strangely abuses those by saying that people of God must not marry. Because of this, some do not wish to give themselves to God, even in the sacrament.

These weddings are the symbol for the wedding of the soul, where we have passed three days of total abandon in nude faith and pure sacrifice, where in death, annihilation, and total loss, the soul is finally taken as spouse. His *Mother* always accompanies the soul because all happens in the eternal Father's heart where Mary, the mother of Jesus Christ, dwells in the place of eternal generation. *His disciples* are there since all saints and angels are witnesses of such a signal favor.

> When the wine gave out, the mother of Jesus said to him, "They have no wine." 4 And Jesus said to her, "Woman, what concern is that to you and to me? My hour has not yet come." (John 2:3–4)

My God, that this is divine! What happens to these nuptials? The *wine gave out* which is the allegory for when the soul loses its power and vigor. All support is taken away; nothing remains. Absolute annihilation exists in a perfect loss. Then the divine Mary warns her Son of their state of the soul, as if she said, "They have nothing." The words of Jesus Christ to his holy mother appear to be rebukes but they are very mysterious. First, if we look at the natural miracle, Jesus Christ says, "*Woman, what concern is that to you and to me*? The union between us is so close, do not you have all you want? You can do everything through me. On this occasion do what you want but do not manifest me yet because *My hour has not yet come* where I begin my apostolic life, waiting for the divine moment. *My hour has not yet come*, because I have to make a much more extraordinary change than the one you want. I will now only change the water into wine, but later my blood into wine. This will be the pledge that I give to the church when I marry her. That wedding will begin with the change of my blood into wine, that will be an eternal memorial that I make of my alliance to the church. Since I marry this church only through my death, I will be a husband of blood, *My hour has not yet come.*"

In the mystical sense, Jesus Christ says to his mother, I have made a union with you so close that I cannot do the same with any other. *What concern is that to you and to me?* Is not my body formed in your blood? In you I was married with human nature in a hypostatic union that will never happen in any other creature. I know what you are asking is that I marry this soul mystically and that I be formed in her. But *My hour has not yet come.* There is one more thing to do before I am formed in her. It is not only that she must be destroyed and annihilated but that she be changed, and that her mortal being be changed into me. As your blood was changed into my flesh, the wine will change in my blood. It is necessary that she be transformed in me but my hour has not yet come yet. However, it will come because I will begin to operate in a clear order that will be seen.

> His mother said to the servants, "Do whatever he tells you."
> (John 2:5)

The first preparation for the spiritual marriage is blind *obedience* to the will of God. We must *do whatever he tells us* without sight, return, or reflection, without hesitation or doubt. The soul then has absolute dependence and blind obedience to the designs of God. If the soul places restrictions on God, she is still not fit for the spiritual marriage. Mary says in this important idea, *Do whatever he tells you* because complete obedience makes us the spouse of the Holy Spirit. It is as if, Mary says, "If you want to be the spouse, your obedience must equal mine which will produce in you the apostolic state."

> Now standing there were six stone water jars for the Jewish rites
> of purification, each holding twenty or thirty gallons. 7 Jesus
> said to them, "Fill the jars with water." And they filled them up
> to the brim. (John 2:6–7)

The *six stone water jars for the Jewish rites of purification* signify the purification of interior souls who are prefigured in the Jews. This purification of the *six jars* show six needed things that we have already said.

These include first, abandonment, death, and annihilation; and secondly, nude faith, pure sacrifice, and total loss. All these are empty things, like the jars. Abandonment empties us of all self-will and propriety. Death deprives us of selfhood. Annihilation destroys us absolutely by losing all the substance of ourselves. Nude faith dissipates all the self-inspired lights. Pure sacrifice evacuates us of individual operations and all use of ourselves for what we want. Total loss takes away our support, subsistence, and other things. The six purifications needed for abandoned souls need to happen before the divine marriage. Then Jesus Christ *fills us with water* which means that he gives the soul a new life, when the emptiness is perfect. This water of new life causes purity, cleanliness, and simplicity which brings a new life without odor, color, savor, or consistence. This new life is without propriety and anything except what the bridegroom gives her and which she is pleased to receive. She is entirely mobile and she has nothing solid to stop her. Therefore, here are the spiritual qualities that prepare the soul for divine marriage and consummation.

> He said to them, "Now draw some out, and take it to the chief steward." So they took it. 9 When the steward tasted the water that had become wine and did not know where it came from (though the servants who had drawn the water knew), the steward called the bridegroom 10 and said to him, "Everyone serves the good wine first, and then the inferior wine after the guests have become drunk. But you have kept the good wine until now." (John 2:8–10)

The soul did not have a new life until after the spiritual resurrection, but now she participates in this life as pure and clean water. She now has all the qualities of water, and has no self-focused, hard qualities. She may flow into God without difficulty. But before this time, she needed to change the water into wine, which means changed and transformed into God. At this same instant, the spiritual marriage is consummated, when the Word takes the soul for his spouse and unites with her. This is more than a simple attachment, for now she unites and changes into God. This is more than being hidden with God for God absorbs her in a true transformation, so to speak, like a wine that we drink. He unites in essence with her. The soul is changed into Jesus Christ and transformed into him by a perfect charity like fire melting iron, making it ardent and burning, as long as it remains in the fire. He transforms the iron by giving it his qualities, without the iron guarding its particulars and allowing the changes. In the same way, Jesus Christ transforms the soul in his charity and love. The bridegroom changes the soul into like essence with him after she passes into him. Paul in his theology tells us to *be transformed* in Romans 12:2. He also writes, *And all of us, with unveiled faces, seeing the glory of the Lord as though reflected in a mirror, are being transformed into the same image from one degree of glory to another; for this comes from the Lord, the Spirit* (2 Corinthians 3:18). He also writes, *Anyone united to the Lord becomes one spirit with him* (1 Corinthians 6:17). This passage of the soul into God, which precedes the transformation, is described in these other words: *Pass into me, all of you, who desire me ardently* (Ecclesiasticus 24:19). How do we pass into God, if not by the flowing of ourselves into him, as he has said? This makes the spiritual marriage, which is a communication of substances, as they pass into one another and become consummated within this total transformation. This perfect union has no distinction or difference but this wonderful operation of union only unites at the end of this perfect transformation. Our spirit seems entirely transformed to clarity in this time of divine action. The memory is perfectly changed and represents only good and holy objects. The will changes into love and entirely burns with love. This is the *first wine* of the bridegroom, but it is different from the last! Then not only the power of the human beings is changed into God but the foundation of the soul is changed into God but now without distinctions between the two.

> Jesus did this, the first of his signs, in Cana of Galilee, and revealed his glory; and his disciples believed in him. (John 2:11)

This miracle represents the spiritual marriage. This is also the first state of the soul that Jesus Christ operates in her. He first takes away the soul's natural weakness which has made her days flow into pleasures and things of the earth which opens the door into evil like corrupt water. Yet the divine power begins charity that animates the person with a secret power and vigor. This makes her operate with the same ease for good that she previously had for wrong. This is why the person converts and tastes the sweetness of the bridegroom, and in her foundation begins to change into wine. This is the *first miracle* that is worked in the soul, that makes the person radiant and manifests the greatness of God before the human being.

> The Passover of the Jews was near, and Jesus went up to Jerusalem. 14 In the temple he found people selling cattle, sheep, and doves, and the money changers seated at their tables. 15 Making a whip of cords, he drove all of them out of the temple, both the

> sheep and the cattle. He also poured out the coins of the money changers and overturned their tables. 16 He told those who were selling the doves, "Take these things out of here! Stop making my Father's house a marketplace!" (John 2:13–16)

Jesus Christ pardons many things, but he will not suffer the profaning of the *temple*. He does not do anything to thousands of sinners who turn to him and who are charged with crimes, but he will not allow commerce in the temple. He wants all temples to be sacred and noble. All the worldly temples are not equal in dignity to the living temple in our interior. Jesus Christ will not allow the profaning of these temples not only by crimes but with commerce. However, human beings may also have an interior *place* of traffic and commerce where they are entirely concerned with creatures in their worldly affairs and not occupied with God. The foundation of the soul is the *house of God* that must be entirely consecrated to God and where we must be entirely occupied with God. The foundation of the soul, if not consecrated, produces the distractions that most people complain of in their prayers. This is because in their spirit and interior they have a continual commerce and walk with things not of God; they are not occupied with God. Jesus Christ is the only one who can stop this trade and commerce in the human soul. Once we give him entry into our heart, he banishes all the rest. He chases out with effort the *sellers of sheep and cattle and money changers*. In these two types of people we see two negotiations. One appears all holy and the other all profane. The one that appears profane are the money changers, while in truth they were only there for the convenience of the offerings. The one that appears holy are the sellers of beef and sheep, which is for the sacrifice.

Jesus Christ wants sacrifice in the material temple and in the interior temple. All places are places of sacrifice, but he does not want us to sell things specific to sacrifice. It is necessary to sacrifice the very means of sacrifice and to leave for Jesus the care of the future victim.

Jesus Christ looks in the heart of people because he himself wants to be the victim. He then acts as priest and victim because the priest banishes an impure victim to substitute in its place a pure, holy, and innocent victim. As a victim, he gives himself and immolates himself as a sacrifice. He does the same in the soul. He sacrifices himself in the soul without the soul distinguishing the sacrifice. He is the victim because he enters the soul in its states. There he is entirely and continually immolated, but in a manner so profound and secret, that the soul does not know this.

Commerce with *money* is a thing entirely of the earth, which sadly may fill and occupy the person. We have to work, yet we do not have to let these things fill our interior life but instead leave the care to God. We must sacrifice, but not reason on this or make an occupation of sacrifice.

Jesus Christ *drove all of them out*, because he wants the temple entirely empty. The commerce and sale of the things involved with sacrifice make noise and tumults and interrupt the sacrifice. Jesus Christ banishes all of this to make sure that his house is a continual *house of prayer*, where the soul does no other thing than to rest in the state of prayer. Jesus Christ does all the rest as a priest who sacrifices and immolates all things.

The last thing that Jesus Christ banishes from the temple is the sale of *doves*. He does not use the whip for this. He says simply, "*Take these things out of here! Stop making my Father's house a marketplace!*" The sale of doves is that the soul does not rest in the state of simplicity but wants to reason on simplicity, thinking this will bring advantages. Yet to be simple is to be infinitely more perfect than to reason on simplicity. This is why our Lord said, "Take these doves for sale out of here and leave the temple empty of all things, and then you will truly be in simplicity of emptiness." But, O divine Savior! Only you can do these things and help us comprehend them. If you do not do this, we only have false imaginings.

> His disciples remembered that it was written, "Zeal for your house will consume me." 18 The Jews then said to him, "What sign can you show us for doing this?" 19 Jesus answered them, "Destroy this temple, and in three days I will raise it up." (John 2:17–19)

Jesus Christ has *zeal* for the holy *house of his Father*. This house is no other than the interior. Scripture refers to his *zeal* through the idea of jealousy. But the Jews wanted to know what *authority* he had to do these things and what *miracle* he was doing in these souls, so they would be certain of the truth of these states. He wanted the soul empty of all commerce that occupied the place of his Father and prevented the making of a permanent home in souls. Jesus Christ said, *Destroy this temple, and in three days I will raise it up!* He was saying that he would establish this state by his death and resurrection. He establishes this in two ways. The first is the death and destruction of the soul which has been described before. In the second, the soul is destroyed by death, loss, and annihilation. God rebuilds her *in three days* because he operates the states, without which the temple will not be rebuilt. He needs the destruction before he rebuilds.

> But he was speaking of the temple of his body. 22 After he was raised from the dead, his disciples remembered that he had said this; and they believed the scripture and the word that Jesus had spoken. (John 2:21–22)

Here Jesus Christ *speaks* not only of his natural *body* but his mystical body. He speaks of each soul in particular, which is a part of the temple. *After having spent many years building the temple*, after it is completely destroyed and overthrown, God restores it in a very short time and makes it infinitely more magnificent and grander than it had been previously. This temple, though, will never be rebuilt except by its destruction.

> After he was raised from the dead, his disciples remembered that he had said this; and they believed the scripture and the word that Jesus had spoken. 23 When he was in Jerusalem during the Passover festival, many believed in his name because they saw the signs that he was doing. 24 But Jesus on his part would not entrust himself to them, because he knew all people 25 and needed no one to testify about anyone; for he himself knew what was in everyone. (John 2:22–25)

It is *after the resurrection* and not before, that we believe the truth of the promises of Jesus Christ. Before the resurrection, the state always appears doubtful and uncertain. But afterwards, we know the truth of the resurrection and the truth of *scripture*, that talks truly and clearly about resurrection.

Jesus Christ wins many people. They *believed in him because of his miracles* but Jesus Christ *would not entrust himself to them*. With people who run to the extraordinary and to be won by miracles, their conversion happens suddenly, but also suddenly stops. Like Jesus, we have to serve everybody but we do not have to trust everybody. We must never stop pursuing the good of the Word in the apostolic state. Although we see many people who seem to give themselves courageously to God, only a few stand firm. But our Lord was not fooled because *he knew all people* and what was in their heart. He knew about their lack of perseverance and how they would convert good into evil and his Word into venom, yet he continued his work. This is the way to be a true apostle by continuing to work in the ministry.

> Now there was a Pharisee named Nicodemus, a leader of the
> Jews. 2 He came to Jesus by night and said to him, "Rabbi, we
> know that you are a teacher who has come from God; for no one
> can do these signs that you do apart from the presence of God."
> (John 3:1–2)

A person like Nicodemus who has greatness of rank, birth, authority, and science experiences a strange reluctance to surrender. When a person is esteemed throughout the world and exposed to the eyes of the people, O the pain to submit is immense! He knows the good and yet cannot resolve to embrace it because he must abandon his feelings and quit his ordinary ways of acting. If he responds to the attraction to seek Jesus Christ and follow his ways based in humility, he must go to search in the *night*, that is to say, when hidden. He dares not declare himself publicly. He is ashamed to participate in the large number of people who seek and follow Jesus Christ. O God! It is difficult when material wealth enters the interior kingdom where you are hidden, O God! Your secrets are great and wise and have only been revealed to the small ones!

Frequently learned people are only attracted by science. Yet, when convinced by the power of the miracles, they do not wish to declare themselves out of concern for what people will say. They approve and esteem spiritual power secretly, but will not confess this in plain day before human beings. Yet they know that the *presence of God* is there and that without God these miracles would be impossible.

> Jesus answered him, "Very truly, I tell you, no one can see the
> kingdom of God without being born from above." (John 3:3)

Who will not admire the conduct of Jesus Christ towards this doctor? Nicodemus testifies that the Jesus' miracles attract him, yet Jesus Christ does not flatter Nicodemus with congratulatory words. Instead, Jesus Christ says, *No one can see the kingdom of God without being born from above.* Jesus was saying to the doctor, "All strong minds cannot doubt the truth of my miracles and doctrine. But to discover the kingdom of God that I came to establish in souls, hidden under my miracles, O, that will never happen unless you are born again."

There are two to know the kingdom of God and experience a new birth. In the first way, we learn that the kingdom of God is within and in the new birth we learn the secrets of the kingdom. The first requires only a renewal of life, a real change that happens when we search for God in the foundation of our soul.

In the second way of knowledge and a new birth, we are annihilated before God and remain in his presence. We let our own spirit and lights diminish and in place of that allow the operations of God. We cease to live in our inclinations and sins and instead live in Jesus Christ and his operations.

In this second way of being born again, the soul after being entirely annihilated takes a new and inspired life. This life is that of the Word, as is explained by Paul who speaks of this new life. In Romans 6:11, he says we are *dead to sin* and that we live in Jesus Christ. In Galatians 2:20, he writes, "It is no longer I who live, but Jesus Christ who lives within me."

> Nicodemus said to him, "How can anyone be born after having grown old? Can one enter a second time into the mother's womb and be born?" (John 3:4)

These kinds of states surprise wise people, even those of good will, because they live naturally within all ordinary rules of science. Some people who believe in general about the two births of which Jesus Christ speaks but very few agree about the way these states operate. They ridicule these states because they are attached to the letter and do not penetrate the meaning of things.

> Jesus answered, "Very truly, I tell you, no one can enter the kingdom of God without being born of water and Spirit. (John 3:5)

Jesus explains this to him, albeit in an obscure way. *No one can enter the kingdom of God without being born of water and Spirit.* Jesus Christ spoke of the sight of the kingdom of God. Now he explains the two births which consists in *entering* the same kingdom. The true knowledge and revelation of the kingdom requires *entering* the kingdom. It is impossible to see the kingdom, if we are not in the kingdom. We need to enter into the interior kingdom according to these two ways that he has said, for us to have a true knowledge.

To enter these two ways, we have to go through *two births*. The first is that of *water*, which is penitence and true conversion which washes and wipes the exterior and purifies by means of the interior. The second birth is done *by the Holy Spirit* which through its life-giving heat reduces the soul to the ashes of annihilation. These same ashes are then reborn into a new human being like a phoenix and by this means enters into the kingdom of God. Our first life is our life purified by the water of grace. The second life is operated by the Spirit, which breathes, vivifies, and makes the soul live, no more in its own sanctified life, but that of God himself.

> "What is born of the flesh is flesh, and what is born of the Spirit is spirit." (John 3:6)

Jesus Christ confirmed by these words what we have just advanced. *What is born of the flesh is flesh.* The carnal human is weak with the miseries of flesh. This needs to be purified by the water of grace. But *what is born of the Spirit is spirit* and *the Spirit* brings the experience of new birth. The human is no longer subject to things of the flesh. This life that emanates from the Holy Spirit is a life entirely spiritual and divine.

> "Do not be astonished that I said to you, 'You must be born from above.'" (John 3:7)

Jesus Christ tells Nicodemus, *Do not be astonished that I said to you must be born from above.* Jesus Christ chooses those who please him for this new birth. He chose Nicodemus who was a doctor to be one of his small ones. This is why Jesus Christ also adds, *The Spirit blows where it will.*

> "The wind blows where it chooses, and you hear the sound of it, but you do not know where it comes from or where it goes. So it is with everyone who is born of the Spirit." (John 3:8)

There are many *winds of the Spirit*. There are breaths of inspiration and the breath that gives life back. We *hear these voices well*, when we are attentive. The soul that listens to God within her foundation *hears his word*, which is not like we imagine as a distinct word, which is what you expect from this strong wind. Instead, God's true word is perfect, pure, and assured, blowing in a divine and small breeze. The other wind is when the soul is in the shadow of death, which is like a profound sepulcher. It is then that she hears this word: *Rise up and go out*. This word is not a distinct word but a very effective one. This word is a wind that animates these ashes and give them life. But even though we hear these two words in very different times, we do not know *where they come from, nor where they go*. We hear them not as individual words. We know the words have happened, but we do not know what will follow and what end they will have. Yet the first words give us strength to walk in the way of God and do God's will. The soul loses herself in God which is the place of her end. Those who are *born of the Spirit* hear his voice and let themselves be moved by the Spirit. Yet we do not see where this motion comes from or what it leads to. We hear the wind without seeing where it comes from or where it goes. We hear and see the good that God makes in these souls.

> Nicodemus said to him, "How can these things be?" 10 Jesus answered him, "Are you a teacher of Israel, and yet you do not understand these things?" (John 3:9–10)

Nicodemus does not understand the truth of the action of the Spirit. They appear impossible to him. This is why Jesus Christ makes a gentle reproach: *Are you a teacher of Israel?* That is to say, "You are a doctor among souls who are destined to be interior, among abandoned souls, represented by the children of Israel, and *yet you do not understand these things.*

These understandings are essential since this is the beginning and the end of the interior! It is a deplorable misfortune that most directors of the interior do not have the experience of God's ways. This is why there are so few interior souls because the directors are not in a state to conduct people and help them in this way.

> "Very truly, I tell you, we speak of what we know and testify to what we have seen; yet you do not receive our testimony." (John 3:11)

Jesus Christ speaks to Nicodemus as a doctor, as he speaks to all doctors. *Very truly, I tell you*, speaking to him and to the souls in whom he reigns, *we speak of what we know*. What we know from our experience is much more certain than science. Nothing is so certain as the experience of a thing. When we study a thing to understand it, the description of it can never equal putting the thing on view. Yet Jesus Christ says here in interior souls and for them, *We know and testify* and prove this *yet you do not receive our testimony*. You do not believe our testimony that we have given you out of our experience.

> "If I have told you about earthly things and you do not believe, how can you believe if I tell you about heavenly things?" (John 3:12)

Jesus Christ assures us that these states of new life in God are also experienced on *earth*. The kingdom of God is not only in heaven but also in our interior kingdom experienced on earth. O divine Jesus! You are very good to explain to us in this way. You show us about the difficulties and doubts that we have as we work in the interior. All that we do in the interior is for the other life. God works in the soul not for *the things of the earth* but for *heavenly things* and our concerns about the divine life. Oh! *How can we believe* and understand?

> "No one has ascended into heaven except the one who descended from heaven, the Son of Man." (John 3:13)

No one may penetrate the secrets of God or enter into God himself *except the one descended from heaven,* Jesus Christ. It is he who ascends by himself and who makes the souls rise with him, hiding them with him in God. For our souls ascend with him into God, when we give ourselves to him and let ourselves be led by him. No one can rise to God except through him.

We can also hear that no one may rise to heaven unless they first descend into the celestial state of light and knowledge of total annihilation, so they rise with Jesus Christ to God, who himself takes the place of the soul.

> "And just as Moses lifted up the serpent in the wilderness, so must the Son of Man be lifted up, 15 that whoever believes in him may have eternal life." (John 3:14–15)

Jesus Christ speaks here of his passion and crucifixion whose brazen serpent was the figure. Jesus Christ *was raised* on the cross, *that whoever believes in him may have eternal life.* Then faithful souls may find salvation in the cross of Jesus Christ and be redeemed by Jesus Christ. But the soul who desperately longs for salvation and does self-works out of weakness still finds salvation in Jesus Christ crucified. All those consecrated to Jesus Christ, who believe and hope in him, *will not perish.* The cross is our sign of deliverance but also what we must suffer. Those who suffer with Jesus Christ and are committed to Jesus Christ crucified, not only will not perish but will *have eternal life.* This eternal life extends not only for the other life, but also for this one, where the soul truly enters into God. Who lives the life of Jesus Christ is already in eternal life.

> "For God so loved the world that he gave his only Son, so that everyone who believes in him may not perish but may have eternal life." (John 3:16)

Oh, the love of God for his creatures! Oh the ingratitude of creatures for their God! *God so loved the world that he gave his only Son* equal to him that he loved as much as he himself. Not only did he give himself, but he gave him into death, so that everyone who *believes in him* and is consecrated to him *may not perish but may have eternal life*. However, some fear to abandon their self to him and say that he does not call everybody to enjoy him and that he does not give graces to all to return to him. He gives grace to everyone but not everyone benefits from this. O Love! You call, give the grace of salvation, and give yourself for salvation. Yet after you give yourself, can we believe that you refuse salvation? Paul says, *He who did not withhold his own Son, but gave him up for all of us, will he not with him also give us everything else*? (Romans 8:32). After this, why don't we hope, attend, and consecrate ourselves entirely to him? Because of our ingratitude, we are still not persuaded of his love. We need to abandon ourselves to him without reservation.

> "Indeed, God did not send the Son into the world to condemn the world, but in order that the world might be saved through him." (John 3:17)

O words that express infinitely much and confound those who doubt the goodness of God! God desires that all human beings be saved, and he wants this even more strongly than we want it ourselves. Jesus Christ did not come *to condemn the world but in order that the world might be saved*. But, O my God! We know that the world of Adam is condemned, but we pray for the people in the world that you came to save so they receive your salvation and not be condemned. The world will only be saved through Jesus Christ. We need to follow Jesus Christ and abandon ourselves to him without reservation. We find our salvation in him.

> "Those who believe in him are not condemned; but those who do not believe are condemned already, because they have not believed in the name of the only Son of God." (John 3:18)

All depends on faith, not only theological faith and virtue but that we believe in Jesus Christ and in all the mysteries, because *those who do not believe* in Jesus Christ in both explicit and implicit ways *are condemned already*. This also applies to those who walk in the interior. Their interior will only advance and subsist according to the measure of their *faith*. It is *faith* that makes the path. Those who have a lot of faith, advance well and persevere infallibly. Those with little faith, advance little. Those with no faith, do not advance at all and leave the way of God. The way of faith is more hidden, small, less flamboyant than that of light, but it is safer.

But what of those who walk in the interior but do not have faith, are they also condemned? Why they do persevere? *They have not believed in the name of the Son of God* and lean on their own industry and not on Jesus Christ. However, he is the only Son of God; no one may participate in God the Father except through him. No one may be interior unless he is a child of God, according to the testimony of Jesus Christ.

> "And this is the judgment, that the light has come into the world, and people loved darkness rather than light because their deeds were evil." (John 3:19)

Jesus Christ *has come into the world* for all people to enlighten them with his light, to animate with his Spirit, and vivify with his life. This is *our condemnation* that people did not want to receive the light of his truth because it *judged their works*. They preferred their darkness, that is to say, their own self-actions and their own light. They preferred their self-centered life over the life of Jesus Christ. Because they do not receive Jesus Christ and prefer their own actions to the ones he would make in them, their *deeds are evil*. They prefer their darkness to his light. The literal truth here is that those who sin, love to sin, and will not suffer the light of Jesus Christ, which is a light of truth that discovers even the smallest mistake.

> "For all who do evil hate the light and do not come to the light, so that their deeds may not be exposed. 21 But those who do what is true come to the light, so that it may be clearly seen that their deeds have been done in God." (John 3:20–21)

All that we do by ourselves is darkness and sin. We can do no other thing but sin. If we say we can do good by ourselves, we are liars. Those who are lovers of their own works, which are the works of sin, *hate the light* and love the darkness, and *do not come to the light* so their deeds may be hidden and not exposed. But those who do *what is true* by being led by Jesus Christ, who is the truth, and moved by his Spirit, which is the Spirit of truth, *come to the light*. They voluntarily expose their deeds to both human beings and to the light of God. They do not fear their deeds becoming known because they confess their sins openly and testify to the goodness of God, giving God all the glory that he is due. They are even glad that their works are known because they do not take any credit. Their *deeds have been done in God*. Only God can do divine works, without which nothing is done. The Word does everything in God.

> After this Jesus and his disciples went into the Judean countryside, and he spent some time there with them and baptized. 23 John also was baptizing at Aenon near Salim because water was abundant there; and people kept coming and were being baptized. (John 3:22–23)

The baptism of Jesus Christ was infinitely more elevated and efficacious than that of John, it would appear, because John had to stop baptizing as soon as Jesus began baptizing. As John sent his disciples to Jesus Christ, it would seem that he sent them to be baptized. Scripture seems to say that John baptized more people in the world than Jesus Christ. All this must be so and is very mysterious.

First, most of those who went to Jesus Christ for baptism had already been baptized by John the Baptist. No one is exempt from repentance except those who have not sinned. They must pass first repent before going to Jesus Christ.

Repentance is where to start. This happens when we leave evil and embrace good, and so we to turn to approach God. Yet special disciplines which are holy and assist salvation are not themselves repentance. They help in separating us from the creature and attaching us to God by a strength of will, supported by the grace that God gives to all of those who ask. No one can go to Jesus Christ without passing through penance. There are many people who go to John the Baptist to receive his baptism, but only a few go to Jesus Christ who alone can support and confirm the baptism of John.

> John, of course, had not yet been thrown into prison. (John 3:24)

Penance has power only for a time, after which it becomes captive, being able to operate nothing more in the soul. This is why scripture says that John only baptized because *he had not yet been thrown into prison*. Penance only serves to drive the soul to Jesus Christ by causing an interior return. This does not happen through austerities. When the soul is led to Jesus Christ, she turns toward him and no longer needs penance which now captive no longer has power to act on the soul.

It is good to explain here about the austerities that are normally called *penances*. I am persuaded that the austerities are necessary at the beginning. The strongest souls the Lord makes are interior souls but these austerities do not help them. The souls must be occupied with God and apply themselves to God in their interior. At the right time, God will take away the austerities because the senses are already mortified.

God subdues her passions and purifies her powers in her and through her; austerities might hurt this. God also takes away the soul's attachment to self-ownership and propriety. We are most unfortunate if we corrupt these holy operations of God. We need to leave behind these austerities or we will not advance. Sometimes when we least expect this, God takes them out of penance and puts them in a state of life which is experienced as perfection.

> Now a discussion about purification arose between John's disciples and a Jew. 26 They came to John and said to him, "Rabbi, the one who was with you across the Jordan, to whom you testified, here he is baptizing, and all are going to him." (John 3:25–26)

John *testifies* himself to Jesus Christ and his testimony is true. If we esteem John, we believe him. Whoever has found Jesus Christ cannot taste anything other than him. Everything else is insipid and even, I dare say, unbearable. The people see that Jesus Christ gives the Spirit, yet if they stop at superficial understandings, they struggle and oppose him. The disciples of John, those attached to exterior penance, are having difficulty entering into the state of Jesus Christ, who is interior penance and profound purification. They oppose him sometimes. But what does John say when asked about his testimony?

> John answered, "No one can receive anything except what has been given from heaven. 28 You yourselves are my witnesses that I said, 'I am not the Messiah, but I have been sent ahead of him.'" (John 3:27–28)

No one can receive anything except what has been given from heaven which means given through Jesus Christ. Everything comes from Jesus Christ and placed in the foundation of the soul. And all the rest is only the bark and not essence. This is why John adds, *You yourselves are my witnesses that I said, 'I am not the Messiah*. John the Baptist means that he cannot communicate the Spirit.

> "He who has the bride is the bridegroom. The friend of the bridegroom, who stands and hears him, rejoices greatly at the bridegroom's voice. For this reason my joy has been fulfilled." (John 3:29)

John shows us that the *bridegroom possesses the soul*. God alone may possess the soul so he is the bridegroom. To God we must go and he guides our soul. Those who are *friends of the* heavenly *bridegroom* may themselves not possess the soul but rejoice at the bridegroom's possession. They participate in the *joy* of the bridegroom and the happiness of the possessed soul.

John *stands and hears the bridegroom's voice* and is ready to accomplish his will. He does not usurp the rights of the bridegroom. If he had some special rights, he would give them to the bridegroom. O true qualities of a worthy Pastor! He guides all souls to the bridegroom and shows them how to please the bridegroom and to be united to him. He listens himself to the voice of the bridegroom, in order to know the bridegroom's will for souls. He stands to signify that he is ready to fulfill the bridegroom's wishes and to let him have all possession of the bride. John is ready to abandon everything to the bridegroom. He is full of joy when he hears the bridegroom's voice speaking to him. O this is justice that the bridegroom has the bride! The friend of the bridegroom makes souls tender to union with him and shows them the shortest way to union. O what joy John the Baptist had when he saw that the bridegroom will unite with souls!

The church also will be the spouse of the bridegroom and unite with him. The church will only find contentment with this union. Through his blood, the church will find freedom after having committed her first liberty to the demon, the enemy of God. O the goodness of the bridegroom! O the ingratitude of the soul! O divine Savior, you receive glory in your union with our souls!

"He must increase, but I must decrease." (John 3:30)

John speaks here as the figure for penance, as the forerunner of Jesus Christ and as the last patriarch who terminates and finishes the ancient law. John the Baptist's light shone like stars in the sky, telling people that the true light of Jesus Christ was coming. The closer the soul grows to God, the more her ways are transformed and changed.

As the precursor to prepare the place for Jesus Christ, John the Baptist must relinquish his place as Jesus Christ approaches. This is also the way that the true pastor must lead. As God takes hold and governs the soul, he must concede his place to God.

The last patriarch, John, finishes the ancient law. As the church grows and increases, the synagogue must concede to the reality of the church.

> He who comes from above is above all; he who is of the earth is earthly and speaks of the earth. He who comes from heaven is above all. (John 3:31)

These words have a very great meaning. John gives a convincing reason why pastors lead souls to Jesus Christ and leave them there. That means that *who comes from above*, that is to say the supreme part of the soul, which is also the center, will possess all that is *of the earth*. This shows the soul what is required of her so that God is pleased. God makes paths of pure love on which to lead the soul. He gives to the soul all that she lacks and gives her everything she needs. To do this, the soul must concede her own place so that God can reign as sovereign. *He who is of the earth is earthly and speaks of the earth*. Everything that comes from us is earthly and unclean. Our words and actions come out of our interior state. If we are still self-involved and Adam lives within us, our words and actions will be motivated by nature as their principle. But if Jesus Christ takes Adam's place, God pours grace into our nature by his pure movements. Then our actions and works will be pure and holy, participating in the principle of Jesus Christ. We remain in Jesus Christ because *he who comes from heaven is above all* leads us and his Spirit is preferred above everything. Everything must be given to him.

> He testifies to what he has seen and heard, yet no one accepts his testimony. (John 3:32)

Jesus Christ himself *testifies* to the soul and saves the soul, according to the will of his Father. He impresses on the soul the reality of pure love which shows us his character and shares with us his knowledge of what he has *seen and heard*. He knows all the will of his Father, as well as the desires and inclinations of the creatures. However, far from receiving the testimony that Jesus Christ gives by his example, words, and inspiration, we reject him. Only Jesus Christ reveals the grandeur of his Father since only he deepened this same grandeur. However, we think that we can know God through our own efforts. We fool ourselves with this. All knowledge of God is only given through Jesus Christ. All other are false testimonies. No one knows the Father except the Son. No one will know the Father except by the Son who imprints the image of his Father on us. If Jesus Christ gives this, we have real knowledge. This is knowledge that he wants to give, yet *no one accepts his testimony* because he destroys the life of Adam within us that maintains the inauthentic life.

> He who receives his testimony sets his seal to this, that God is true. (John 3:33)

Jesus Christ expresses his *testimony* both in the Word of his gospel and in his person. Jesus Christ did what he said or testified. To receive the testimony of Jesus Christ, we must practice his teachings and his example. He makes yet another testimony in the expression of himself in the foundation of the heart of the person who *receives it*. He imprints in the heart who he is and this imprinting spreads into the person's external actions, giving the grace to do what he did. So, the *testimony* is a *seal* because the testimony is Jesus Christ himself. That seal is *on the heart and on the arm*, as the bridegroom says to the bride (Song of Songs 8:6). On the heart, so that everything is consecrated to God, so that he may not depart. On the arm, so that all of our actions be for his glory.

This double *testimony* and *seal assure us that God is true* because he who confesses the truth of God within welcomes the sovereign being of God within. His self-ownership now leaves. He confesses this truth in his heart by the experience he has of God in himself and in the foundation of his soul. He also witnesses to this in his actions and by his dependence on the will of God and by the exactitude by which he practices what he confesses. This makes everyone see the advantage of his confession.

No one may know the truth of God unless he receives the testimony of Jesus Christ. No one may receive this testimony unless he gives himself to God's will, the observance of his laws, and abandons himself to the movement of his Spirit.

> He whom God has sent speaks the words of God, for he gives the Spirit without measure. (John 3:34)

Jesus Christ is *he whom God has sent* to earth to save human beings and to testify to the truth of God. He was able to testify because all truth is within him, as he assures us that he is the truth. This truth did not come to remain hidden but to be manifested. Only the Word can manifest Truth. The Word of God came to be *announced*. This truth is the same *Spirit* of truth that is in Jesus Christ for *he gives the Spirit without measure* within his people. In the fullness of God is an infinite truth which he kindly gives us proportioned to our weakness.

According to the testimony of John, Jesus Christ brings the fullness of *grace and truth* to human beings (John 1:17). But human beings will only have this plenitude if they let this Spirit flow in them. They must banish error and the lies inspired by the same demon who inspired

Adam. In his beautiful day of truth, Jesus Christ dissipates our lies hidden in darkness and shadows.

> The Father loves the Son and has placed all things in his hands. (John 3:35)

These two ideas include all the spiritual life: *The Father loves the Son* and is uniquely pleased with him. God can only be pleased with people through Jesus Christ. This is why proprietary people are the object of God's charity. Everything was created through the Word and without him nothing was made. God the Father can only love his Word and image in people. The more that we represent this beautiful image and the more we give place to the Spirit of the Word flowing within us, the more we please God the Father. He can only be pleased by people who bear the image of his Word and his Spirit.

God loves people so much that he gave his only Son to the power of death for human beings. He sees in all human beings the remains of the image of his Son and though the image is almost obliterated, this does not fail to attract the love of the Father. He sent his Son to recreate the image in human beings so the Father sees in the human being the image of his Word and loves them. The Father's wrath against human beings is entirely appeased because Jesus Christ is entirely exposed to the eyes of God the Father. This has disarmed God's wrath and illuminated his charity in favor of human beings.

The death of his Son reestablished the image of God. Humanity had erased the image of God in order to procure a strange and blunted life, opposed to the life of the Word. The divine Savior wanted to die in order to destroy by his death this miserable life. As we keep in view God's superabundant love, we let God destroy this miserable life so that we have a place for the premier life of the Son of God. He died to communicate new and abundant life to us, as he himself said, *I came that they may have life, and have it abundantly* (John 10:10).

This abundant life of Jesus Christ retraces in us in a perfect way the image of God. The abundance of this life and the perfection of this image attracts the Love of God the Father to the human being in a wonderful way.

The second thing comprised in this verse, is that God *has placed all things in his hands* of his Son, giving him all power on heaven and earth. He has assured us of this, *All authority in heaven and on earth has been given to me* (Matthew 28:18). God the Father wants his Son to exercise his power for us and to lead us according to his will and that human beings obey him. Many do not want to do this.

We must abandon ourselves to the way of the Word, to remain in his power, to remain entirely with the master, giving him all the rights that we claim for ourselves. These are the rights that God has given to Jesus Christ for humanity. He can only love them as much as they allow him to use these same rights. Only through giving Jesus Christ our rights will he remake us in his image. Jesus Christ uses his power in our interior. In this way, we give Jesus Christ full power to act and stop our self-directed action which usurps his rightful place. We submit to his power and abandon to his way.

We live in death so that he can communicate his life. We rest immobile and without self-directed action so that he can retrace his image in us. We are dead inside for any self-action, but vigorous externally to act in dependence on the will of God. When we live for self, we prevent Jesus Christ from having his rights. This is why it is absolutely necessary that we renounce ourselves and our own operations to follow him.

> Whoever believes in the Son has eternal life; whoever disobeys the Son will not see life, but must endure God's wrath. (John 3:36)

This passage confirms admirably all that has been said. *Whoever believes in the Son* gives a place to the Spirit to act in the interior and who embraces in his exterior the purest maxims, that is to say *eternal life*. This eternal life is no other than the life of the Word, which is communicated to those who believe. Jesus Christ says this in the present tense, *Whoever believes in the Son has eternal life*, that is to say, the moment that he believes in the Son, he receives the power to exercise his mission. From this moment he has life and eternal life through the communication of the life of the Word. This *life* of the Word flows within the soul as life eternal, exempting and delivering from eternal death of sin. Oh, the state of faith and abandon! This is the true good that is preferred to all others. Scripture does not say that he who believes and trusts in his own works but he who believes in the Son has eternal life and trusts in him.

Whoever does not believe in the beloved Son and who does not believe his testimony when he says that all power has been given to him, and who will not let him exercise his power, usurps the Son's rights. He is a liar who will not see life, because he will not abandon his conduct to the Son and also opposes others doing this also. He will have neither knowledge nor experience of eternal life. He does not discover the Son's goodness or the beauty, because he will never receive this. Because of this, *the wrath of God endures*. God can only live in the human being in what there is of his Son. But to the contrary, all the traits of the Son are erased in the human being due to his fault. He would not let himself be repaired by the divine Word. God no longer sees what will attract his love and pleasure, so the human being is deprived of this by his fault. Indubitably *his wrath* and his indignation *remain on him* where the Spirit and Word should be. Those who are not penetrated by the love of the Son necessarily experience God's wrath.

To have the charity and love of God living within us, as Jesus Christ himself says, *Those who love me will keep my word, and my Father will love them, and we will come to them and make our home with them*. To do Jesus' will is to allow oneself to be led, taught, and animated by Jesus Christ. Whoever does not do this, does not do his will. If we do not do his will, God does not live within him and he does not have life. Instead of the love and pleasure of God, his share is God's wrath.

> Now when Jesus learned that the Pharisees had heard, "Jesus is making and baptizing more disciples than John" 2 —although it was not Jesus himself but his disciples who baptized— 3 he left Judea and started back to Galilee. (John 4:1–30)

Some people will always disapprove of Jesus Christ. It suffices to announce his power and reign to be facing disapproval and contradiction. The Pharisees who are attached to the exterior and superficial bark of matter maligned the testimony of Jesus Christ in favor of John. They could not suffer the progress Jesus Christ made by having more followers than John. This is why John said, *He must increase, but I must decrease*.

Many people give themselves to Jesus Christ because of his sweetness. This is what attracted the envy *of the Pharisees*, although Jesus Christ does not make these conquests immediately by himself, but through the way of his *disciples*. Then Jesus Christ withdrew from them. He withdraws from people who place obstacles in the way of his kingdom.

> But he had to go through Samaria. 5 So he came to a Samaritan city called Sychar, near the plot of ground that Jacob had given to his son Joseph. (John 4:4–5)

O mystery more wonderful than all other mysteries about the truth of the interior! As soon as Jesus Christ withdrew from the country of the

Pharisees because they were against him, he came *near the plot of ground that Jacob had given to his son Joseph*. If we pay attention to the book of Genesis, we see that Jacob was the father of abandoned souls and that his son Joseph was a child abandoned to providence as seen in the mystical explanation of his life.

So when Jesus Christ was persecuted among people who are attached to scruples of the exterior, but do not give a place to the spirit of Jesus Christ, he withdraws. But where does he go? He goes to the plot of *Jacob*, leader of abandoned souls, and Joseph, who was abandoned to providence for a longtime. After having had an excess of humiliations, Joseph was filled with glory and happiness! Ah! When we are abandoned to providence, we pass through similar states! The hand of the Lord is not too short to save and he acts in our favor.

> Jacob's well was there, and Jesus, tired out by his journey, was sitting by the well. It was about noon. (John 4:6)

All these circumstances are ravishing. In the earth of Jacob, the heritage of abandoned souls, there was a well, the source of water discovered by Jacob called *Jacob's well*. Jacob had known the truth of abandonment because he had lived this way. The way of abandonment was his children's inheritance and he had discovered this source. But why did Jesus Christ *sit* here? To show that he was the source of the water in the well and all the graces given to abandoned souls to save them. *Jesus was sitting by the well* to purify the water. We come to Jesus Christ to find the true source of living water and abandon ourselves to him. He confirms and seals us through our abandon and puts us into a new and perfect state, making the ancient law flow continuously into the new, as it is written in St Matthew. Jesus Christ came to consummate, perfect, and perpetuate this abandon. This is why *he was sitting*, practicing what the patriarchs had done, to repose in the living water. Then he perfected and sealed all these states. He himself paid the price for them, and at once surrendered the spring of living water. All the patriarchs had hoped to see this spring on earth, for which they had searched, but which could only be found in Jesus Christ. He substituted himself for the patriarchs, bringing perfection to this state not only for the past but also for the future. His perfection remains in perpetuity.

Jesus Christ *was sitting* there, *tired out by his journey*. And how tired you were, O divine Savior, of the long way you had to go without finding abandoned souls? You were tired of seeing the ingratitude of the people and forced to withdraw. The holy patriarch Jacob intensely desired God because of the promises made to Abraham. Now after so many centuries, his descendants force Jesus to withdraw. This fatigue of Jesus indicates the hardships and pains that he takes to seek sinners. O divine Savior! You tire yourself out looking for sinners after having made the infinite path between God and human beings to descend from heaven to earth to find human beings. But we often prevent sinners from approaching our Savior and we make his approach to them almost inaccessible. O sinners, go to Jesus Christ! As long as you have the sincere will to stop being sinners, he will receive you with pleasure. He has tired himself out looking for you. He wants you to give yourself to him and to search for him. When we search for things with pain, the happier we are to find it. O sinners, seek for your Savior! You will be glad to find him, since he seeks you himself.

> When a Samaritan woman came to draw water, Jesus said to her, "Will you give me a drink?" (John 4:7)

O Love! You knew that this sinner would come to draw from these waters. That is why you were sitting there to have the pleasure of giving this to her. This *woman came to draw water*. This is the first step of conversion and absolutely necessary. She leaves the city of her sin and goes to the well to draw water. Scripture does not say that she drew water but it was not up to her to do this. But that she *came to draw water*, putting herself in that state. Jesus was on the edge of the well because he himself was the source of living water, who would quench her thirst. He did not want her water to come from the earth. *Jesus said to her, Will you give me a drink?* O the designs of love! To encourage this woman to ask him for a drink, he says this first. It is true, O my Savior! You were encouraging the woman to ask for a drink. Yet you asked her because you wanted to give her a drink. And what a drink, O Love! Did you want her to give you this? Alas! Our friendly and fatigued Savior says, "I have searched among the chosen people, among my own dear people, for abandoned souls, but I do not find many who let me have access to their soul. You let me clean your soul so you can pass into me and you serve me food and water. *Give me a drink*, O woman, so that I have the pleasure of quenching my thirst not only among my people, but among strangers. I desire to let everyone participate in this happiness. O woman, I desire to enter into conversations with sinners. I desire to reveal hidden mysteries in the interior. Give me a drink. I satisfy my thirst with you. I am fatigued with searching for souls with whom to commune."

> (His disciples had gone to the city to buy food.) (John 4:8)

This blow, which seemed unexpected, is a blow from the will of God who ordains this. The greatest things happen in a natural manner. Appearing haphazard, these are the true blows of providence. Jesus Christ's *disciples had gone.* Why did they need to go to the city and why did they not remain with him? O Love! You wanted conquest of this soul! You wanted to testify to this poor soul in a discourse about love. This excessive love toward this woman would have scandalized the apostles. They would be incapable of understanding the tenderness of his love and the ineffable communication he has with her. O truly happy woman who listens to the voice of Jesus Christ who shows favor by speaking with her! Jesus Christ grants you the grace of hearing.

> The Samaritan woman said to him, "How is it that you, a Jew, ask a drink of me, a woman of Samaria?" (Jews do not share things in common with Samaritans.) (John 4:9)

This poor Samaritan woman is astonished that she receives so great an extraordinary favor for which she had not hoped or merited. She only admires the goodness and sweetness of his word and the impression of love which he makes on her heart. She feels raised and supported, and she does not know what to say. His arrows have penetrated her heart at the most profound part of the soul. She feels the difference between his words and the words from other human beings whose words make no impression on the heart. She expresses her astonishment and begins to receive a small ray of mystery which she does not understand. So, she says, "*How is it that you, a Jew, ask a drink of me, a woman of Samaria,* for Jews would consider our water corrupt? I have corrupt doctrine and sin. If Jews of a less purity than you have no commerce with the Samaritans, because of the difference in their ceremonies, how would you with your pure character speak with me? I have a different faith than you and my life is not pure." O Woman, you will soon be taken to a different state. However criminal your sins have been, you will soon speak to Jesus Christ about them and they will be entirely forgiven. We hear our Savior's heart for us and he assures us that he is our salvation. When we go astray, he looks for us. His pure Word, so powerful, intimate, and sweet, puts us in a state where we listen for salvation. O who can resist the sweetness and the power of his attraction? All the chains that hold us break and the soul attaches to Jesus Christ through the power of his Word. O hearts who deprive themselves this good by not listening to the Word, are you not guilty, unhappy, and worth of compassion?

> Jesus answered her, "If you knew the gift of God, and who it is that is saying to you, 'Give me a drink,' you would have asked him, and he would have given you living water." (John 4:10)

If you knew, O woman very fortunate to hear this, *the gift of God* and what it holds, you would be astonished. The little I have given you has already raised you up. Ah! I want you to know my gift because this infinite gift communicates to you my Word. O woman, Jesus Christ says, if you knew the gift of God my Father, who gives me as a gift to humanity, you will be placed in a state of joy.

Jesus Christ himself is the source of graces and fullness of life. O woman, if you know this without doubt, you would ask *Give me a drink*. O if you had enough fortune to understand this, he *would have given you living water*. This *living water* is no other than himself. He would have given you participation in his life or rather, he would become your life. The water flows easily in the one who drinks it, like the Word flows easily into the soul who listens. O souls, if you knew the gift of God, the gift of the interior, through which the true Spirit of Jesus Christ is communicated, O! Jesus Christ expresses the desire that you enter into his way. If you ask for his grace, he will give you living water, which is himself. He wants you to be part of his union. You will have a cup of water from the source of life, overflowing with superabundance, into you and others. You alone, divine Savior! Only you can give this living water, yet we do not want to draw it from you. This is the just complaints that Jeremiah expresses: *They have forsaken me, the fountain of living water, and dug out cisterns for themselves, cracked cisterns that can hold no water* (Jeremiah 2:13). This is what is ordinarily done. We leave the source of water, Jesus Christ, and do not let ourselves be possessed by his Spirit to be led, moved, and animated by his life. We amuse ourselves in a thousand ways. All these amusements are without value and fruit, because they are broken and cannot contain the very waters of grace.

> The woman said to him, "Sir, you have no bucket, and the well is deep. Where do you get that living water?" (John 4:11)

She asks this not in defiance, but as a request for instruction and understanding about what she should do. Showing a profound respect for him, she calls him *Sir* which shows her lack of natural aversion frequently known between Jews and Samaritans. She has heard the divine word through Jesus Christ. Oh, if we only put ourselves in the state of speaking and listening to Jesus Christ, we would become attentive! The word *Lord* shows a certain sovereignty that he acquired over her, as if saying, "Lord, I feel myself instructed by you. Lord, I know you have made a conquest of my heart. Lord, I love your authority over me, and I am forever attached to you; you have a right over human hearts and we submit to you with joy. You, Lord, do not make a conquest of the heart through violence, but always with freedom. We do not resist your sweet charms. We follow freely, agreeably, voluntarily and infallibly. Your charms are sovereign that are little known and tasted. O, who would not surrender to you! Who would want to defend herself against you? O Lord! Though I am Samaritan and you are a Jew in appearance, I see how good your reign is, that I am ready to leave all that I am to obey you without reservation. O Lord! You already rule my spirit and heart; send me this *living water*. You desire to possess me and I desire that you do this because there is a great mystery contained in your word. I know it is true, but I cannot understand the meaning because of my ignorance. I see that *you have no bucket, and the well is deep. Where do you get that living water?* I desire this water."

The woman was still taking things materially but she was being raised up and did not know what she was doing. O woman, this water is Jesus Christ. He is the fountain and source of living water. Everything comes from him. Oh, quickly ask him for this water. He desires to give this to you. Do you not see that he presents himself to you? Can you not see that this friendly conqueror has paid the price? He has been wounded by blows and when he is wounded, he says, *You have ravished my heart, my sister, my bride, you have ravished my heart with a glance of your eyes, with one jewel of your necklace* (Song of Songs 4:9). He enflames the heart to whom he gives love and then receives love in return. O love that is always reciprocated, how fortunate you are! O mutual woundedness, what an advantage you give! O inexhaustible source! You are only fully satisfied with your fullness, when the soul is drowned in your overwhelming plenitude! You are like a burning fire near the water. You only illuminate and enhance to bring the soul to drown in you! O inventions of love! O ways so charming!

O ungrateful hearts, you do not get caught because you do not consider the beauty of this love and do not accept the sweetness of these words! You say that grace is not strong enough within you. Grace is always strong and vigorous, and even felt, at least at the beginning, but not always efficacious. Grace can enter your soul only by two doors of seeing and hearing Jesus Christ but you close both of them. Alas! How you would be charmed? What charms that open the hearts of others closes yours. Your eyes are sick and the beautiful sun makes you full of sorrow and does not heal you. You are deaf to his charming voice. David seeing the hardening of people's hearts, which he properly calls idols, did not fail to speak up about these hearts. He said: *They have mouths, but do not speak; eyes, but do not see. They have ears, but do not hear; noses, but do not smell. They have hands, but do not feel; feet, but do not walk* (Psalm 115:5–7). Here is the figure of sinners. God gave them a spirit but they blind themselves with their own light. Not seeing the true light, they do not surrender to God. God gives them a heart to hear and receive his word, but they do not want to taste or hear it. Their heart is only occupied with things of the earth. Full of love for themselves, they have no place for God. They have hands, which is to say, the ways to practice the virtues but they are too occupied with things of the earth. They do not work to acquire heaven. They have feet to walk, that is to say, the way to advance more and more toward God, yet they use their feet only for their desires and affections of their will. Their thoughts are only of their own spirit and to advance toward things of the earth. They take a way entirely contrary to that which they should.

> "Are you greater than our ancestor Jacob, who gave us the well,
> and with his sons and his flocks drank from it?" (John 4:12)

This woman still wants to know the way of our Lord, who is *greater than our ancestor Jacob*. She does not compare Jesus to Jacob making him equal or even less. If she had regarded Jesus Christ as a human being, she would have seen him as less than Jacob. But she wants him to declare to her heart that he more than a human. *Are you greater than our ancestor Jacob, who gave us the well*? O woman, what do you mean by that? The source of the living water, Jesus Christ gives the well and the fountain to all those who want to drink it and share with their children. He nourishes and feeds them with water and bread. He gives waters to both Israelites and Christians in the desert. He drinks these waters and gives this fountain of living water to the Holy Sacrament on the altar where he gives himself as food and drink. He shares his crosses and reproaches with us. He gives a pasture for his flocks. If we understand this *water* as the source of graces, Jesus Christ, the Word of God and the source of *grace and truth*, distributes all of them (John 1:14).

> Jesus said to her, "Everyone who drinks of this water will be thirsty again, 14 but those who drink of the water that I will give them will never be thirsty. The water that I will give will become in them a spring of water gushing up to eternal life." (John 4:13–14)

Jesus Christ explains the difference between the water on earth and the water of grace. All water *changes things*, but the holy water of grace causes a satiation with the full truth. The water of grace brings contentment and satisfaction to the soul at the right time. These waters bring holiness and desire for the source of grace. When the soul drinks these waters, the capacity of the soul is expanded. They clothe us in an abundant grace from the divine source.

In contrast, the waters of the earth do nothing to satisfy our thirst. This is why Jesus Christ says that those who drink this water will thirst again because they are from the earth. Jacob, the father of abandoned souls, communicates the water of grace to his children. The efficacious way of the grace of abandon leads us quickly to the end. Jesus Christ is the way and the end. As the way, he causes our changes but as the source and the end, he causes abundance and plenitude. His water overflows and changes life and brings desire with his plenitude. A person who lives in this water with its superabundance has no more thirst.

Yet this causes problems for some people who pamper themselves with this self-centered abundance and became full of abundance that is not from the source. They experience a certain spiritual drunkenness. They know that there is a more perfect grace which is from the source of God himself. Yet their self-centeredness makes them feel as if they are losing themselves little by little.

To understand, we first know that the loss of all desire comes from the source. The more she approaches the source, the more she loses her desires and she changes. This is difficult to understand. She does not understand why the desires are missing or why the soul is empty. To explain this, we will use the same comparison of water. A person drowns in lots of water. This water suffocates and she will lose her power and gradually will be deprived of life. The abundance of water surmounts life, weakens her, and she dies. It is the same with the divine source. When this comes into the soul, she knows a grand abundance that little by little weakens the soul of her self-centered life, the life of Adam, which subsists in her. Eventually she does not perceive her self-centered plenitude, but she has been emptied of this. She perceives an emptiness and a weakening of all desires. She does not know what to attribute this to. She does not feel the plenitude that causes desire for things. She is like a person who has lost her taste for food. But it is abundance of the divine source that causes this and not a problem. However, she does not understand this.

The abundance of the water of grace changes us. The soul feels then its abundance and faith. This plenitude of God may feel like an emptiness, yet the soul desires this, because this death truly gives life. God only gives death to what truly occupies the place of life. To the extent that this self-life leaves, the abundance of divine life takes its place. This abundance of life chases out propriety and causes its death. The soul does not perceive directly the divine life that makes its self-life die yet perceives the death of its self-life and this is what causes the mischief.

Jesus Christ assures the Samaritan woman that *Those who drink of the water that I will give them will never be thirsty*, because this water is entirely made of the Word. Whoever receives the Spirit of the Word is perfectly ravished, because all the emptiness is filled with the sovereign good. All desire is gone. After having procured a death of self-ownership, then the water *becomes in them a spring of water gushing up to eternal life*.

And how is this done? This soul no longer lives, but Jesus Christ lives within her. After having died to self, and giving this place to the divine, the soul becomes herself a source of life. The soul herself becomes a spring with living water discharged in abundance and rejuvenates in eternal life. She returns to the One and the soul has a plenitude of divine life, a life of immortality. She will never lose this without a terrible infidelity which will not happen. She enters in this moment into life eternal, although it is the beginning of the day and still a mixture of light and darkness. In eternity, though, the light will be like noon. This is why in the Song of Songs, the bridegroom says to his spouse, *Tell me, you whom my soul loves, where you pasture your flock, where you make it lie down at noon* (Song of Songs 1:7). This source of water, like the day, gradually rises in the soul and reflects eternal life upon it, guiding the soul to eternal life or rather giving a plenitude of the Word to her.

> The woman said to him, "Sir, give me this water, so that I may never be thirsty or have to keep coming here to draw water." (John 4:15)

O woman, you are blessed to ask for this water! Jesus speaks to her out of respect, and she reacts in faith, even as he says incredible things. She asks for the water that she *may never be thirsty*. As she says, so I may not *have to keep coming here to draw water*. As if she had said, "Lord begin my conversion, that it may be so perfect that I never draw from terrestrial waters, and that I am never corrupted by the pleasures of the earth. Give me water so abundant, that I do not have the trouble to draw from the water of Jacob, that is to say, that I no longer work by these holy ways." Finally, she says, "That I may never be thirsty for the waters of grace, communicate this plenitude to me abundantly." The Samaritan woman is a spiritually disposed soul, like most of the souls in this Gospel of John who spiritually surrender.

> Jesus said to her, "Go, call your husband, and come back." (John 4:16)

Jesus Christ begins to grant her request by skillfully identifying the source of her corruption which will always harm her unless she detaches from this. He makes her see the necessity of leaving the sin. He puts his finger on the wound with sweetness and goodness, in order to heal her. Oh, the goodness of God to engage with sinners! Oh, real pastors and priests, imitate Jesus Christ. Some are cruel to sinners and engage only to anger more. Yet there is a directness full of sweetness that helps them love. This is the way of Jesus Christ, who loves sinners. He takes precautions to touch their wounds with his sweet medicine and goodness. He only touches them if they agree to sweetly separate from their sins. Then they have more pleasure leaving their sins than committing them. Oh, if fathers of souls do this, they would attract them by sweetness! Then sinners would ruthlessly turn away from sins without returning to them, because the direct involvement is seasoned by sweetness. To engage with sins might feel cruel but Jesus Christ's sweetness heals. The soul, charmed by his sweetness, only wants Jesus Christ.

> The woman answered him, "I have no husband." Jesus said to her, "You are right in saying, 'I have no husband'; 18 for you have had five husbands, and the one you have now is not your husband. What you have said is true!" (John 4:17–18)

With sweetness Jesus heard this woman's confession. The woman only partially confesses when she says, *I have no husband*, but Jesus naturally says the rest. He gives her a warning with complete naturalness and makes her aware that he does not ignore her sins. He tells her with true light her circumstances that she cannot deny. Nothing is hidden from Jesus Christ who reveals here that he is the Messiah. She says, "He is the

Messiah. He told me everything I did." By telling her that she has spoken the truth, he encouraged her to tell the rest.

> The woman said to him, "Sir, I see that you are a prophet. 20 Our ancestors worshiped on this mountain, but you say that the place where people must worship is in Jerusalem." (John 4:19-20)

The woman knows he is a prophet by entering the revelation he gave her. She uses this to educate herself in the necessary things of the world which is *worship* and how to do this. Oh, if we are touched by God, we will be converted and instructed in how to worship. God is worthy that we reserve everything for God. This prayer goes to God only and not to creatures. Oh, if we worship, we pray, and if we pray, then we worship. Perfect prayer is worship. This is the prayer made at the beginning of the world. This is the prayer that the holy kings made in the stable. It is this prayer that the woman desires to learn, prayer that shows her the way.

Prayer is nothing else but a simple, formal, and substantial act that recognizes God as worthy of praise. This is a sovereign honor that knows the ultimacy of God and regards God for God's sake. The believer worships in a profound annihilation before the majesty of God.

We worship in the body by our exterior actions and in our soul by interior faith. The worship of the body is a posture of humility before the majesty of God. The body does nothing but to rest in this state. The soul worships in a state of annihilation before the grandeur of God and remains in a profound abasement before this sovereign Being. The more profound the annihilation, the more perfect is the worship. This woman knew that she was to adore the majesty of God. Everyone who knows there is a God knows to worship God who merits our submission. But most do not know how or where to worship God. The woman wanted to learn this, and we also must be instructed in this. Jesus Christ takes pleasure in teaching the woman and us about this. Listen to his response.

> Jesus said to her, "Woman, believe me, the hour is coming when you will worship the Father neither on this mountain nor in Jerusalem. 22 You worship what you do not know; we worship what we know, for salvation is from the Jews." (John 4:21-22)

Jesus instructs about the place of worship saying, *The hour is coming when you will worship the Father neither on this mountain nor in Jerusalem*. They will not worship in the temple because he will make a new C=hurch and a new way of worship. They will not worship on the *mountain* in a certain place but he will have a *continual worship* in all time within us. The human heart must be in continual worship before the sovereign Being. Instead of a place, the *mountain* signifies an elevated state of being. God does not ask for extraordinary things, but instead asks for our simplicity of heart and spirit.

Then Jesus Christ adds, *You worship what you do not know*. In our ignorance, we love what we do not know. This signifies that knowledge and reason are not necessary for worship. I do not speak here of knowing there is a God and what we owe him, but who he is in himself. We may attempt to reason about God and say that love supposed previous knowledge. Creatures love other creatures out of knowledge, yet loving God is different. God is within us and we do not need to know him distinct from ourselves. Do we know our soul and how it animates our body? We do not know this. We know that we have a soul, yet are ignorant about the rest. In regard to interior life, we understand more through experience than knowledge. Through God's operations in the soul, we experience, taste, and feel God, and through this, know God. But suppose that we think that knowledge is necessary. I say, that if we have the knowledge of God through the light of reason, the less we know him. The more people try to get to God through the light of their knowledge, the blinder they become through their own lights. Their ideas move them away from the one they thought they knew. The means of knowing God in this life, and the knowledge necessary for worship is *annihilation*. God reveals himself to the *little ones*, but no one can know him by himself. If God does not give himself to us, all our efforts are vain and futile.

No one can know God except through Jesus Christ. This is why he adds, speaking of himself, *We worship what we know, for salvation is from the Jews*. We need to go to Jesus Christ, so we may know the Father. We abandon ourselves to his guidance. Only he can reveal the Father. We cannot know God the Father by our own efforts, but we can receive his adorable infusions, which are essential truth. Jesus Christ teaches us the truth, and through this at the same time, we receive salvation.

Jesus Christ teaches how and where we must worship. He shows us the true way to worship, which is why he adds:

> "But the hour is coming, and is now here, when the true worshipers will worship the Father in spirit and truth, for the Father seeks such as these to worship him." (John 4:23)

Jesus Christ assures us that *The hour is coming and is now here.* There is not a word in scripture more useful than this. Certainly, Jesus Christ taught this prayer to the apostles. This was the prayer of the early Christians who were united by heart and soul. The time *is now here*, because Jesus Christ had begun. He had already come in plenitude, or all the earth will enter into a plenitude of the Spirit, as all the earth will one day be connected with the only Pastor. When there will be only one flock, they will be animated by one Spirit, which is the Spirit of the Word. This adorable leader flows continually on his members in the happy times following the time of the Antichrist. In these times the abyss will be closed and the dragon chained. Then there will be no sickness or death because everyone will receive the influences of this adorable leader.

Then in this wonderful order *the true worshipers will worship the Father in spirit and truth* by an annihilation of their own spirit, which happens when they worship continually in their interior, which is the source and principle of exterior worship. Exterior worship should be a realization of the worship of the spirit which should be done in all times and places throughout the world. The sick and those working can worship, even in their sickness and work. We carry within ourselves in all times and places the way of worship and sacrifice, which is within ourselves. The Spirit of God shows us how to worship. Jesus Christ assures us that the *Father seeks* this interior worship. When it comes to worship, exterior worship has no value unless it participates in the interior. It is the same with prayer and sacrifice which we do ourselves. The only sacrifice with merit is that of Jesus Christ who offers himself as the victim and sacrifice. He gives us the benefit of his sacrifice and we enter into the Spirit of his sacrifice.

God desires us to worship in *Spirit*, as well as *truth*. Spirit and truth are connected one to another. We cannot worship in *Spirit* if we do not worship in *truth*. In worship we recognize God's sovereign power. Worship is an annihilation in Spirit and a continual regard for God which does not turn away from God for any other object. This is why the cult of the Holy Virgin and the saints is not called worship, because they are only relative and not God. The worship of God contains reverence for the Virgin and the saints. We worship God alone who alone is the recipient of our worship. While we worship God only, we venerate the Holy Virgin and the saints. Honor and respect for the saints comes from God. The more the saint is annihilated, the more the saint is holy, because as the Holy Virgin said, God regards our lowliness and humility. As the mother of God, Mary had a profound annihilation. Saints are not full of their own spirit, but that of God. When I honor God, I honor the saints who are in God, yet I do not worship the saints.

Christians abuse the adoration of the saints and appear to forget God to attach themselves to the saints. They call for the invocation of the saints, as if they were their savior. The saints did not die for them. Paul says this to the people at Corinth in 1 Corinthians 1:12 *Each of you says, "I belong to Paul," or "I belong to Apollos."* Paul asks them if Paul died for them. Because of their ignorance and lack of understanding, the people fall into disputes. The church should rid itself of these abuses because it gives some people reason to wander away from the faith. I have seen a great number of people in the city turn their backs on the Holy Sacrament and yet pray before a statue of the Holy Virgin. This shameful practice dishonors the Holy Virgin who wants only glory given to God. She can be honored only by those who give the glory to God. This is why the church so divinely explains the worship that is due to God only, and the saints are only relative to the worship of God. This is why if our wandering brothers and sisters have even a little justice, they would see that the pure, clean, and sincere church lives in their hearts and sentiments. The worship of saints is not part of the church and should not be attributed to the church.

There is another difficulty that is good to mention here. We are called to unity and union with God, and God gradually turns our multiplicity into unity over a very long time. During this time, we may notice our powerlessness to think and pray on the saints. This happens, though, because God operates in them and they must leave all for God. God does this for two reasons. Changing our multiplicity into unity, we leave worship of saints behind. First, if God did not draw us out of both good and bad things, we would always remain in multiplicity and weakness. Our souls would not be united to God but remain divided and dispersed in the world. We would never find the divine union. Secondly, the soul should see only God and makes the soul turn away from all objects that turn her away from God. Because of this, she unites with God keeping her gaze on him and never leaving. In this way God gives us pure perfection without any division. Those who have interior rapport with God unite with him. This is *worship in Spirit*, in reunion with the Spirit of God. In this worship, the soul has knowledge of the grandeur of Mary and the mercy of God to the saint, and the holy operation of God within. Ah! If we knew this admirable way to honor saints! We would not have so much trouble leaving certain devotions, when God invites us to leave devotions to the saints and apply it only to him. We see that the saints are more honored by this and how they participate in our unity with God. Only there do we find the saints who participate with God in perfect union. Jesus Christ asks this of his Father, *As you, Father, are in me and I am in you, may they also be in us* which extends from unity with God (John 17:21). God seeks those *who worship him*. Even if they worship only a little, God takes pains to find them.

Worship God in truth is what he wants from us. We enter into his truth which is that he is and that he is everything. He holds everything that is within him. This only happens in annihilation, in which the creature gives everything to him and confesses the truth that all is in God, giving him the homage that he is due, and not taking anything away from him.

We must therefore worship God *in truth* and leave everything to him and take nothing for ourselves, allowing him to work in us. We then work only according to his movement and his will. As David says, he was *nothing before God* and that his substance was annihilated before God (Psalm 38:6). O God! If we are in this state of truth, we are happy! We need to turn to God and accept his perfection.

> "God is spirit, and those who worship him must worship in spirit and truth." (John 4:24)

After Jesus Christ shows the way to worship God, he gives the reason why we must worship this way. He says, *God is spirit*, a pure and penetrating spirit that melts the heart and penetrates what is most hidden. We must worship God according to who he is but we do not need to worship with a particular body posture or in certain words. Whoever says he loves God is worshipping. Some people even say no words yet truly worship. Worship is a recognition and homage of God's sovereignty through annihilation and abasement. To worship in spirit means being occupied with God alone. God melts our hearts, and we let him discover our heart, hiding nothing from him. In prayer we show God our annihilated spirit and give pure homage to his Spirit. We worship God who is Spirit in spirit and in truth.

> The woman said to him, "I know that Messiah is coming" (who is called Christ). "When he comes, he will proclaim all things to us." (John 4:25)

The woman understands the truth that *The Messiah is coming*. She understands that Jesus Christ comes first on the earth and then in the soul. In both of these comings, *He proclaims*. On the earth, he proclaimed through his words and his example. This is why we must follow what he says and imitate what he does. In the soul, *He will proclaim all things to us*. We must listen and understand what he says. A disciple who wants to speak with his Master must give him the time to speak or he will never be instructed. Most Christians never listen to him. They are content to offer some vocal prayers without paying attention to him. They believe that this satisfies everything and that they have worshipped God. However, if Jesus Christ is going to teach us, we must pay attention to his instructions. It says in his Word that God wants, seeks, and desires those who worship God in Spirit. We can only worship him in this way that he desires, by surrendering ourselves to God and remaining silent before his majesty. We notice that simple people who have never been taught by anyone are taught to worship in this way directly by God. Because of this, we are convinced of the truth of this way. All the people that are taught directly by God have no other master than the Holy Spirit and walk in this way. They are distinguished by the cross, extraordinary piety, patience, tranquility, and sweetness. Every soul that is led by the Spirit of God experiences this. Those who do not experience this are souls who are full of self-love, or who do not want to leave, renounce, and submit their spirit and self-ownership to that of God. Or some are addicted to the pleasures of the senses and love the disorder and violence of creatures. But for those who want to submit, their minds are captivated by Jesus and they renounce themselves entirely.

> Jesus said to her, "I am he, the one who is speaking to you."
> (John 4:26)

It is he, the Messiah, who has the right to speak to our heart. Jesus say, "O woman, since you listen to my voice with the ears of your body and your heart, know that *I am he, who speaks to you.*" Only he can speak in this way. When someone speaks and we are touched, we must conclude that God speaks by their mouth. This is why when he sends his prophet he says, *Speak to the heart of Jerusalem* (Isaiah 40:2). It is the mark of a mission and he only delivers the word. God speaks through that person when the word penetrates through the heart. But when the word does not soften the heart, then it is a sign that this is not Jesus Christ who speaks. Though the word may not make conversions in the present, it is always effective in the future. Some have their hearts touched but, after consulting reason and nature, they do not respond. Others are convinced at the very time that he speaks, and they enter into his Word. After this, they leave everything, because they see others are contrary to the Word. This is easily proven in Jesus Christ's parable of the seed. When Jesus Christ's Word falls among the rocks, it does not grow. Instead it dries up right away because there is no foundation and interior. Another time the seed falls among thorns. These are people who let the word into the interior, but because of their external occupations, they erase the interior. The seed that falls into the road is not received because of the unjust commerce with other people. Another seed falls into good earth. We see there, that the word truly has a godly effect in the soul. This is a soul with a foundation and an interior. This delighted and ravished soul bears fruit and is disengaged from things of the world.

> Just then his disciples came. They were astonished that he was speaking with a woman, but no one said, "What do you want?" or, "Why are you speaking with her?" (John 4:27)

Good and simple souls who have little experience are *astonished* and shocked at small things. These souls remain surprised but they suspend their judgment. Advanced people are surprised at nothing because they penetrate to the truth in all things. We can wish that all people behave as did the apostles, who suspend their judgment about what the servants of God do, as opposed to the common order who condemn what they do not understand. They judge everything and judge the best actions as if they were criminal. Two types of people judge in this way. Corrupt people condemn, because they believe all the world is like them. They interpret innocent actions as ones of malice. A second type of people condemn out of a secret pride that makes them condemn others and only approve themselves. They have a limited idea of virtue and everything else seems to them false and frequently as sin. Yet people who are truly of God leave everything as it is and judge nothing.

> Then the woman left her water jar and went back to the city. She said to the people, 29 "Come and see a man who told me everything I have ever done! He cannot be the Messiah, can he?" (John 4:28-29)

This woman became the first missionary. As soon as we know Jesus Christ, and he has spoken and won our heart, we want to let everybody know. How does she let them know? She leaves the water and her water jar to trust in God alone and be filled with the infused water, the living water, that Jesus Christ communicated to her in his words and promises. After she has left her own way, she invites everyone to come participate in such a great good and publicly confesses her faults. She admits that Jesus Christ in a moment *told her everything she had ever done*. She concluded that he was the *Christ* who comes to bring salvation. He only can work such a great salvation in the soul.

> They left the city and were on their way to him. 31 Meanwhile the disciples were urging him, "Rabbi, eat something." 32 But he said to them, "I have food to eat that you do not know about." 33 So the disciples said to one another, "Surely no one has brought him something to eat?" 34 Jesus said to them, "My food is to do the will of him who sent me and to complete his work." (John 4:30–34)

After a word from a simple woman, the Samaritans *left the city and were on their way to find Jesus*. This is faith that answers the vocation. God uses a woman, and indeed a sinful woman, to make her an apostle at the moment of her conversion. If they had reasoned like the others, they would have said, "This is a woman saying this, and a woman who has lived a bad life. We must not believe her." But they say nothing like this because the woman is sent on her mission by Jesus Christ. In speaking she impressed on their hearts the same Jesus Christ, or rather, Jesus Christ uses the words of this woman.

The disciples of Jesus Christ invite him to *eat something*. They did not know he had other food and that even in fasting, he was full. This food was the salvation of these people. But, O Love! These disciples lack understanding. They do not comprehend the healing you give out of your generous charity. They did not know what your food and drink was. O God! Your food was these souls. And how were you nourished on these souls? It was in changing them. Jesus Christ attracts and converts them and does not leave them until they are lost in him. O Love! We are your food, as you are ours! Finally, so that we have no difficulty in passing into you and becoming lost in you, you want to pass into us and nourish ourselves with yourself. O Savior! Your food was to *do the will of your Father* so that human beings are saved. You bring our salvation. This is the *work* of redemption and creation, which is the will of the Father. Jesus Christ desires this with ardor. O souls who are lost and wandering in the ways of injustice, it is up to you to give Jesus Christ this food. He nourishes us with himself, if you want to be nourished, and this food is reciprocated.

> "Do you not say, 'Four months more, then comes the harvest'? But I tell you, look around you, and see how the fields are ripe for harvesting. 36 The reaper is already receiving wages and is gathering fruit for eternal life, so that sower and reaper may rejoice together. 37 For here the saying holds true, 'One sows and another reaps.'" (John 4:35–37)

Jesus Christ speaks here of the people are *ripe for harvesting* and ready to be reaped, because they are ready to be converted and to receive his word. He speaks also of the *fruit* that the apostles have in their work. Jesus Christ came to sow and reap. This is why he said, *One sows and another reaps* for he thought then of the salvation he sows for all humanity by the effusion of his blood and that his apostles would reap.

> "I sent you to reap that for which you did not labor. Others have labored, and you have entered into their labor." (John 4:38)

Here Jesus Christ confirms what he has said and makes them see that they are already reaping what has been sown either by himself or the Prophets. Conversions are very easy in souls that are already prepared. God almost always works in this way. Many souls are converted by the ministry of the word yet do not advance for lack of help. Then God sends a person in the same place who completes what is begun, and who enter into souls in a way most perfect. This is then very easy.

> Many Samaritans from that city believed in him because of the woman's testimony, "He told me everything I have ever done." (John 4:39)

Many well-disposed people believe in the word that is announced by this simple *woman* because they have been prepared. God has often used women, and even women who are sinners, to show his truth. He used Mary Magdalen to announce to the apostles his resurrection. She served as an apostle and as a wise director to guide souls to Jesus Christ.

> So when the Samaritans came to him, they asked him to stay with them; and he stayed there two days. 41 And many more believed because of his word. 42 They said to the woman, "It is no longer because of what you said that we believe, for we have heard for ourselves, and we know that this is truly the Savior of the world." (John 4:40–42)

Everything we learn about the interior, and all that we may say, never equals the actual experience of it. A person who listens to God speaking within her, learns more by the words God speaks, than through all the words of the preachers. Those who have experienced the sweetness of the presence of God within themselves, cannot but help but say that what they taste or experience goes beyond all they can say. O you, who always doubt what we tell you about the ways of God, who believe that this is formed by imagination, work to have this happy experience. You will be charmed by the advantage that you have. You will say then that experience is the test and proof of this.

> Once more he visited Cana in Galilee, where he had turned the water into wine. And there was a certain royal official whose son lay sick at Capernaum. 47 When this man heard that Jesus had arrived in Galilee from Judea, he went to him and begged him to come and heal his son, who was close to death. 48 "Unless you people see signs and wonders," Jesus told him, "you will never believe." (John 4:46–48)

Nothing is so opposed to the faith as the constant desire for assurance. Many people behave in this way. Although their path is good, their way is not pure or pleasing to God. God makes some wonders in their favor, but they have trouble receiving them because of their weakness. Some people with elevated social status or birth follow only outward signs and have trouble following the obscurity of faith.

> The official said to him, "Sir, come down before my little boy dies." 50 Jesus said to him, "Go; your son will live." The man believed the word that Jesus spoke to him and started on his way. 51 As he was going down, his slaves met him and told him that his child was alive. 52 So he asked them the hour when he began to recover, and they said to him, "Yesterday at one in the afternoon the fever left him." 53 The father realized that this was the hour when Jesus had said to him, "Your son will live." So he himself believed, along with his whole household. (John 4:49–53)

The words of this royal official *Sir, come down before my little boy dies* show both faith and lack of faith. He had faith enough to believe that Jesus Christ could heal his son, yet he did not believe that Jesus Christ could revive his son if he were dead. There are many people with such faith to deal with their defects or seek very limited perfection. They do not believe they can have a strong faith, so they ask for only ordinary grace and not extraordinary grace. There are sinners who believe that God pardons only minor sins. They do not believe that God pardons sins, such as Cain's sin in murdering Abel. *My iniquity is too great to be forgiven.* (Genesis 4:13). As soon as they enter into trouble, they despair or go into wildness and libertinage. Because the goodness of God is infinite and larger than our weakness, we must not put limits to our confidence in God. When we have a sincere desire to be converted to God, no matter what sins we have committed, God's goodness is more powerful than those sins. The same truth holds us in our desire for perfection. We must always strive for more perfection, hoping that God will give us the necessary grace for this. We do not need to look at ourselves and our weakness, because we do not rely on ourselves. We know we are foolish. Instead, we rely on God's goodness and his sovereign power. When we look for perfection, we are not looking at extraordinary things, for this is pride. There is a difference between the grand and the perfect. Being grand is an extraordinary favor, like visions, revelations, exaltations, ravishments; these are extraordinary and eminent graces. They are grand but they are not the perfect which is to tend to death and annihilation. Perfection is to let God be everything and to let everything be taken away, if we have anything. We then enter into smallness, abjection, and let everything go into the hands of God. We abandon ourselves to him without reservation and allow our own lights and inclinations to be taken away. We let God's will be substituted instead of our own will.

The son of the *royal official* was healed. God sometimes grants miracles to those of a beginning faith because this fortifies their faith. To show this, the Gospel adds, *He himself believed, along with his whole household.*

> After this there was a festival of the Jews, and Jesus went up to Jerusalem. 2 Now in Jerusalem by the Sheep Gate there is a pool, called in Hebrew Beth-zatha, which has five porticoes. (John 5:1–2)

This figure of a pool shows well both repentance and the interior state. For repentance, it shows a pool that heals all the maladies that sin has caused in the soul. There are *five doors*, that is to say, five entries or different ways to convert. The pool is also the figure for the interior life, the place where we find healing for all kinds of sickness. It is the pool for washing in purification and the healing for all those who abandon themselves to their Shepherd and follow his way like sheep. There are *five doors* which are five ways of being introduced into the pool. Those who want absolute healing must not be willing to stay in the rooms but must go into the pool. The *five doors* which are ways to be introduced are reading, meditation, affection, actions, and general external practices. All these ways are good ways through which we approach the pool, but they are not the pool. If we have a good disposition hoping for an entire and perfect healing, we will still not be healed unless we get into the pool.

> In these lay many invalids—blind, lame, and paralyzed waiting for the stirring of the water; 4 for an angel of the Lord went down at certain seasons into the pool, and stirred up the water; whoever stepped in first after the stirring of the water was made well from whatever disease that person had. (John 5:3-4)

The stirring of the water is done in two times. First, when it pleases God to move the foundation of the sinner's soul to bring him to repentance. This is the *first* movement of the heart which *infallibly heals* and converts. But if the person lets this movement pass, there will only be an appearance of conversion and not a real one. When this happens, these souls desire to be converted, but in their sickness, they hardly make any effort. They wait for the movement of the water or for some help. They do, though, have an advantage over other sinners, which is even though they are sick, they are in a position to be cured.

The other movement in the water in an interior soul can only happen in the repose of contemplation and in sweet tranquility, and who believes that everything is consumed in her by the great calm that she experiences. All of a sudden, the Angel of the Lord comes to disturb this calm and peaceful foundation. We feel then that everything that seems to be extinguished, awakens. The strong agitation becomes all the stronger because the tranquility was profound. It is then a strong grief to the soul and almost insupportable. Those who have not tasted this peace have an appalling pain with disorder. They live in trouble which finally hardens their heart. But some after a long and profound peace experience this strange agitation, O, this is more unbearable to them than death. If they are faithful to throw themselves first into the pool with total abandon, they will be *made well from whatever disease that person* has. But if they do not do this, they will not be healed.

There are some who never abandon themselves and yet try to return to their previous state of peace. This is entirely impossible. The only way to be healed and radically purified is to throw oneself into the pool. They say, "Since this soul is so peaceful and tranquil, what good is it to trouble the water?" Yet she was peaceful because she did not feel her pain and her propriety. She was purified externally, but the calm was only on the surface while evil was in the foundation. Because of this, the Angel troubles the water and the soul must throw herself into the water. If the disorder returns and the evils are not healed, it is because the abandonment was not complete and total and she only *waited in the hall*. The healing was not perfect because there was not total abandon. Whoever throws himself into the pool with total abandon was completely healed of whatever illness he has.

There was no cure except for those who *stepped in first after the stirring of the water*. We must follow our first instinct and throw ourselves in at the first movement of the water without doubt, hesitation, or fear of drowning because if we wait, we may start reasoning whether we will abandon ourselves or not. If we do not abandon ourselves, we will not find the healing.

> One man was there who had been ill for thirty-eight years.
> (John 5:5)

There are two types of illnesses that are long-term. The first illness happens to sinners who languish with an envy for healing but do not search for a way there. Without help, they remain in their illnesses. Secondly, the other illnesses are when an Angel troubles the water, but far from abandoning herself to God, she seeks all the ways to get out of the illness. Her disobedience intensifies everything, far from helping. She resists the sickness, instead of suffering the sentence. I have known people who remained ten or twenty years in this way and failed to find someone to help throw them into abandonment.

> When Jesus saw him lying there and knew that he had been there a long time, he said to him, "Do you want to be made well?" 7 The sick man answered him, "Sir, I have no one to put me into the pool when the water is stirred up; and while I am making my way, someone else steps down ahead of me." (John 5:6–8)

Jesus Christ addresses the man and asks him, *Do you want to be made well?* First, this shows that consent and will is needed for healing. Secondly, Jesus Christ shows that he himself is the pool that heals of all ills. In whatever situation we are in, if we know how to abandon ourselves to him, he will entirely heal us. The response of the poor, sick man is admirable. He says that he has remained for a long time in this illness, because *no one* has helped *put me into the pool*. Almost all the slowness of the spiritual life comes from the fact that no one is found who knows the way of abandonment and who can throw the soul into the pool. Jesus Christ often pities those who have no one to help them. He puts himself in their way to show them the way, after having received their consent.

Jesus said to him, "Stand up, take your mat and walk." (John 5:8)

Jesus says to him. *Stand up*, which means, "Get out of your painful rest and take a contrary route. The rest has supported you. It is now necessary that you carry your rest with you and support yourself." Sometimes, the soul is supported, sustained, and rested in its repose. Another time, he carries his rest everywhere. She no longer rests in her rest, but she rests in her walk. She bears the same repose that sustained her.

> At once the man was made well, and he took up his mat and began to walk. Now that day was a sabbath. 10 So the Jews said to the man who had been cured, "It is the sabbath; it is not lawful for you to carry your mat." 11 But he answered them, "The man who made me well said to me, 'Take up your mat and walk.'" (John 5:9–11)

We only go into abandonment according to the will of God, who *makes well* from all illnesses. *To take up your mat and walk* is to enter into the freedom of the children of God, where the walk does not interrupt the repose, nor the repose interrupt the walk. We find many people who oppose this last state and say that "You must not leave your rest because it is against the will of God." Yet we must leave the general will of God to enter into the particular will of God. The healing is the sign that he is going the right way into the particular will of God. This is why the man has no other response to those who object against him, except to say, *The man who made me well said to me, "Take up your mat and walk."*

> They asked him, "Who is the man who said to you, 'Take it up and walk'?" 13 Now the man who had been healed did not know who it was, for Jesus had disappeared in the crowd that was there. 14 Later Jesus found him in the temple and said to him, "See, you have been made well! Do not sin anymore, so that nothing worse happens to you." (John 5:12–14)

After Jesus healed him, *he disappeared*. The healed soul was astonished that he disappeared *in the crowd*. His opponents want the man to give a reason for his new state and he has no reason. They ignore that the man is healed, and how this healing was done. Jesus Christ presents himself a second time, telling the man that he is completely healed but that he must be faithful, or the second evil could be *worse* than the first. Evils and infidelities that are committed after receiving the great graces of God are much more dangerous that the crimes of the greatest sinners.

> The man went away and told the Jews that it was Jesus who had made him well. 16 Therefore the Jews started persecuting Jesus, because he was doing such things on the sabbath. (John 5:15–16)

The most holy actions are frequently interpreted as evil. When envy and jealousy intermingle, it closes people's eyes to the grandest divine actions. They then complain about certain formal external actions that are not essential. On the Sabbath, people were to abstain from all servile work and sin, yet with this man's healing, they changed this to include abstaining from all good works. By doing so, they transgress against the Sabbath which should bring glory to God. We also should not do this. When some hear of the repose of God in contemplation, they want to keep it with exactitude and religiously and not interrupt it for anything in the world. Yet, we must leave contemplation for action as soon as God makes his will known about this. Jesus Christ acted on the Sabbath and in the people's eyes, transgressed on the Sabbath. He acted on this day because he was the Son of God. He showed that what was a rest for a human being was an action for him. The more our interior repose, the more God acts in us and for us. The more profound our repose increases the intensity of God's actions within us. This is what made Jesus Christ take pleasure in healing on the Sabbath, to convince us that when we repose in God, it is then that he heals our evils with much care.

> But Jesus answered them, "My Father is still working, and I also am working." (John 5:17)

Jesus Christ speaks here of the exterior and interior actions of the Trinity. God in all his interior operations is always *still working*, since he is constantly producing his Word. His Word acts also continually with him. This mutual action of the Father and the Son produces the Holy Spirit. This continual action of God in himself does not interrupt for a second the rest that he takes in himself. In his exterior operations, he acts continually in favor of human beings, but this action does not interrupt his repose.

Jesus Christ protests that he is *also working* with his Father in favor of human beings. He wants human beings to let him work in them, and he said this in response to the opposition he faced. He does not cease to act and operate in souls, provided they let him do this. When a soul is placed in an apostolic state, she participates in the action of God, so that her repose is not stopped by her action nor her action stopped by her repose.

> For this reason the Jews were seeking all the more to kill him, because he was not only breaking the sabbath, but was also calling God his own Father, thereby making himself equal to God. (John 5:18)

Truth is tolerated or believed by only a few people because they take the declaration of truth for pride or impiety. Jesus Christ declares that he is the *Son of God* and then the demons threaten him. Truths so very pure and sublime as these can only be revealed by truth itself. Jesus Christ declared himself the truth that he was the Son of God. Human salvation depended on this. He did not want the demons, the Father of Lies, to declare that he was the Son of God because people would doubt the truth of this since it was manifested from the Father of Lies. The demon, then, tried to destroy the belief that Jesus Christ was the Son of God. That is why Jesus Christ forbade the demons to say he was the Son of God. Instead, Jesus Christ tells them he is the Son of God.

> Jesus said to them, "Very truly, I tell you, the Son can do nothing on his own, but only what he sees the Father doing; for whatever the Father does, the Son does likewise." (John 5:19)

After Jesus Christ makes it known that he is the Son of the eternal God, and equality reigns between the Father and him, he speaks of the shared actions that he has with the Father. Jesus Christ speaks of himself as both God and man. As God, Jesus Christ does *only what he sees the Father doing* and does *whatever the Father does*. As human being, *the Son can do nothing on his own* but he does everything God does and lets himself be led by God's action. As Word and image of the Father, he perfectly represents all that the Father is does and does everything that he does, and he may do nothing that the Father does not do. What does he see his Father do? He sees that his Father happens entirely in him. The Son does the same and by this action the Father and the Son are reciprocated. The Son is doing only what the Father does, and they produce conjointly the

Holy Spirit. Jesus Christ as God-man still does what he sees his Father doing. And like his Father, he also himself occurs in the Holy Sacrament on the altar. In all the works of the Father, the Son does them with the Father, as has been explained. Everything was made by the Word, and nothing was done without him.

> "The Father loves the Son and shows him all that he himself is doing; and he will show him greater works than these, so that you will be astonished." (John 5:20)

Jesus Christ is speaking here again as man and God. As God, *the Father loves* necessarily his Word, as the Word necessarily loves the Father. This reciprocated love proceeds from God with God's charity, love, and knowledge. All this is one God with one indivisible essence, there is an entire distinction of three persons. The Father necessarily loves his Son and *shows him all that he himself is doing* and all that he is. Everything that happens in the Father, happens in the Son. And as human being, the Son *will show him greater works than these* showing to holy humanity the operations of divinity, which puts all angels and human beings into astonishment and admiration. He also speaks of the considerable miracles that he has done.

> "Indeed, just as the Father raises the dead and gives them life, so also the Son gives life to whomever he wishes." (John 5:21)

Jesus Christ speaks here of the many kinds of resurrections. The first resurrection was in the creation of the world, where God gave life to a dead form. Other resurrections are from sin to grace, from natural death to a new natural life, and the death of Adam to the life in God. But although God the Father operates all these resurrections, they are also operated by the Word. God the Father does this only with the Word, and the Word does it only with the Father. If the Father has a divine authority to do his will without anything resisting him, likewise the Son does his will and *gives life to whom he wishes*, the Son has the same right to communicate the same life he receives from the Father. But to whom does he communicate it? *To whom he wishes*. He does not look at the merits of the creature, but he looks at his goodness and the mercy he wants them to have.

> The Father judges no one but has given all judgment to the Son. (John 5:22)

As soon as the Word became flesh, God gave him the right to judge, because Jesus Christ has satisfied God the Father for the sins of human beings. God the Father is superabundantly satisfied, he no longer has any judgment to make for human beings, because the human beings are in Jesus Christ who paid all their debts. Therefore, Jesus Christ will judge them because he has every right to judge them. He will judge them if they abused the application of his blood to them, or whether they refused to apply his blood to them. For when they offend God, they mainly offend Jesus Christ. They do not only offend him as redeemer, but as judge. However, if this judge is full of mercy for the redemption of souls for whom he gave his blood, he is also full of fury and indignation against souls for their inconceivable malice in refusing and abusing his graces. But for those who are not filled with malice, and have only weakness, they are not to fear or be discouraged. They must trust in their judge who loves them excessively and who has been willing to pay their debts with his blood and life, covering their weakness from the eyes of his Father. Therefore, they can go to him with complete trust. But sinners with complete malice have a reason to fear through their offense to find his rigorous justice. They will see that it is up to them to benefit from such an infinite mercy or to abuse it. In abusing it, they will see with fright that his mercy has changed into indignation. The greatest sins that are committed in the world are the abuse of God's graces. If Jesus Christ has the power to judge, it is only because his Father gave it to him, for the Son has nothing that was not given by the Father.

> "So that all may honor the Son just as they honor the Father. Anyone who does not honor the Son does not honor the Father who sent him." (John 5:23)

God wants all the nations to recognize Jesus Christ as God and *to honor the Son* the same as *they honor the Father*. The Trinity was honored before the incarnation. Jesus Christ speaks here of the truth of his divinity, and those who honor only God without honoring the Son, do *not honor the Father*. God is not able to be honored by those who dishonor the Son and abuse his blood and his merits.

> "Very truly, I tell you, anyone who hears my word and believes him who sent me has eternal life, and does not come under judgment, but has passed from death to life." (John 5:24)

O words very consoling, which alone would suffice to prove the truth of all that has been advanced! Jesus Christ swears that those who *hear his word* in the foundation of the soul, and *believe the truth of Jesus Christ*, his mission, and the truth he came to proclaim, has *eternal life*. This eternal life is the life of the Word that is communicated to those who listen. Those who listen to his Word receive a flow of his life. With the Word's life and animation, the believer *does not come under judgment*. And even more, Jesus Christ does not judge those marked by his seal.

Jesus Christ assures us that those who believe and listen have already passed *from death to life*, have passed from the death of sin to the life of grace and have passed from interior death to interior life with God.

> "Very truly, I tell you, the hour is coming, and is now here, when the dead will hear the voice of the Son of God, and those who hear will live." (John 5:25)

O divine Savior! Uncreated Word, Incarnate Word, Mediating Word, Word which is heard in the heart of human beings! All good depends on hearing the Word, and all evil comes from not hearing. However, many do not listen. Jesus Christ speaks here of two types of *dead* who must *hear his Word*: those dead through sin and those dead in the mystical state. The dead through sin must be placed in a state to listen to the word of God. The ears of sinners must be closed to the voice of enchanters: the demon, the world, and the flesh. If they want to hear the voice of God, they need to listen to his adorable voice which gives life. There are also mystical deaths in which the believer has heard your voice many times, and yet the voice stops in what seems an entire deprivation. But when they are dead in the sepulcher, they *hear the voice* which is adorable in their dark tomb. The voice of the Son of God communicates an entirely divine life. O love of God! O what is it that has come, that the dead listen to you and hear your voice!

> "For just as the Father has life in himself, so he has granted the Son also to have life in himself." (John 5:26)

This passage confirms the others. No one *has life in himself* except God, who gave life to Jesus Christ, man and God, to have life in himself in the hypostatic union. All other beings may only have life as they participate in him. They have no life of their own. All lives emanate and flow from the life of Jesus Christ. The Word *has life in himself*, which he communicates to human beings. He only communicates this life, though, to those who want to receive it. He communicates more or less life, according to the greater or lesser place in the soul into which this life flows. The more emptiness there is, the less obstacle there is for this life to flow into the soul. Therefore, the more we see the necessity of letting Jesus Christ live, act, and operate in us, the more we give up our self-inspired action and let Jesus Christ live in us.

> "And he has given him authority to execute judgment, because he is the Son of Man." (John 5:27)

This passage shows the generous and excessive goodness God has for human beings which makes human beings without excuse and complaint toward him. If God as holy, just, and perfect God judges human beings, the judgment will be rigorous based on who God is. But God has given his rights to judge to Jesus Christ and gives him *authority to execute judgment* because being both Son of Man and human, he bore our weakness and languor. He does not judge us as God, but according to our weaknesses as human being. Because finally he himself had no weakness, but he bears ours and understands this. O judgment very just and sweet brought together in love!

> "Do not be astonished at this; for the hour is coming when all who are in their graves will hear his voice." (John 5:28)

So we cannot doubt the truth of the mystical resurrection, as well as the bodily resurrection at the end of the world, Jesus Christ assures us that the *hour is coming when all who are in their graves will hear the voice of the Son of God*. After having spoken of death, he speaks of another state, which is that of *the grave*, which is a state more desperate because there is more hope for one who is simply dead, rather than one in the grave, reduced to power and annihilated. However, finally there is no reason in either place to the truth of this state, however desperate it appears. Jesus Christ assures us that the *hour is coming when all who are in their graves will hear the voice of the Son of God*.

There are many graves. One is sin, the second of grace, and the third is the natural grave. The voice of the Son of God is heard differently in each type of grave.

There are two types of sinners in graves. One hears the voice of the Son of God and converts. The others do not want to benefit from this. The first hear a voice of pardon and the last a voice of anger. Both are in the grave, which means a long habit of sin. The first convert, while the last ones get worse. Also, our Lord does not say in this place, as he does in other passages speaking of death, that all those who hear his voice have life because many hear but do not receive. If they have new life, they have new sins, because of the abuse they make to the graces of God.

There are two kinds of graves. The first are contained in themselves as a grave where they live separated from the commerce of creatures. There in peace and tranquility they listen for the voice of the Son of God, who attracts, instructs, and separates them from others. This voice animates them, giving them interior life, while also giving them exterior death. The second grave happens in the soul after an interior death or a profound annihilation and a lack of perceived graces from either God or creatures. She only thinks of staying in her grave when she hears the voice of Jesus Christ who gives new life. There are many other states of obscurity which the souls experience as dark dungeons but we are not speaking of them here.

This passage supports well what is said of Jesus Christ in Matthew 4:16 and Isaiah 9:2. *The people who sat in darkness have seen a great light, and for those who sat in the region and shadow of death light has dawned.*

> "And will come out—those who have done good, to the resurrection of life, and those who have done evil, to the resurrection of condemnation." (John 5:29)

This passage explains the natural resurrection, which I forgot to explain in the other verse. So *those who have done good*, according to their state and what God asks of them, are *resurrected to enjoy God* but *those have done evil, are resurrected to condemnation*. This interprets the state of sin. The soul is resurrected for the life of grace if she does the good proposed to her. But she is resurrected for the state of condemnation if she uses grace for a greater vigor for evil.

This passage merits an explanation. When we hear that in the interior the soul must be dead and passive, it is incorrectly believed that the soul may not do good works in this state or do the will of God. To the contrary, the more dead we are in our interior, the more good we do in our external state. It is true also that we do not have the desire for thousands of things that we had formerly wanted. These goods would draw her out of her state and out of the will of God. God takes away the desire for these strange goods, and he lets her do only what he wants her to do. When she is in conformity to God's states, he carries her to do the work.

> "I can do nothing on my own. As I hear, I judge; and my judgment is just, because I seek to do not my own will but the will of him who sent me." (John 5:30)

Jesus Christ is God and as both man and God, he could do nothing on his own and without his Father. He was inseparable from his Father. Even more, everything he has comes from his Father because his origin is in his Father. As a man, he judges according to intelligence given to him from divinity. *My judgment is just*, because in judging he does not look for his own interest, or his own will, but he looks for *the will of him who sent me*. But to do the will of his Father, Jesus Christ has a divine will, which is necessarily the will of his Father. The will of the Father and the Son are the same, which is their love produced in God. Jesus Christ as God has no other will than the Father and as man, he has his will entirely free, and infinitely freer than any other human. However, his will was submitted to the divine will. He only wants what God wants and does this. This is what happens in the Garden of Gethsemane, when he says *Not my will, but your will be done*. We see here the freedom of his will, and yet the necessity of submitting to the Father's will.

Those who claim that an annihilated soul does not have freedom are mistaken. After annihilation, the soul is freer than ever to do what God wants. The soul has given everything to God and little by little conformed to God's will, until God unites with her. O when the soul has no more will, she becomes happily lost in God but this in perfect freedom. Because the soul is advanced, she wants only what God wants. This is a reward from the sacrifice of her own will and not a fault of her own. This is a most abundant liberty to be lost in the will of God called mystical annihilation, a happy necessity where the soul finds the will of God. This is beyond ordinary grace which a person may resist. We may always want or not want the grace of communal order. Separated from the will of God, she remains in an inferior and animal will with an appetite for good or pleasure, and a repugnance for pain. Yet we find that the will of the spirit has more power than the will of animal which must be submitted to the spirit. For the annihilated soul, dead and lost in God, there is no other will than that of God when the transformation is done.

> "If I testify about myself, my testimony is not true. 32 There is another who testifies on my behalf, and I know that his testimony to me is true. 33 You sent messengers to John, and he testified

> to the truth. 34 Not that I accept such human testimony, but I
> say these things so that you may be saved." (John 5:31–34)

Jesus Christ teaches us not to judge him. Because he is God, the testimony that he gives to himself is true, yet to testify to himself was not worthy of him. This is why he adds, *There is another who testifies on my behalf*. He was referring to his Father who called his Son the well-beloved, as well as to John who *testified to the truth* of who Jesus Christ was.

Not that, adds Jesus who was God, *I accept such human testimony* because I know the truth by myself and do not need human testimony. *But I say these things so you may be saved* and believe in me based on faith, since your weakness and blindness lead you not to believe in the works that I do.

> "He was a burning and shining lamp, and you were willing to
> rejoice for a while in his light. 36 But I have a testimony greater
> than John's. The works that the Father has given me to complete,
> the very works that I am doing, testify on my behalf that the
> Father has sent me." (John 5:35–36)

O divine Savior, John was a lamp who illuminated you as holy! This is why he was *burning and shining*, though he was not the source of the flame. Yet as a shining light, he showed the way to the true light, which is you. O God! Humans *rejoiced* in the brilliance of John the Baptist's light. People enjoyed and were raised to his ardor. O Jesus Christ, because John was a small light in comparison to you, he was more accessible to them. But instead of using this light, which only served them as a means of going to you, they stopped at it, amused themselves with it, and recreated themselves in it without passing out of it. They would have always remained there, if God did not through his love and power, stop this light and offered sovereign light. Then they were obliged to go to you and abandon themselves to your way. For this reason John died and had his head cut off when Jesus Christ began to preach and appeared like the light of the full day, compared to the lamp which was used during the night but was useless in the day. This is why the death of John and his eclipse was a *testimony* to Jesus Christ who works in souls, as the day gives clarity and by the testimony given to people who he is. Those who see the day, and do not ignore it, and go on to say it is day, have no trouble announcing, *Day to day pours forth speech* (Psalm 19:2). Also, Jesus Christ says that his works *testify on my behalf that the Father has sent me* and that he draws light from the Father. Spreading this light, Jesus Christ announces in the day the light of his Father and the light of truth gives evidence to him.

> "And the Father who sent me has himself testified on my behalf. You have never heard his voice or seen his form." (John 5:37)

In this verse, Jesus Christ proposes himself as the *voice* and *image* of the Father. The people had desired to see God, to resemble him, and to hear his oracles. As God cannot be represented in images, they had formed God according to their fantasies and had made idols. Jesus Christ, who is the faithful and perfect image of the Father, has come himself to show human beings so they do not make more images of God for themselves to worship. So he came as image. This is why he says, *You have never seen his form* but you yourself have formed his image. But Jesus says, If you desire to see God, look at me, receive me, and worship me. Then you will worship the image of God without idolatry. Until me, you *have not heard* the word of God and neither have you heard God's oracles. The Word of God is not a formed or articulated word. All formed words are sometimes expressions of his will, at times expressed by an angel. But the Word of God himself is substantial and engenders himself externally in the mystery of incarnation. He expresses this substantial Word internally in the foundation and center of the soul.

Jesus Christ says to the people that they have not heard his voice and that he has come so they hear it. O if we are faithful to listen to Jesus Christ, and to consider it often, we will be very happy! Because when he speaks to the soul, he engraves his image on our soul when we consider it. Truly we cannot make an image of God to worship, because there is no form of divinity except Jesus Christ, the image of the Father, who has come to repair in us the image of God. This image has been disfigured within us, so this divine Word became man and took a nature and a form that can be represented. It is a laudable, just, and useful thing to represent him both in the natural and in his mysteries that remind us of the obligations we have to him. When we honor these images and understand them spiritually, we do not worship them. Instead we see the figure shown with the affection of the adorable original. Our wandering brothers have made a very great mistake in wanting to exclude these painting that show our Lord suffering and working for us. Yet they keep the statues and effigies of their fathers and benefactors, and do not allow disrespect to be shown to them. How much more should they show respect to paintings of our divine Savior? They are also wrong to accuse us of worshipping them.

Since it is true that one always passes from the literal object to the meaning it represents, we learn in catechism how to interpret these images. If ignorant people misunderstand these images, we cannot hold the church responsible for this. Through the pictures of the saints, we preserve the history of their lives, and the memory of all they have done and suffered for God, so that we love their example and also do great works. As God lives in them and they participate in his glory, we joyfully honor the figures of those who God honored. We see God in them and them in God but we do not make a cult out of this. The honor we give them returns to God.

Since we are on this subject, we should address an issue solved by more simple people: losing the image of Jesus Christ and the saints, as described by St Angele de Foligny (chapter 26 in new edition, p. 290). They cannot think or remember the image of Jesus Christ because of being absorbed in a general way, that excludes all distinction. God attracts them to union with him and they pass past the image to be united at the sensitive center. There they have a certain facility for union with the saints, to invoke them without an image. In the church we pray an invocation to the saints, but God wants to reduce the soul little by little into unity, simplifying the soul so that God can multiply her, uniting with God only. When the soul is one with God, nothing is distinct with God, but only God himself, with sacred humanity, the Holy Virgin and all the saints in God in an admirable manner and a very real goodness that does not happen when separated, distinct, and perceived. This lostness makes trouble at the beginning, but if the soul is faithful to remain abandoned in all things, the soul finds God in a charming and ravishing manner.

> "And you do not have his word abiding in you, because you do not believe him whom he has sent." (John 5:38)

If we *believe* in Jesus Christ and the operations his Word does in us, and we let him act within us, if we listen attentively to him, *his word abides in us*. The Word of God is no other thing than God himself, the Word always working. The Word always works when the soul remains with him in a permanent way. Before this, the Word comes but does not stay.

Many who hear that God works in the soul are troubled and scandalized by this, believing that this takes away the creatures' correspondence and actions. No, assuredly, this is not how it works. God works and operates in the soul with sovereignty more or less according to the degree of her annihilation. The correspondence between God and the soul grows and changes. In an annihilated soul, God is the only power. At the beginning of the correspondence, the soul is entirely active, impressionable with a very strong operation. As the soul advances, God becomes the master and acts with more strength. The soul corresponds to God in a strong way with tranquility by giving a place for God's operations. God having taken over, the soul does nothing but follow. Because the action of God is infinitely more noble and strong than that of creatures, the person acts with more strength when passive before God than when she acts under her own strength. When she becomes in a state entirely passive, she receives the operations of God. She receives God's communications without any work on her part but not without correspondence with her. When the correspondence between the soul and God becomes more refined, the soul receives God's operations freely and voluntarily. The soul corresponds by not opposing it. Then God creates the interior.

When God works in the soul, he gives goodness to the soul who then applies it to the external world. She does then with faithfulness and perfection. The passive state is in the interior and receives all that God communicates. The soul then acts externally according to the communication received that shows her the will of God. God gives the interior all that he pleases, and the soul freely receives the operations of God. Yet the operations of God are not always sweet and gentle and are frequently painful and distressing. Yet the soul receives even these interior communications with approval and acts on them externally in the will of God with complete dependence on the Spirit. She executes what God commands. A King who commands others as master to do his will does not exclude telling others what their actions should be. The commandment is received passively, but the execution of it is active. She is free, but she does not have a choice or her own will involved with this. Instead, she follows the commandments of the King, which are frequently contrary to her own inclinations.

It should be noted that there will come a time for the soul who has given herself freely and voluntarily to God, that God accepts her liberty and will, which has been given freely. Then the soul becomes without freedom and will. Then God makes the last tests for this soul, which consume her in the crucible of purification. If she needed a will for these things, she would never give it, and she would use her will to resist God. Because her self-will is strengthened, she is placed in a torment that surpasses her natural power. This is an unconceivable thing.

God strengthens her troubles and if they last for a long time, finally the grandeur of these troubles increases, and the strength increases, and it becomes necessary to die. If this was not the case, the soul would never die the mystical death. To the contrary, she would use all her power to conserve her life. We can use some comparisons. For example, a soldier engages freely. But when he is engaged, he is no longer free. If he were free, how many times would he leave despite his commitment, with all that he has to suffer? A person may give himself up to death, yet a natural repugnance to this would stop this. We throw ourselves into the sea with its ruthless element, which we cling to all we can, until the waves become more irritating, and the soul's force ever weaker, we give up, perish, and die. But the mystical death gives the soul an admirable resurrection that morally speaking, the soul has no longer the freedom for evil, she has done all that God wants her to do. This is explained enough to make this intelligible to other places where it is discussed.

> "You search the scriptures because you think that in them you have eternal life; and it is they that testify on my behalf." (John 5:39)

Christ said that he is the Word of God, yet they do not want him to stay with them. This is because they do not believe in him. Ah! If we have a little faith, we give a place to the Word to stay in us, to let the Spirit of the Word dwell in us. He adds, *You search the scriptures, because you think that in them you have eternal life*. But you do not discover my truth in the scriptures and use this truth to go to me, because all the scriptures give a true testimony that I Am and the Father gives me power over souls. However, in place of submitting to me, and receiving the testimony that the scriptures give about me, each one interprets this in their own fashion. Oh, if we have our eyes opened even a little to penetrate the holy scriptures, we could see all this so well without any doubt! But as we are blind, we are in the most profound darkness when the day is the brightest. We do not see the light even in the light. David said to God, *In your light we see light* (Psalm 36:9). See the truth of Jesus Christ in the light of scripture which makes the true experience.

> "Yet you refuse to come to me to have life." (John 5:40)

Jesus Christ is justified in what he says here. We seek life everywhere, except in him. We seek life in death, but we do not seek life in the author of life. We need to *come to him to have life* with eagerness and ardor. Jesus Christ came for us to have life abundant. It is useless that we spend so much effort seeking life outside of God, but we do not go to God and Jesus Christ.

> "I do not accept glory from human beings. But I know that you
> do not have the love of God in you." (John 5:41–42)

Jesus Christ assures us that he does *not accept glory from human beings* since essential glory only comes from the Father. Only through grace do human beings give God glory. But why did Jesus Christ say? *I do not accept glory from human beings. But I know that you do not have the love of God in you.* Oh, the grand sign of the love of God is to work to extend his kingdom and to bring God glory. Those who do not love God, do not know God. Those who glorify God, love God. They let him decide all things. They may be miserable and poor, yet they are delighted to be nothing because this furthers the everything of God.

> "I have come in my Father's name, and you do not accept me;
> if another comes in his own name, you will accept him." (John
> 5:43)

This is what usually happens. When someone comes *in his own name*, which is a sign that he lives fully as a creature in the ways of the world, he is *accepted*, applauded, and approved. But those who *come in the name of God* and have no other desire than to procure glory for God, and to make him known and loved, are *not received*.

> "How can you believe when you accept glory from one another
> and do not seek the glory that comes from the one who alone is
> God?" (John 5:44)

Oh, if we had only a little faith, we would not seek *glory from one another*, which is only dirt! Instead, if we look at God, we work to establish God's Spirit in human beings and use everything for God. We would not look for approval from human beings. Horrible blindness! If we speak of these things, we are received badly. Creatures will not suffer that which destroys him.

> "Do not think that I will accuse you before the Father; your
> accuser is Moses, on whom you have set your hope. 46 If you
> believed Moses, you would believe me, for he wrote about me.
> 47 But if you do not believe what he wrote, how will you believe
> what I say?" (John 5:45–47)

We put our whole trust in things not of God and do not trust God. Some *set their hopes on Moses* as if he had any power in himself instead of trusting God. Moses cannot save us. Those who hope in him attach themselves to the letter of the law and reject the spirit. They do not receive Jesus Christ and what he means. Instead, they call out to creatures for spiritual directors, as if they were God. We must trust in God only.

Some ignorant Catholics trust only in the intervention of the saints and this is spiritual abuse. They place their trust in the saints and not in God. This is absurd. Our prayers to the saints can be compared to temporal power. If I ask a worldly Lord for help, ultimately, I am petitioning the King over the Lord for assistance. If I receive the help I need, I will have the obligation of grace, that does not prevent my heartfelt love and gratitude for the one who made this possible. We think in the same way about the intercession of the saints. If we pray to a saint and believe that they intercede for us before God, we know at the same time that the help only comes from God. Yet sadly, some pray to the saints and believe that the help only comes from them. In the Mass, instead of thinking that the Lamb without stain is sacrificed for them, they think only of the saints and ask for help from them only. This is a spiritual abuse. This dishonors the saints whom they wish to honor. The church needs to correct these faults, though it is difficult to purge these faults.

> After this Jesus went to the other side of the Sea of Galilee, also called the Sea of Tiberias. 2 A large crowd kept following him, because they saw the signs that he was doing for the sick. 3 Jesus went up the mountain and sat down there with his disciples 4 Now the Passover, the festival of the Jews, was near. 5 When he looked up and saw a large crowd coming toward him, Jesus said to Philip, "Where are we to buy bread for these people to eat?" 6 He said this to test him, for he himself knew what he was going to do. (John 6:1–6)

Jesus Christ often tests our faith and trust, though he knows what will happen. All the good he does to creatures is decided because of his goodness. God has calls that are absolute vocations and calls to us, as well as conditional calls. Our doubts and hesitations happen for the most past because we think of God as being in time. This is not true because God is equally present in all time and places without confusion and succession of time. Knowledge accompanies God's predestination and does not diminish any part of the human being's freedom. God knows everything and sees all equally without any difference in time. God sees things as they are, and they are as he sees them because he is able to see them as they are. He knows things as they are and as they will be. For example, we see a dead body but that does not mean that we caused the dead body. We say that God can prevent this, which is true, but he does not have to prevent it. He gives the human being freedom. God can use his authority and does this in whom he pleases. In others, he does not and lets them have their freedom. He gives them sufficient grace to make a good use of their freedom. This grace invites the will to do good and stop evil yet grace does not act violently against their will. God does not use force to constrain the freedom, except where God acts within God. But in the ordinary course of human freedom, and if the human being accepts the grace offered, she has a germ of grace that produces other graces. This first grace attracts others. As soon as in our freedom, we accept and live the grace, we are given more graces, building upon the first. The contrary is also true. If we refuse the first grace, we will also lose other graces. God sees the success of his graces and his goodness is even greater than his gifts. He has the knowledge that human beings abuse his gifts, yet he does not cause this. God gives the grace and we have no excuses if we abuse it. This is why God says, *I call heaven and earth to witness against you today that I have set before you life and death, blessings and curses. Choose life so that you and your descendants may live* (Deuteronomy 30:19). When a person is dying of thirst, we offer him water. If he refuses to drink, then he causes his own death. It would be inexcusable not to offer the water but if he dies, we did not cause it. This is the same with Jesus Christ who came to offer his blood to save us from our sins. This is why he says, *Drink you all of this*. He gives, offers, and commands us to drink, yet not everybody drinks. Jesus Christ has given his life for us but we must choose to participate.

> Philip answered him, "Six months' wages would not buy enough bread for each of them to get a little." 8 One of his disciples, Andrew, Simon Peter's brother, said to him, 9 "There is a boy here who has five barley loaves and two fish. But what are they among so many people?" (John 6:7-9)

In the two response of his disciples, we easily see how little faith they had, though one had more faith than the other. Philip saw the thing as impossible and Andrew had his doubts. They looked at this issue in the human way, though they were persuaded in their foundation of the power of God. Jesus gives a figure of a wonderful distribution of bread that multiplies continually, without his power or goodness being diminished. He always satisfies superabundantly. When Jesus fed the multitude, he also clearly signified the nourishment he gives us in the Eucharist, as the Gospels say. His word causes an immediate nourishment when it is received in the soul. This is so much goodness here that the soul cannot contain all of it.

> Jesus said, "Make the people sit down." Now there was a great deal of grass in the place; so they sat down, about five thousand in all. 11 Then Jesus took the loaves, and when he had given thanks, he distributed them to those who were seated; so also the fish, as much as they wanted. (John 6:10–11)

We need to notice the order that Jesus Christ follows in the distribution of his nourishment. First, *Make the people sit down.* This signifies the repose of contemplation, where the soul receives abundant graces of God. Then *he distributed them to those who were seated* the divine nourishment of both the Eucharist and the immediate Word. In the Eucharist and divine repose, the human is prevented from being a worker of iniquity because God banishes this from his table when he says, *Go away from me, you evildoers* (Matthew 7:23). The first repose and the cessation of evil works, accompanied by the life of charity, suffices for the rigor needed for the reception of the Holy Eucharist. But the interior repose of the soul is the perfect disposition needed for the eating of the adorable bread of the Eucharist. The church does not require this, but she wants all her children to have this. No one can receive the bread of the immediate Word unless it arrives in the repose of the center. This is a word that God makes when the soul is in the repose of contemplation. God acts in her but according to the limitations of the creature. This action requires the repose of interior action without asking for the central repose which happens when the soul falls into nothingness and finds union with God.

Scripture adds, he distributed *the fish, as much as they wanted.* The bread signifies the plentitude of essential grace. The fish signifies the plenitude and satisfaction of delectable things. But besides what grace is in inside her and fills her, she also has sweetness. Grace can be without sweetness, but sweetness cannot be without grace.

> When they were satisfied, he told his disciples, "Gather up the fragments left over, so that nothing may be lost." 13 So they gathered them up, and from the fragments of the five barley

loaves, left by those who had eaten, they filled twelve baskets. (John 6:12–13)

There are many circumstances to notice here. First, Jesus tells his disciples, *Gather up the fragments left over* and there were as many baskets as there are apostles which signifies the power they would have of distributing and multiplying the Eucharistic bread. It says they *filled twelve baskets*. The apostles must be full so they have enough to give and distribute around the world. And to make us see that Jesus Christ offered this as a sign of the power given to the apostles to multiply his body in the Eucharist, it is not said that the apostles gathered the fish, which is the sweetness of grace, but only the bread. It says this because it shows that the apostles were given the power to distribute both the bread of the Eucharist and the bread of the Word.

When the people saw the sign that he had done, they began to say, "This is indeed the prophet who is to come into the world." (John 6:14)

Jesus Christ's extraordinary miracles had helped the people recognize him and sincerely express their faith in God. They truly know him now. His nourishment sustained them by passing into the most intimate part of themselves. Only God can communicate knowledge of himself. All the rest are weak ideas that fade almost as soon as they appear.

When Jesus realized that they were about to come and take him by force to make him king, he withdrew again to the mountain by himself. (John 6:15)

The soul tastes in herself this charming nourishment. Then disgusted by the things of the earth, she desires nothing more than to make Jesus Christ perfectly *king* within herself. This is why after Jesus Christ having commanded us to ask that his kingdom come, commits us to ask for the super-substantial bread. He knows that once we have this nourishment, we may desire *to make him king* to put him in possession of his kingdom in us. Without this, we will always resist. When we have been filled with the good nourishment that he gives, in this moment we choose him as King, and we submit to his sweet kingdom.

But if we only pretend that the goal of Jesus Christ is to reign in us, how does it follow that *the people wanted to make him king*? Oh, this is mysterious! Then the people understand Jesus Christ in the human manner. They want him as an external king but his kingdom is not of this world. He wants to reign in the interior and wants his kingdom to extend in the heart, as well as the body. Almost all Christians are like these people. They want to give God their exterior, but they keep and remove all their interior. This is why Jesus Christ hides himself. Because he wants to possess the foundation and heart, and he gives himself only to those who make him master.

> When evening came, his disciples went down to the sea, 17 got into a boat, and started across the sea to Capernaum. It was now dark, and Jesus had not yet come to them. 18 The sea became rough because a strong wind was blowing. (John 6:16–18)

If Jesus is absent or we want to walk without him, two things happen. First, we walk in the *dark* and the *strong wind blows*. When we walk in the darkness, the beautiful sun is hidden. When he is absent, the night appears. When he withdraws, the shadows take the place of the light. But when he appears on the horizon, the shadows dissipate. It is you, O Love! Who causes the light and the dark! Alas! Why do you do this? Since the one who does not follow you, or from whom you withdraw, enters first into darkness. There are two types of darkness, as there are two types of absences of Jesus Christ. The first absence is the darkness of sin. Sin causes his real absence and distance in the obscurity of death. This darkness of death always deprives of light and never gives it back.

The second absence is one caused in interior souls like the darkness of night and signifies the advance of the sun's return. The darkness cause by the absence of Jesus Christ in interior souls causes night and obscurity, but not a total deprivation because the beautiful sun is always present, though hidden from our eyes. Jesus Christ removes the light from the superficial powers, so it spreads into the center! Then the soul is never brighter in reality, though she seems dark to herself. When we experience this absence, we know there is a real presence. It is he that causes the darkness and not the soul. This experience serves the soul, without harming it, by testing the soul and strengthening the faith.

The absence of Jesus Christ causes the effect of making rough waves and raising a tempest. There would be little to suffer in this last darkness if the sea were calm. We cannot walk in this night because he raises a frightful tempest. The passions awaken and become irritated. So we do what we can and do our best to find calm. But alas! All the efforts of the creature are useless, if Jesus does not appear! If he appears his presence dissipates the darkness and calms the mutinous waves. He is not long in coming, as it is added in scripture.

> When they had rowed about three or four miles, they saw Jesus walking on the sea and coming near the boat, and they were terrified. 20 But he said to them, "It is I; do not be afraid." 21 Then they wanted to take him into the boat, and immediately the boat reached the land toward which they were going. (John 6:19–21)

The soul attempts to advance without success and Jesus Christ pities her and appears. What consolation is this for the soul? She becomes astonished and *terrified*, both at the promptness of the appearance of Jesus Christ and the relief this brings. Secondly, she knows she is powerless in her efforts, yet she fears that this is a deception. This is why Jesus Christ assures the soul and says, *Do not be afraid*. O sweet word, very efficacious word, that puts peace combined with pleasure into the soul when she receives the divine Savior in her entire heart!

This expression that the disciples *wanted to take him into the boat* shows the contentment this brings the soul. They leave their rowing and let him act in all their heart. Also, the scripture adds that as soon as Jesus Christ entered the boat (for the other gospels say that he entered the boat), that *immediately the boat reached the land toward which they were going*. O divine Savior! When you operate in the soul, you guide and take possession of the soul who leaves the work of rowing and promptly advances; now she flies rather than walks. Those who do not believe they can make progress because they are not doing the work of walking or rowing, are very much mistaken. They advance even without work or trouble.

> The next day the crowd that had stayed on the other side of the sea saw that there had been only one boat there. They also saw that Jesus had not got into the boat with his disciples, but that his disciples had gone away alone. 23 Then some boats from Tiberias came near the place where they had eaten the bread after the Lord had given thanks. 24 So when the crowd saw that neither Jesus nor his disciples were there, they themselves got into the boats and went to Capernaum looking for Jesus. 25 When they found him on the other side of the sea, they said to him, "Rabbi, when did you come here?" 26 Jesus answered them, "Very truly, I tell you, you are looking for me, not because you saw signs, but because you ate your fill of the loaves." (John 6:22–26)

There are many different connections in these verses. First, these people are actually *looking for Jesus* when they are lost, which differs from Christians of this century who pass their whole lives distant from Jesus Christ without looking for him. These people in the scriptures use the means that Providence provides for them to find Jesus Christ. They are faithful without neglecting the way, so find him quickly. He was absent from them only to test their faith and love. But if he was hidden, the more he attracts them in a secret and profound way. These are the ways of love. He follows so that he is followed; he hides himself so he will be sought. He is absent so that the desire for his presence is doubled by losing such a great good.

But if the circumstances are remarkable, the response Jesus Christ makes to them is also very remarkable. He says, *"Very truly, I tell you, you are looking for me, not because you saw signs* or other extraordinary things, *but because you ate your fill of the loaves."* Oh, it is true that everyone does not feel and taste this in the foundation. As long as the people experience the mercies of God as superficial, then the effects of his mercies are also superficial. But when the soul tastes the celestial bread, the substantial Word, the divine Word in the profound places of the soul, then she loves God, and she wants to search everywhere for him. She does not want to live a moment separated from him. We need to observe that Jesus said that *they ate their fill*. Notice that the communication had been in the most profound part of the will, that causes a perfect satisfaction. But before the soul experiences such a great good, she cannot find anything on earth that will satisfy her. Another way to search for Jesus Christ with ardor is in the Holy Eucharist which is useful and necessary for the interior and for the advancement of souls. Oh, if we take communion with required dignity, only one communion is needed to make us passionate about Jesus and obliges us to search for him with intensity. Oh, if we knew what interior people taste in communion! Others are deprived through their fault of this great good! Oh my brothers and sisters, whoever you are who will read this, I encourage you to work to become interiors, or you will miss an ineffable happiness.

There are very good interior souls who after having the liveliest feelings of ardor in the Holy Eucharist, but when they are deprived of the feelings, they have incredible pain. The sentiment of love and ardor has been taken away but not the truth of love. God permits this to purify them from amusing themselves with the sweetness of grace, that causes them to turn away from the true faith. In pain, she redoubles her faith.

This is the best state and advances the soul, not through tenderness, but through very useful purgation. In this time, they should take the Eucharist more frequently which will help them.

> "Do not work for the food that perishes, but for the food that endures for eternal life, which the Son of Man will give you. For it is on him that God the Father has set his seal." (John 6:27)

Jesus Christ communicates to us forms of nourishment to us, that we must work to acquire. This is very easy to do, since it is only a matter of receiving food that he promises to give us.

Of the two nourishments, he speaks first of his sacred body that he promises, which is a nourishment *that endures for eternal life*. Following this, he assures us in verse 52 that she who eats the bread lives eternally. Therefore, this bread is his flesh. His promise shows his plan proving that he gives us his adorable flesh for nourishment. He here shows us the connection between *food* and nourishment with the bread that we eat. Jesus Christ blesses us with the actions of graces and distributes them *in his bread*. He promises that his promises are effectual. Jesus Christ puts his consolation and blessing into the bread which changes into his proper flesh. He says that the Son of Man gives you this nourishment. We have been blessed by Jesus Christ himself, multiplied by a great miracle, so that no one would be lost. So, if the promise that Jesus Christ gave only included ordinary bread, he would have promised less than he did here and would not have urged them to work only for the food that gives eternal life. He says *The Father has set his seal* of divinity on Jesus Christ; therefore, his humanity is also sealed and consecrated.

The other way of hearing this passage is in the mystical sense, which is to *work to acquire this substantial nourishment* which means eternal life is communicated to us. This is a communication of the life of the Word, that flows into us when we give the Word a place within us by the loss of ourselves. Then the actions of God are substituted for our own actions, stopping our own actions so that God acts, stopping our being so that God's being is there. Jesus Christ promises to give his substantial life to us mystically. It can only be given to the one who works to acquire this but this requires dying to self so Jesus Christ lives in us. The *Father has set his seal* which is his will that the Son is the life of all people because *In him was life, and the life was the light of all people* (John 1:4).

> Then they said to him, "What must we do to perform the works of God?" (John 6:28)

These poor people did as most people do and believe that they must *perform* and do the works of God. These people think that they must be active and are deceived about this. Instead, God works in them and there are no obstacles to the *work of God*. It is God's work and not ours.

> Jesus answered them, "This is the work of God, that you believe in him whom he has sent." (John 6:29)

This is why Jesus Christ makes this admirable and useful response. *The work of God* is not that we work ourselves but that we *believe in him whom he has sent* for the work. The more we let him do it, the more it will be done. We believe that he can and must do every action; on our part, we abandon ourselves to his action. God only asks that from us.

> So they said to him, "What sign are you going to give us then, so that we may see it and believe you? What work are you performing?" (John 6:30)

All the people in whom Jesus Christ wants to operate see some extraordinary thing that will show and distinguish his operation. As long as Jesus Christ leads by the extraordinary, we allow ourselves to be led. Because the things that surprise, attract us. But when it comes to entering the little path of faith, Oh, we defend ourselves against this. If we do see something extraordinary, we see this way as of God. This is why they say, *What sign* and what testimony do you have that God operates in us? *What work are you performing?* How then do we stop our work to let you work, they say in themselves to Jesus Christ, since we do not see what you do and nothing assures us.

> "Our ancestors ate the manna in the wilderness; as it is written, 'He gave them bread from heaven to eat.'" (John 6:31)

We always resort to what is miraculous and extraordinary to guide our lives. However, all this is nothing compared to the real state of joy in God and not his gifts. The gift of manna was only a figure of the body of Jesus Christ that was to be given as a bread descended from heaven. Likewise, all the extraordinary things of which so many cases are made, the gifts, visions, and revelations are only shadows and figures in comparison with the real rejoicing of God himself, even in the obscurity of faith.

> Then Jesus said to them, "Very truly, I tell you, it was not Moses who gave you the bread from heaven, but it is my Father who gives you the true bread from heaven." (John 6:32)

Jesus Christ is the real and true *bread* that the eternal *Father* gives us. *It was not Moses who gave you the bread from heaven*. All that was done in the ancient law was only the figure of what was to be observed in the new. Manna was the figure for the true bread from heaven, Jesus Christ, who gives the true gift of bread. Jesus Christ assures us: God the Father gives you the true bread from heaven and not Moses.

First, the Father gives the bread, which is truly understood in the Holy Eucharist. Mystically the Father gives us his Spirit and life in his Word; no one can give it except him. Neither the law nor exterior ceremonies may give this but God can. This life of the Word makes an intimate and real union between God and the soul, a wonderful mélange of the espoused soul and her bridegroom. They flow together and are lost in a sacred union and transformation in God, where the life of the Word is communicated.

Secondly, the Holy Eucharist is truly and really the body of Jesus Christ, the true bread from heaven and a gift that the eternal Father made to us by giving us his Son. If the manna given to the Israelites signifies and points to the true bread from heaven, as is said by the words of Jesus Christ, then the real bread is grander and more perfect than the manna. But if the bread of the Holy Eucharist is only bread, as our brethren say, then the manna is greater than the bread from heaven. The manna then becomes the true bread from heaven and the reality on the altar is only a gross figure of it.

> "For the bread of God is that which comes down from heaven and gives life to the world." (John 6:33)

Jesus Christ confirms here what has been said: *the bread of God*. Yes, may there be bread of God! *The bread of God is that which comes down from heaven*. Who came down from heaven? According to the testimony of Jesus Christ, it is not only the Son of Man who came down from heaven. This bread of God also descended from heaven *gives life to the world*. Who gives life and gives it abundantly! It is not only Jesus Christ who descended from heaven. The bread descended from heaven and the bread gives life. Therefore, the bread is Jesus Christ.

> They said to him, "Sir, give us this bread always." (John 6:34)

These people made the request to Jesus Christ because they thought he was talking about a material loaf, as he had distributed and multiplied in the desert. This is why they ask him, *Sir, give us this bread always.* They were like the Samaritan woman who was asking for water.

> Jesus said to them, "I am the bread of life. Whoever comes to me will never be hungry, and whoever believes in me will never be thirsty." (John 6:35)

But finally, that they do not take this for literal bread as distributed in the desert, or the living water of grace that he promised to the Samaritan woman, he explains in terms that they understand that he is speaking about Eucharistic bread. *I am,* he says, myself *the bread of life* who gives life. There is no question that he is not the bread distributed in the desert. The promise I give to you is of another nature. I myself am the bread of life. *Whoever comes to me will never be hungry* because I give full satisfaction. But to show that he speaks of the state of faith that unites the soul to him, he adds, *Whoever believes in me will never be thirsty,* making the difference between the union of spirit and faith, that he promised to the Samaritan under the figure of water and between the Eucharistic bread.

> "But I said to you that you have seen me and yet do not believe." (John 6:36)

Jesus Christ tells them that though they *have seen me* in the flesh, and though he communicates himself to them in the Eucharist in the following centuries, they do *not believe* in him. They have seen his external operations both in his works and in his miracles, yet they do not believe. If the evidence of these works does not create belief in them, how will they enter into the way of nude faith?

> "Everything that the Father gives me will come to me, and anyone who comes to me I will never drive away." (John 6:37)

Jesus Christ assures us that everyone that *the Father gives me will come to me.* The greatest sign of predestination is the knowledge given to come to Jesus Christ who is the way, the truth, and the life. All those who come to Jesus Christ in this special way are predestined and know him. All these souls go to the Father through Jesus Christ. At the same time, Jesus Christ assures them that he *will never drive them away.* Oh, this is so consoling!

But where does it come from, O divine Savior, that many people complain about your rejection? Two types of people feel that they are rejected. First, some people do not look for Jesus Christ where he would be found. That is why they believe themselves rejected. However, we have an infallible oracle that Jesus Christ will never reject those who come to him. Those who come to him will be received. Secondly, some good souls feel rejected but God loves them dearly. He tests their faith and abandon to increase their love which has been weakened by pleasure. Their love increases in deprivation. Jesus Christ does not reject them but, to the contrary, he calls to them.

> "For I have come down from heaven, not to do my own will, but the will of him who sent me. 39 And this is the will of him who sent me, that I should lose nothing of all that he has given me, but raise it up on the last day." (John 6:38–39)

Jesus Christ assures us that he came *down from heaven, not to do my will*, speaking of his human will, *but the will of him who sent me*. This is the one indivisible will, for the Father has no other will than that of the Son, and the Son has no other will than that of the Father. Their will and essence are both indivisible.

The will of God, who gave us his only Son as the price of our ransom, is that we might be saved, and that the Son *should lose nothing of all that he has given me*. After this, how can we not abandon ourselves to him? We hope. Jesus Christ promises us that he *will raise on the last day* all those whom the Father has given him. He speaks here not only of the general resurrection, but again of the mystical resurrection. When everything appears to be lost, then Jesus Christ comes to save, as he himself promises, *For the Son of Man came to seek out and to save the lost* (Luke 19:10). The more complete the death, the more perfect is the resurrection.

> Then the Jews began to complain about him because he said, "I am the bread that came down from heaven." 42 They were saying, "Is not this Jesus, the son of Joseph, whose father and mother we know? How can he now say, 'I have come down from heaven'?" (John 6:41–42)

The Jews only regarded Jesus Christ's common exterior and not who he was. In these murmurs they doubt what Jesus Christ says about himself as the bread that descended from heaven.

The same thing happens today. We look at only the outside of the servants of God and not who they are. Those who are the most advanced in God have the most common exterior. God hides his treasures in an earthen vessel, that is to say, in a common and simple life. Those who do not know this are foolish. God takes pleasure in hiding himself in the soul.

> Jesus answered them, "Do not complain among yourselves. 44 No one can come to me unless drawn by the Father who sent me; and I will raise that person up on the last day." (John 6:43–44)

Jesus Christ attracts others to the spiritual life yet it is impossible to come to Jesus Christ as the way, unless *drawn by the Father*. God himself, our center and our end, draws us continually to him. We need to give a place to this attraction by a sincere and true return and by a strong meditation. Very frequently God attracts us into our depths, but we are in a place contrary to where God wants us to go. Even more, God's attraction is sweet and he does not violate the freedom of human beings. If we oppose this attraction, we will never be able to feel or follow God. The spouse says, *Draw me after you and let us make haste* (Song of Songs 1:3). God draws us by the center and foundation of our heart. We must follow all the powers of his attraction. But to know and discern these attractions, he must live within our heart.

Those who come to Jesus Christ through the way of his attraction, enter into these states. Those who die like him and with him, he invariably *resurrects on the last day* because the day of mystical resurrection is a day that lasts eternally because there are no more days after this. It is the last day because after this the days of our proper life are passed away.

> "It is written in the prophets, 'And they shall all be taught by God.' Everyone who has heard and learned from the Father comes to me." (John 6:45)

To arrive at this state of mystical resurrection, we must belong to God and be *taught by God*. Those who have been taught by God, listen to him and speak. This is why Jesus Christ adds that those who have *heard and learned from the Father* and listen in their foundation *come to him*. God speaks the Word. The person penetrated by God's sweetness will arrive at Jesus Christ and will abandon himself to Jesus Christ without reservation so he may possess him. When we listen to God in prayer, we are shown how to seek the true path which is Jesus Christ himself. Those who know Jesus Christ through the Word of his Father have Jesus Christ imprinted in their soul. This is infinitely better than we could do by all our own reasonings and ideas.

"Not that anyone has seen the Father except the one who is from God; he has seen the Father." (John 6:46)

Jesus Christ shows us that no one can know God *except the one who is from God*. No one can know the Father except the Son who proceeds from him. The Father looks at the Son who continually shows us the Father. So the Son sees and knows the Father, since the Father knows the Son. This knowledge makes a mutual love as grand as the infinite knowledge. It is not the same with us. We are taught not by knowledge but by the Word. The Word is knowledge and word and works in souls with all these effects. This is why we must listen. The soul must be lost in God, so some reflections of the love of God fall on her. All this works in the center of the soul, when the three powers are reduced into unity by the way of pure love.

"Very truly, I tell you, whoever believes has eternal life." (John 6:47)

Jesus Christ teaches us that this life *of faith* supplies knowledge. This is why he says that *whoever believes has eternal life* because pure and nude faith communicates the life of the Word, which is eternal life. O happy faith, infinitely more secure in itself than all knowledge, although a soul frequently has doubts, uncertainty, and fear because of neutrality toward you and ignoring your treasure. They do not know how great you are! Pure and nude faith, so sure and certain in itself, only gives assurance to those who have this.

There are two types of faith. One supports the testimony, while the other is stripped of testimonials. It is difficult to explain this. There is a great difference between the object of faith and the possession of this same faith. For example, the pure and nude faith that I have in God is always certain of God's side. The faith that I have is a mystery always assured in the truth of this mystery. There is no doubt or uncertainty. The characteristic of this faith in regard to its object is to be certain in its truth. It is not the same with the faith that is possessed. I am assured by the certainty of faith that God is all-powerful, and he may do anything he wants and if I abandon myself to him, I will be led according to his will. This faith is very certain in regard to God. However, in the application of my faith to my situation, I am uncertain if it is God who leads me and if I know his will. My doubt and ignorance of all that concerns me is greater, so that I am stripped of all support. I hope against all hope and the more my faith seems to be destroyed in regard to me, because it is destitute of support, the more it is pure and assured for the side of God.

> "I am the bread of life. 49 Your ancestors ate the manna in the wilderness, and they died. 50 This is the bread that comes down from heaven, so that one may eat of it and not die." (John 6:48–50)

Jesus Christ after having spoken of the faith and its certainty, says how it is necessary to believe this great mystery that is revealed. Our errant brothers and sisters misunderstand this mystery by thinking of this as only a figure of speech. Jesus Christ assures us, *I am the bread of life* that communicates life. If he had only spoken of faith, he would have remained with only faith. But to show the relationship between faith in him and the truth of the mystery, he shows two different traits and interrupts his discourse to explain this. Therefore, Jesus Christ is the bread that communicates life. How does he communicate this? By eating. He speaks of a thing that is eaten by the mouth of the body, as manna was. The sacrifices of Jesus Christ were real sacrifices. When Jesus Christ wills to accomplish these sacrifices and gives reality to these things, did he do it in figures of speech, images, or in faith? He did it in reality and in truth. If Jesus Christ is a real sacrifice, I say that he is really given to eat, as the Israelites really ate manna that is not just a figure. If Jesus Christ does not really come in the Eucharist, there is not a real death. If he comes in the Eucharist, there is a real death in the Eucharist. We know this because he has told us that he surrendered himself to death as he really did, and as scripture assures us. He also assures us in explicit terms that he gives himself to us to eat. Therefore, he has done this and scripture testifies this. How can we doubt this? Even more, Jesus Christ says that he is the bread of life that communicates life. If the bread is not Jesus Christ, it is not living but he is dead. If the bread is dead, how can it communicate life? The bread cannot be interpreted as literal nourishment because such a small amount of bread cannot nourish the body. We cannot question that the bread is the living body of Jesus Christ. Therefore, this bread is for the life of the soul and not the body.

The next passage shows that Jesus Christ speaks of the life of the soul when he says, *Your ancestors ate the manna in the wilderness, and they died* by their sins and this manna did not communicate to them a certain principle of life that stopped them from dying. It also did not bring them a germ of immortality. But, he says, "*I am the living bread.* It is

I, I am here with my body, my flesh and my blood that is descended from heaven. It is I myself who is the bread. I am the bread." Not only those who see him have life, but those who eat him. He wants to be eaten so they do not die. O wonderful advantage of the holy communion! What good you produce and what a difference you make for those who commune frequently with those who commune rarely? Jesus Christ is not only to be worshipped, but to be eaten.

> "I am the living bread that came down from heaven. Whoever eats of this bread will live forever; and the bread that I will give for the life of the world is my flesh." (John 6:51a)

Jesus Christ is not content to say only that the bread *comes down from heaven* but says that he is the living bread and he is present. He leaves no doubt about this. Then to provide further clarity, he adds, *I am the living bread*. This is not only a bread that communicates life, but an alive bread that is himself. Was the bread that the ancestors ate in the desert alive? Assuredly not. Therefore, this was not the bread that Jesus Christ promised because the bread that he promised was always living, as Jesus Christ always lives in the Holy Eucharist.

> "Whoever eats of this bread will live forever; and the bread that I will give for the life of the world is my flesh." (John 6:51b)

Could anything be more expressive and could we blindly doubt after this? Does not Jesus Christ seem to have answered in advance all the objections that could be made and all the persecutions that the demon raises against the adorable Sacrament? We either believe that he wanted to fool us, or we recognize the truth of Jesus Christ in the holy Eucharist. If Jesus Christ says that he *will give his flesh* and does not do this, then this is injurious to his goodness. The one who gives his life to save us, would he try to fool us? He tells us, *My flesh will be given for you*. He clearly promised this without any intention to deceive. To say that he could not do this is clearly blasphemy since he is God and all-powerful. To doubt his power is to doubt his divinity. Does he not say that all power on heaven and earth has been given to him? If all power has been given to him, he is able. Not willing to deceive us, he acts in good faith and did this for us. If he gives his own flesh to death, I must conclude that he gives his own flesh to eat. When he says he gives his flesh to eat, this is not a figure of speech.

Finally, so that we have no doubts, we must examine all the places and circumstances of this passage. *Whoever eats of this bread*, he says, *will live forever*. But what bread do you give that will produce such great effects and that you promise us? *The bread that I give is my flesh*, my own flesh, not a borrowed flesh, not just a figure of speech, but really my flesh, the same flesh *that I will give for the life of the world*. So that if I do not give it to eat, then I do not give my flesh for the life of the world. So all hope of salvation is vain. Our errant brothers and sisters cannot say that he gave his flesh only to the apostles, since he promised it to all those for whom he died. He died for us all, so he gives us all his flesh, yet we are the ones who must eat it.

> The Jews then disputed among themselves, saying, "How can this man give us his flesh to eat?" (John 6:52)

Some have problems in believing that Jesus Christ will give his flesh for them to eat, yet his promises about this are clear. The purest maxims of the gospel, the ones most necessary for salvation, support his words. Did Jesus Christ say this with such clarity, repeat it so many times and with such power, so we could doubt it? Any person who reads this, even if not a Christian, would say that if the gospel is true, we are persuaded of the truth of the Eucharist. There is no middle ground here. If we believe the gospel, we must believe that Jesus Christ gives his flesh for us to eat. When Jesus Christ promises his flesh, he promises bread. The flesh has the form, figure, and taste of bread in the holy Eucharist.

> So Jesus said to them, "Very truly, I tell you, unless you eat the flesh of the Son of Man and drink his blood, you have no life in you." (John 6:53)

If Jesus Christ had said that his body was only a figure, when the Jews had raised these difficulties, he would have disillusioned them by saying, "This is only a figure of my body." Or he would have assured them that this eating was done only by faith. If it is only done by faith, then what are we eating? If only by faith, what rapport does the morsel of bread have with the body of the Son of Man, if the Son of Man is not there? But Jesus Christ, far from disillusioning them, swears by this truth. He intensified the meaning by again asserting the truth of his words. *Very truly*, says Jesus Christ, *I tell you, unless you eat the flesh of the Son of Man*, his own flesh, *and drink his blood, you have no life in you*. He means, You will be alive in the natural life, but you will not have life in yourself, because you will be deprived of the author and source of life.

Jesus Christ desires to communicate himself to human being for their salvation. He wanted them to participate perfectly in the Word which became flesh and became God and man. He wanted to make this human-God life for all people for whose favor he had come. This can be done appropriately by eating, otherwise the union is quite superficial. Therefore, Jesus Christ wants to unite with human beings, not only with his character of a human being, but with his quality of both human and God. This plan is worthy of God full of love and goodness. Who can doubt the goodness of God who was delivered to death for us? And if he did not regard it beyond him to die as a criminal on a cross, not only to save human beings, but to testify to his love for them, can we doubt his goodness? The Son of God clearly has a positive plan for us.

> "Those who eat my flesh and drink my blood have eternal life, and I will raise them up on the last day." (John 6:54)

In this passage, Jesus Christ clearly repeats what he has explained before and removes any doubt about this. He tells us of the infinite goodness of God and his power. Therefore, *Those who eat my flesh and drink my blood have eternal life*. We must therefore eat his flesh to have eternal life.

> "For my flesh is true food and my blood is true drink." (John 6:55)

Jesus Christ takes care to establish this truth. After having said that we must eat his flesh and drink his blood to have life, he assures that *his flesh is true food* and *his blood is true drink*. We are witnesses of his truth. We either believe that we eat his flesh or we believe that Jesus Christ is lying. Jesus Christ wants to give us his flesh to eat and his blood to drink so he can give us life.

> "Those who eat my flesh and drink my blood abide in me, and I in them." (John 6:56)

Jesus Christ promises a true union that he makes with the soul who receives him. As the soul remains in him, Jesus Christ changes the soul by her eating of his adorable flesh. The soul *abides in him* and is gradually transformed into him. O happy advantage produced by the reception of the adorable Sacrament! O those that deprive themselves of this are to be pitied because they deprive themselves of a great good!

> "Just as the living Father sent me, and I live because of the Father, so whoever eats me will live because of me." (John 6:57)

Jesus Christ proves this truth about his real presence in the Eucharist by his divinity and his mission on earth. Jesus Christ says, *As the living Father sent me* shows the truth of his mission and he continues, *I live because of the Father* which is the true and certain generation of the Word. *So whoever eats me will live because of me.* The Father gives and communicates his own life to the Word. The Son lives only by his Father and so they have only one life united by an indivisible essence. This life distributed equally between the three persons without difference, however each person has a function their own that makes a real distinction of people without a division of life, having in all a perfect equality. The Word lives with God the Father, who passes entirely into the Word without losing his own personhood. Whoever receives Jesus Christ experiences something similar. Jesus Christ passes into the soul, and truly communicates his life with both his humanity and divinity to him. The soul who receives this life lives with Jesus Christ and because of this, also lives with God the Father. Those who eat the flesh of the Son of God, live by him and with him, as the Son lives with the Father.

> "This is the bread that came down from heaven, not like that which your ancestors ate, and they died. But the one who eats this bread will live forever." (John 6:58)

Jesus Christ confirms the truth of what he has said, although he saw that this was not being received by his people who were now leaving him. Even with this rejection, he continued to say this and now in even stronger terms.

> He said these things while he was teaching in the synagogue at Capernaum. 60 When many of his disciples heard it, they said, "This teaching is difficult; who can accept it?" (John 6:59–60)

Here the disciples show that they have no doubt that Jesus Christ is speaking of his own flesh. Because they understand this as his carnal flesh, this appears *difficult* and strange to them. They are not yet thinking through the mystery of the transubstantiation. Oh, Jesus Christ loves us so much as to give us his living body! His love planned this giving of himself under the appearance of bread.

> But Jesus, being aware that his disciples were complaining about it, said to them, "Does this offend you? 62 Then what if you were to see the Son of Man ascending to where he was before?" (John 6:61–62)

Jesus Christ sees that his disciples are *scandalized* by this truth and confirms here the truth of the ascension and says that they will be scandalized by this wonderful mystery. *What if you were to see the Son of Man ascending to where he was before?* He speaks here of the infamy of his execution, which as it is written, that the Son of Man must suffer and then ascend to his glory. Those who cannot bear the truth of eating of his body, cannot bear the truth of the ignominy of the cross. Those who understand truth through faith recognize easily the passion of Jesus Christ and the truth of the Holy Sacrament. Jesus Christ says that the cross will scandalize the Jews and be a folly to the Gentiles. Here he says the same thing of the Eucharist.

> "It is the spirit that gives life; the flesh is useless. The words that I have spoken to you are spirit and life." (John 6:63)

Jesus Christ addresses the human carnal interpretation when he says *the flesh is useless*. We are not to look at this mystery from the perspective of flesh. This is why he says that the *spirit gives life* and the spirit is in his flesh. We do not eat his mortal flesh but flesh animated by his Spirit which communicates life. The Jews regarded this only as a mortal nourishment. Therefore, he adds, *The words that I have spoken to you are spirit and life*. This means, "If you eat what I give to you, you will receive the Spirit and life, which will be communicated to you, because the Spirit and life are in the bread." This is not material bread but a bread that communicates life.

> "But among you there are some who do not believe." For Jesus knew from the first who were the ones that did not believe, and who was the one that would betray him. (John 6:64)

It takes faith to believe what Jesus Christ had said. He shows them how needed faith is before saying what should be the subject of their faith. After saying this, he reproaches them for their little faith, *There are some who do not believe* this mystery. He still makes them see that they need faith to believe him. If this mystery were not true, and this was only a figure or representation, what was the need to predict this so long ago, to scandalize all the world, and to lose his disciples for a thing of little consequence? Jesus Christ could have said that he wanted to be remembered by the Last Supper with a piece of bread and a sip of wine. The Jewish religion already did these observances with bread and wine. The people had seen so much already in the miracles of Jesus Christ and the multiplication of the bread and wine. Jesus Christ could have only spoken of his flesh and did not have to say that the bread was his flesh, and that by his death he was giving salvation to human beings. He could have said, "I give you bread, which is a figure of my body and the representation of my passion. You will have life when you eat this because it is a memorial of my passion." But instead he says directly that this is his own flesh and we must have the faith to believe this. In which place does he say that this is only a figure? He uses no negative propositions but only affirmative ones. To show the truth of this promise, Jesus Christ confirms this before he dies. He really gives what he really promised. Just as he promised he would give his body, he gave the body he had promised, when he said, "This is my body which is given for you." We see the conformity of the promise with the gift. He says, "This bread I give for the life of the world." When he gives what he promised, what does he say? "This is the body which is given for you." Therefore, the gift conforms with the promise. Is there any reason to doubt?

> And he said, "For this reason I have told you that no one can come to me unless it is granted by the Father." (John 6:65)

It is because of their lack of faith that Jesus says, *No one can come to me*, listen, follow, and believe in me *unless it is granted by the Father*.

> Because of this many of his disciples turned back and no longer went about with him. (John 6:66)

It is a strange thing that a truth so useful and a great testimony of love from Jesus Christ that attracts the whole world cause many disciples to *no longer go about with him*. Instead of using faith and letting it captivate their reason, they let reason measure their faith. As they had only a gross understanding, they turned all the words of Jesus Christ into a carnal interpretation.

> So Jesus asked the twelve, "Do you also wish to go away?" 68 Simon Peter answered him, "Lord, to whom can we go? You have the words of eternal life." (John 6:67–68)

Jesus spoke openly to his apostles. What he said to people in parables and enigmas, he explained to his apostles in secret. Seeing that some disciples were leaving as soon as he told them a truth beyond the ordinary, *Jesus asked the twelve, Do you also wish to go away?* Simon Peter, who was already a model of faith for the apostles, answered him, *Lord, to whom can we go. You have the words of eternal life.* Jesus Christ from his generosity gives us eternal life.

Jesus Christ arrives in the same way in our interior life. When Jesus Christ leads us by the easy way, sustained by his miracles, we see before our eyes evidence and assurance of our faith. We follow Jesus Christ with a good heart, and but when he leads us into a pure faith, we leave this common way. In our pure faith, we exercise our faith with light and testimony. We leave everything for this.

> "We have come to believe and know that you are the Holy One of God." (John 6:69)

St. Peter adds, How could we doubt the truth of your promises, because *we have come to believe and know* two things. *You are the Holy One of God.* As such, out of your excessive love, you came to save and redeem us. We find nothing extraordinary in your testimony about this utterly generous love. As the *Son of God*, you can do all things. Thus, we may not hesitate in things that seems to exceed the range of our reason, because we do not measure actions based on what we think, but we look on them from the perspective of your love and your omnipotence.

> Jesus answered them, "Did I not choose you, the twelve? Yet one of you is a devil." 71 He was speaking of Judas son of Simon Iscariot, for he, though one of the twelve, was going to betray him. (John 6:70–71)

Jesus Christ says not to be surprised if his disciples had left him, because he *had chosen the twelve* and *one of them is a devil*. This disciple was not content to leave Jesus Christ as some others did; instead, he betrayed Jesus Christ who was even then testifying of his love. This is why evil Catholics are worse than heretics. They are not content to leave Jesus Christ as the others, for lack of faith in the words of Jesus Christ. But in believing the truth of this mystery, they use this testimony of love, the greatest that ever was, to betray Jesus Christ and deliver him into the hands of sin, his mortal enemies.

> After this Jesus went about in Galilee. He did not wish to go about in Judea because the Jews were looking for an opportunity to kill him. 2 Now the Jewish festival of Booths was near. 3 So his brothers said to him, "Leave here and go to Judea so that your disciples also may see the works you are doing; 4 for no one who wants to be widely known acts in secret. If you do these things, show yourself to the world." 5 (For not even his brothers believed in him.) (John 7:1–5)

It appears that Jesus Christ is fleeing death, even with his testimony that he desired death so much. Oh! It is that Jesus Christ waited for the ordained and eternal decree for his death. The people closest to Jesus benefit the least from him, for relatives frequently thwart the pious. We receive the harshest persecutions from those who are closest to us. Only rarely do those who converse with the servants of God, and spend all their days with them, believe their words. We should not be surprised when the most holy people are condemned by those who should support them because Jesus Christ was treated the same way.

> Jesus said to them, "My time has not yet come, but your time is always here. 7 The world cannot hate you, but it hates me because I testify against it that its works are evil. 8 Go to the festival yourselves. I am not going to this festival, for my time has not yet fully come." (John 7:6–8)

The time for Jesus Christ *had not yet come*. He waits for the hour ordained by his Father to voluntarily surrender to death. But for those who commit iniquity, their *time is always here* because they act according to their whim and do not consult the divine moment. This is the difference between a soul abandoned to the will of God and those who are not. Those who are abandoned to the God's will do not act independently of the movements of grace, while the others follow their own will in all things. This is why Jesus Christ adds, *The world cannot hate you*, because you are part of the world and support its ways. *But it hates me because* far from approving, I condemn the world, and *testify against it that its works are evil*. For you, who do not fear anything, *go to the festival*. But for me, who only want to do the will of my Father, *I am not going to this festival, for my time has not yet fully come*. He said this because he knows that it was in a festival that his time would be accomplished.

> After saying this, he remained in Galilee. 10 But after his brothers had gone to the festival, then he also went, not publicly but as it were in secret. (John 7:9–10)

Jesus Christ seems to contradict himself here. He says, *I am not going there* but then he went. However, we must notice that he does not say, *I will not go* but *I am not going* because my time has not come. He is dependent on the movement of grace and will not precede the divinely ordained moment. But when his time came, when the order of providence says to leave, he leaves. Jesus Christ does only the will of God in even the slightest action. We look at the providences of his life. When he was a child, God gave the orders to St Joseph how to raise Jesus Christ. Even then following providence, Jesus Christ lived the life of a little child. When he became great, he still followed providence step-by-step.

> The Jews were looking for him at the festival and saying, "Where is he?" 12 And there was considerable complaining about him among the crowds. While some were saying, "He is a good man," others were saying, "No, he is deceiving the crowd." (John 7:11–12)

There is no state as exposed to criticism and persecution as the apostolic state. In a hidden life, we are sheltered well from persecutions. But when one is destined to help others, they are exposed to censure from all the world. *Some approve, others condemn.* Those who approve today, will condemn tomorrow. The true apostle must despise the praise and ignore the blame. Since Jesus Christ was condemned, who would be ashamed to be condemned? Since Jesus Christ, the chief of all the apostles, passes for a deceiver, why are we surprised at being treated the same? Since Jesus Christ could not please people, should we be surprised that we cannot please them?

> Yet no one would speak openly about him for fear of the Jews. (John 7:13)

Some simple people understand truth and justice, but others do not listen out of fear of those in authority. They do not acknowledge the goodness of others, because they want to please the Princes of the world. Such was the fate of poor David, when King Achish replied to him, *I know that you are as blameless in my sight as an angel of God, but you do not please the Princes* (1 Samuel 29:9) Also, out of fear of others, Pilate handed Jesus Christ over to crucifixion.

> About the middle of the festival Jesus went up into the temple and began to teach. 15 The Jews were astonished at it, saying, "How does this man have such learning, when he has never been taught?" 16 Then Jesus answered them, "My teaching is not mine but his who sent me." (John 7:14–16)

The Jews were filled with admiration at the teaching of Jesus Christ who convinced and astonished them. Yet their hearts were hardened and he did not win them. How many people are convicted by the truth and yet only resist the power of the teaching? They arm themselves with spikes like a hedgehog to repulse everyone who approaches them so they cannot be won. They fight to resist the blows of grace. How many people are convinced in the truth of the interior way and yet do not want to follow?

The Jews were *astonished, saying, How does this man have such learning, when he has never been taught*? They saw well that it was an infused wisdom which cannot be replicated. But because of their hardened disposition and the obstacles they put in the way, they do not either go into the truth or persevere in the way. They see his goodness but lack the courage to follow.

Jesus Christ assures that his teaching *is not mine but his who sent me*. Being himself the Word of the Father, his words are those of his Father.

> "Anyone who resolves to do the will of God will know whether the teaching is from God or whether I am speaking on my own." (John 7:17)

The soul that is consecrated, devoted, and abandoned to the will of God knows well the truth of these words. The effect produced in the soul do not allow any doubt. But to know this teaching through experience, we must submit and be abandoned to all of the will of God, who guides us through his will. Our only work is to do the will of God. As soon as we are in submission to the divine will, we hear the language in our heart.

> "Those who speak on their own seek their own glory; but the one who seeks the glory of him who sent him is true, and there is nothing false in him." (John 7:18)

The main quality of a true apostle is *they do not seek their own glory*. Also, they do not speak for themselves. But in bearing the word of the One who sent him, he seeks only the glory of the One who sent. So if preachers bear little fruit, it is because they speak for themselves. They have only a studied word and look for their own glory. They want to please human beings and receive glory from them. But those who do not speak for themselves but speak through the power of the Spirit and say what the Spirit suggests, bear much fruit. They do not seek their own glory and *there is nothing false in them* because injustice consists in robbing God of the glory due him in order to have glory for themselves.

> "Did not Moses give you the law? Yet none of you keeps the law. Why are you looking for an opportunity to kill me?" 20 The crowd answered, "You have a demon! Who is trying to kill you?" (John 7:19-20)

Those who sustain the letter of the law while banishing the spirit, frequently become *violent* and break the law. They condemn those who break the laws in order to do something better, but they do not condemn those who break the laws to do evil. An example, if a person misses a sermon because there is something more important to God, and something considerable that God wants done, all the world cries out against her and says she has broken communal laws. If another misses a sermon for entertainment, no one says anything.

The Jews tell Jesus Christ that he *has a demon*, because he reveals the plans they have in their heart that only they know. Surely there is no cross like the one produced by the apostolic life.

> Jesus answered them, "I performed one work, and all of you are astonished. 22 Moses gave you circumcision (it is, of course, not from Moses, but from the patriarchs), and you circumcise a man on the sabbath. 23 If a man receives circumcision on the sabbath in order that the law of Moses may not be broken, are you angry with me because I healed a man's whole body on the sabbath? 24 Do not judge by appearances, but judge with right judgment." (John 7:21-24)

Evil happens in superficial condemnations because we *judge* only according to a small external factor rather than how things are in themselves. We look only at the *appearance* and not at the reality. If it is permitted to do a good action on the Sabbath, why is it not permitted to do a better one? O God! You say well that you do not judge the way human beings judge! Oh, human beings are unjust in their judgments and will be astonished to see that they condemned the better things, while approving things that God condemned!

> Now some of the people of Jerusalem were saying, "Is not this the man whom they are trying to kill? 26 And here he is,

> speaking openly, but they say nothing to him! Can it be that the authorities really know that this is the Messiah? 27 Yet we know where this man is from; but when the Messiah comes, no one will know where he is from." (John 7:25–27)

What stops us from benefiting from the mission of Jesus Christ, or of apostolic souls, is that we have to let our ideas be transformed about what makes a person apostolic. If we see qualities we are not used to seeing, then we begin to believe that they are not sent by God. For if Jesus Christ had all the qualities of being the Messiah, if he did the works that the Messiah was to do, then why did they not believe in him? Because they falsely claim that *no one will know where the Christ is from*. This is plainly contrary to scripture, which says that the Christ must come from David and be born in Bethlehem.

> Then Jesus cried out as he was teaching in the temple, "You know me, and you know where I am from. I have not come on my own. But the one who sent me is true, and you do not know him. 29 I know him, because I am from him, and he sent me." 30 Then they tried to arrest him, but no one laid hands on him, because his hour had not yet come. (John 7:28–30)

Whatever judgment is made of the preachers of the gospel, and whatever is said about them, they must never stop *teaching* and fulfilling their ministry; they must not be concerned with success. Jesus Christ continued to teach, despite the judgement made against him. A true apostle can only expect insults for the blessings they give. A cross is the crown and the end of the apostolate.

How does our Lord say this? *You know me, and you know where I am from*. Did these people really know who he was? They know him only according to the flesh and to his temporal generation, and not according to the eternal. So he makes them go higher so that they may comprehend the good and know his origin. Then they will know, *I have not come on my own* because he has been sent on his mission from on high. *The one who sent* on the earth sent him to preach. But the people's minds are dull and cannot comprehend the truth of Jesus Christ according to his divinity. However, Jesus says, *I know him, because I am from him, and he sent me*. No one may know the Father except through him. Many people believe that they know Jesus, but they do not. If they knew him, they would truly surrender and live by his maxims. We often know apostolic souls only from their exterior, but we do not penetrate their interior principles by which they live. They know this well, because they feel the presence of the One who makes them act, and they cannot ignore that everything comes from him.

Scripture adds, *Then they tried to arrest him, but no one laid hands on him, because his hour had not yet come.*

People who are consumed with passion to procure the salvation of others are the object of hatred, envy, and jealousy. Yet people cannot always do the harm they want to do, because the hour of the apostolic soul has not yet come. When the hour has come, O God! It seems that you join with their persecutors and you fortify those opposed to them. But until the time has come with the moment of divine permission, all the bad will has no effect.

> Yet many in the crowd believed in him and were saying, "When the Messiah comes, will he do more signs than this man has done?" (John 7:31)

In the midst of the harshest persecutions, there are always some people who keep the faith, but these are usually the simple people in the *crowd*. The others are entirely opposed out of their self-love and their lack of docility. These people for the most part are not won over, even by extraordinary things.

> The Pharisees heard the crowd muttering such things about him, and the chief priests and Pharisees sent temple police to arrest him. (John 7:32)

Jesus Christ did not have stronger persecutions than those the *Pharisees* made against him. These proud and haughty spirits did not want to enter the way of Jesus Christ. They could not suffer that simple people entered into it and diverted them as much as they can. Not content to do only this, they persecuted Jesus Christ and those who listened to his preaching. The Pharisees agreed among themselves how to do this, trying to stop him from working in souls, and attempting to extinguish his kingdom.

> Jesus then said, "I will be with you a little while longer, and then I am going to him who sent me. 34 You will search for me, but you will not find me; and where I am, you cannot come." (John 7:33-34)

Jesus has *a little while longer* to stay with these people persecuting him. He still has time to win and convert them by his excessive goodness.

He stands in favor of the souls who benefit from him. When our Lord sends apostolic souls in places where they are persecuted, he stays for a little while, obliging his apostles to stay in places of persecutions, so they can win people for the sake of others. But then they *go to the one who sent* them and leave the place that would not receive the grace of the Word. Yet there comes a time when they *will search* for him to learn from him, but they *not find him* because they did not want to take advantage of him when he was with them. He comes to them like lightening, but because they have not taken the path, they seek Jesus Christ and do not find him.

They search for him outside of themselves, but they do not search where he wants to be found, their interior. This is why he says, *Where I am, you cannot come* because you do not take the path. You take an entirely opposed way. God is inside of us where he wants to be found. That is where he wants to be searched, found, and loved. That is where God wants to communicate with us. But we are only able to go to him if we follow him on the way he leads. We must leave the self-centered way where we are filled with only the love of self. We must be entirely interior, yet we are entirely exterior.

> The Jews said to one another, "Where does this man intend to go that we will not find him? Does he intend to go to the Dispersion among the Greeks and teach the Greeks? 36 What does he mean by saying, 'You will search for me and you will not find me' and 'Where I am, you cannot come'?" (John 7:35-36)

The Jews do not understand Jesus Christ's discourse, because they interpret his words interpret literally and to the letter. Because of this confusion, they will not find Jesus Christ. Not separated from them, he was in the midst of them, but they could not find him. He is also in the midst of our heart, but we cannot find him if we do not search in our heart.

We may not *go where he is*, because he goes to his Father through the cross, death, losses, afflictions, and persecutions. We want to go to places with pleasure, joy, and life. However, no one may follow Jesus Christ except through the cross and self-denial. If we take a contrary route, it is impossible to arrive at Jesus Christ, as he himself says, *"If any want to become my followers, let them deny themselves and take up their cross and follow me* (Matthew 16:24). Instead, we seek more wildness while pretending to follow Jesus Christ, rather than renouncing ourselves. Jesus Christ attracts us, but we do not want to follow his attraction. If we do not find it, we are not looking well for it, because we fear that when Jesus Christ approaches us, he brings the cross, contradictions, pain, suffering, and affliction.

> On the last day of the festival, the great day, while Jesus was standing there, he cried out, "Let anyone who is thirsty come to me." (John 7:37)

Jesus Christ is always ready to be found. Scripture says that *On the last day of the festival*, at a time when the world is crowding into the temple to see him, *he cried out*, so that all the world could hear. He invites all the world to come, *Let anyone who is thirsty come to me*, if anyone desires salvation and thirsts for eternity, *come to me* and drink. "I am the inexhaustible source of all you desire and you will drink it in with abundance. Come and drink continually! O ineffable happiness! We may always have joy in such a great goodness! It is up to us to tap into such a treasure, too immense for us to understand. Yet we let ourselves die of thirst rather than drink this living water. O Love! O ungrateful hearts of the creature, to be full of the mud of the earth, yet refuse this clear and clean divine water, the water from the source!"

> "And let the one who believes in me drink. As the scripture has said, 'Out of the believer's heart shall flow rivers of living water.'" (John 7:38)

Oh, to know the advantage of faith and the inconceivable happiness of the soul who goes to God by the way of faith! Those who believe in Jesus Christ and follow the way he gives them, drink from the source of life. By having done this, a *river of living water* is formed in them and *flows* to others. This is the apostolic state, in which the Spirit fills the person with *life-giving* water which flows to others, but this source is only communicated by faith.

> Now he said this about the Spirit, which believers in him were to receive; for as yet there was no Spirit, because Jesus was not yet glorified. (John 7:39)

This scripture tells us that the *Spirit* is communicated through faith, which is the Spirit of the Word, *which believers in him were to receive*. This Spirit flows and is communicated in the soul by the Word. If the Spirit is not received, Jesus Christ is not. To receive the Spirit, the soul loses all propriety, self-interest, and self-motivated action, in order to remain open to the actions and flowing of the Spirit of the Word that gives honor and glory to Jesus Christ in all things. Jesus Christ is truly glorified in us by our annihilation that gives God the glory. Our annihilation stops our self-action so that God can work.

> When they heard these words, some in the crowd said, "This is really the prophet." 41 Others said, "This is the Messiah." But some asked, "Surely the Messiah does not come from Galilee, does he? 42 Has not the scripture said that the Messiah is descended from David and comes from Bethlehem, the village where David lived?" (John 7:40–42)

It is an astonishing that the people fall into the same fault that their leaders have made. In Jesus Christ, they see the truth and solidity of his state and principles, yet they stop, believing false circumstances. They do not want to believe in Jesus Christ, because they believed he was from Galilee and not from the house of David. They falsely concluded that because of this, Jesus was not the Christ. If they had examined all things well, they would see that he was the Christ. If the leaders made known to others that Jesus Christ was from Bethlehem, and, combined with witnessing his astonishing works, they would have known he was the Christ.

The same is true when interior Christians are judged. Leaders doubt them based on faulty information. When judging people, the truth needs to be found out. The first lie prevents the truth from being seen.

> So there was a division in the crowd because of him. 44 Some of them wanted to arrest him, but no one laid hands on him. (John 7:43–44)

Falsely persuaded, the people divide over the truth of Jesus Christ and doubt him. They want to arrest him, based on a lie. The leaders hide the fact that he is from Bethlehem so that the people will not believe. This harms the people because it stops the Spirit from flowing into their souls. Their efforts, though, are useless. They cannot stop Jesus Christ from doing what he wants. *No one laid hands on him* because he is always victorious, despite the persecutions.

> Then the temple police went back to the chief priests and Pharisees, who asked them, "Why did you not arrest him?" 46 The police answered, "Never has anyone spoken like this!" (John 7:45–46)

It usually happens that those sent to take and fight against Jesus Christ, are themselves taken and won because it is difficult to resist the

Word spoken by the mouth of God. This is why the Word is well compared to a two-edged sword. It destroys any obstacle in its way with an extraordinary power. All the souls in whom this Word is heard have a certain "je-ne-sais quoi"—a power against which no one may defend themselves. This is why these people say, *"Never has anyone spoken like this!"* The apostolic souls in whom Jesus Christ has truly spoken also gain this quality of speaking like no other, because they have an authority in their words that raises others and an unction that wins others.

> Then the Pharisees replied, "Surely you have not been deceived too, have you? 48 Has any one of the authorities or of the Pharisees believed in him?" (John 7:47–48)

This is a terrible passion. When a person is persuaded of the truth, they accuse her of being *deceived*. When a simple person has good faith, persons in authority accuse and fight against her. The Pharisees themselves say that none of them have let themselves *believe in him*. We do not read in the Gospels that Jesus Christ won the Pharisees. Their science, pride, self-love, propriety, self-esteem attachment to their own light, stopped them from being won and loved by Jesus Christ.

> "But this crowd, which does not know the law—they are accursed." (John 7:49)

Oh, the pride and esteem of human reasoning! To believe that simple people who go straight to God from the sincerity of their heart are *accursed*, because they do not think like Pharisees! However, it is certain that God has said, *Those of blameless ways are his delight* (Proverbs 11:20). The eyes of God are constantly on her to lead her. Why do they say then that these blameless ones are *accursed*? What ignorance and pride inspires the Pharisees! These people know so little. What they know is like nothing compared to what they do not know.

> Nicodemus, who had gone to Jesus before, and who was one of them, asked, 51 "Our law does not judge people without first giving them a hearing to find out what they are doing, does it?" (John 7:50–51)

Nicodemus is the only scholar who knew Jesus and supported him yet did it in a hidden way. Scripture says that he *had gone to Jesus before* under the darkness of night. Pride and concern for human respect stops the other leaders from declaring themselves for Jesus Christ. Nicodemus does let these other leaders see that they are misusing the law here because the *law does not judge people without first giving them a hearing.* The same thing happens today. People are condemned without a hearing based on false reports and imagination. They are not judged by the truth.

> They replied, "Surely you are not also from Galilee, are you? Search and you will see that no prophet is to arise from Galilee." (John 7:52)

The response of these leaders shows their prevention of the truth and ignorance. If Nicodemus takes the part of truth, they accuse him also of being from *Galilee.* They tell him to examine the scriptures, as if he were ignorant. These self-serving leaders accused Jesus Christ of being from Galilee rather than acknowledging he was from Bethlehem. People looking out of pride have only eyes to condemn and not to examine the evidence. Nicodemus is silent, perhaps out of timidity, but maybe not to move them farther away from Jesus Christ. Nicodemus was not won over by their speeches, but he did not strongly defend Jesus Christ. Some were not convinced to be against Jesus Christ because scripture adds, *Then each of them went home,* which means to the same disposition they previously had (John 7:53).

> While Jesus went to the Mount of Olives. 2 Early in the morning he came again to the temple. All the people came to him and he sat down and began to teach them. (John 8:1–2)

If Jesus Christ took the time to pray, why do we not do imitate him, if our occupations do not hold us back from prayer? Jesus Christ went to the *Mount of Olives.* This is mysterious. It shows that when we want to pray, we need to leave places of activity. The tranquil exterior favors and contributes to the tranquil interior. The name *Mount of Olives* means a place of peace, because the prayers of Jesus Christ were tranquil and peaceful. The more we pray in peace, the more we approach the prayer of Jesus Christ. He chooses peaceful places for prayer to show that his prayer brings reconciliation with his Father. All that Jesus Christ did on earth was done in favor of human beings. There this immense river of divine peace flows on humanity. This divinity touches the humanity and the inferior part with a torrent of wonder. Jesus Christ obtained this prayer for human beings so we can participate in these ineffable delicacies. Human nature may receive these admirable communications. Oh! It is up to us to be part of it. Peace both exterior and interior constitutes the whole thing.

Jesus Christ leaves this mountain of prayer and peace to go *again to the temple*. Pastors and priests must only teach what they have drawn from prayer. They must be filled before they spread the Word. Oh if they did this, they would have a better effect!

> The scribes and the Pharisees brought a woman who had been caught in adultery; and making her stand before all of them, 4 they said to him, "Teacher, this woman was caught in the very act of committing adultery. 5 Now in the law Moses commanded us to stone such women. Now what do you say?" (John 8:3–5)

The Pharisees always had a zeal against sinners, because they wanted an exact observation of the law without looking at the purpose of the law, which was to save the lost. However, if their intentions had been right, they were right to condemn this woman, because adultery was the greatest of crimes.

There are two types of adultery: adultery against God and adultery against human beings. Adultery against God is the most criminal. If Jesus Christ had not called the Pharisees an *adulterous nation* and an illegitimate race, one would say I said this in a reverie (Matthew 12:39). However, this is true. The human heart is made for God alone and must be subjected to him. Whenever we remove our heart from God to give it elsewhere out of vanity or avarice, the heart commits adultery. The Pharisees loved themselves with a disordered love, and, because of this, did not love God. Their heart was prostituted to a demon and vanity. They believed they had a chaste body and could condemn others. They asked that this woman be *stoned*. They did not see that their adultery was more criminal than hers was. The Pharisees actually merited a more rigorous execution than she did.

> They said this to test him, so that they might have some charge to bring against him. Jesus bent down and wrote with his finger on the ground. 7 When they kept on questioning him, he straightened up and said to them, "Let anyone among you who is without sin be the first to throw a stone at her." (John 8:6–7)

The Pharisees had no other plan in this interrogation than to *accuse Jesus Christ*. This is the ordinary conduct of proud people to try to trap simple people. The response of Jesus Christ overwhelmed and surprised the Pharisees. He *wrote with his finger on the ground*. Jesus Christ wrote first about their adultery, which was infinitely more dangerous and enormous than that of the woman. This is more dangerous because if this is not discovered, this does not correct itself. This is more enormous because it does not regard God but only other human beings. The adultery of the Spirit is a form of idolatry and more criminal than that of the body.

While Jesus Christ condemns the spiritual adultery, he still does not tolerate the physical adultery. Adultery of the body is an abomination, but it is easier to heal than spiritual adultery. What he writes in the dust of the earth is not retained. Adultery of both kinds is hideous, bringing shame and horror. The enormity of this brings the knowledge that this is criminal. The sins of the Spirit bring great confusion, yet they can be seen as virtues. Instead, they intensify evil. We pile up crime after crime, believing that we pile up virtue after virtue. This evil is without remedy because we ignore the sickness. Instead, we look at the remedy as evil. This is why Jesus Christ says, *Let anyone among you who is without sin be the first to throw a stone at her.* This word of Jesus Christ brings an efficacious light that makes them bewildered but they do not discover the truth of what he says. Jesus Christ also revealed this to them as they hid the sins of the body out of shame. The light of Jesus Christ's sun could not heal them. This is why he *once again* writes on the ground.

> And once again he bent down and wrote on the ground. (John 8:8)

Jesus Christ wrote both the sins of the body and of the spirit on the ground. As they were easily discouraged, they withdrew.

> When they heard it, they went away, one by one, beginning with the elders; and Jesus was left alone with the woman standing before him. (John 8:9)

These circumstances led to the entire conversion of this woman, as soon as she was brought to Jesus Christ. Oh if we bring sinners to Jesus Christ, they will be delivered from their misery. Jesus Christ has such strong and sweet attractions, that when we only approach him, we are disengaged little by little from all the rest. This woman is separated from creatures and *alone* with her God. Oh true and whole conversion! The sins of this woman had a criminal engagement with creatures and her conversion is a total separation with creatures and she *remained alone* with her God. But how does she stay *standing*? This indicates that she was relieved of her fall. *Standing before him* shows that she was already converted and turned toward her God. Oh if we took this basis for conversion, we would soon be perfect! Then we would turn and conversion would be perfect, so the soul would remain alone, separated from creatures and close to her God.

> Jesus straightened up and said to her, "Woman, where are they? Has no one condemned you?" 11 She said, "No one, sir." And Jesus said, "Neither do I condemn you. Go your way, and from now on do not sin again." (John 8:10–11)

Jesus asks this woman, *Where are these people who accuse you? Has no one condemned you?* They do not wish to condemn because God showed them in a moment what they were, and they did not want to condemn a person less criminal than they are. If we are even a little enlightened about ourselves, we would not easily condemn others. At times others wish harm for their brother, particularly if he does not do their own spiritual practices or austerities. They might have a reformed exterior so they feel the right to condemn others. They speak out wildly against others, particularly while consuming alcohol. O that they would be placed in the light of truth! They will then see their own severe evils that need healing. Not only do they condemn people who are innocent and just before God, but also accuse those who are already converted.

The sweetness of Jesus Christ toward this woman is wonderful. He assures her that these uncharitable people do not condemn. Also, our infinitely-good Jesus Christ, does not condemn her. I do not know why we frighten sinners so much when they go to Jesus Christ. Under the pretext of humility, we dismiss the words and actions of Jesus Christ. O sinners, come to Jesus Christ! In him you will find your sanctification. You will hear these words from his mouth, *Go, do not sin anymore.* These words are efficacious so that the sinner does not only remain detached from sins, but also from the inclination for sin. Oh, those who listen to these sweet words are happy!

> Again Jesus spoke to them, saying, "I am the light of the world. Whoever follows me will never walk in darkness but will have the light of life." (John 8:12)

After Jesus pardons this woman and tells her to sin no more, he assures her that he is the *light of the world*. To have this true light, we must go to him or we will always remain in darkness. Jesus Christ is the true and essential light, the light of truth. Because he has knowledge of the Father, he has the splendors of the Father's glory and represents in the natural world the Father's truth. All humanity must go to him for light.

He wants all sinners to come to him for light, yet most do not do this. Jesus Christ came for the sinners, as it says in Isaiah and Matthew, *The people who sat in darkness have seen a great light, and for those who sat in the region and shadow of death light has dawned* (Matthew 4:16). Jesus Christ brings light to shine on sinners who walk in the shadow of death.

Then he enlightens those who *follow* him as the way and *walk* in the path that he has traced. This is why he adds, *Whoever follows me will never walk in darkness*. Jesus Christ enlightens them with the truth. In the first degree, through a full and sincere conversion, the soul approaches Jesus Christ and conforms her steps to his. She follows him as the Way and conforms herself to him, walking in his footsteps. In the second degree, Jesus Christ enlightens the soul with his Truth and makes their will united. She receives knowledge of God and not of the creature. With this light of truth, the soul does not stray or walk in darkness, but in joy her will unites with God and knows God throughout her being. The soul enters into the truth of her nothingness and confesses that God is everything.

After the soul is enlightened in this way, she leaves the darkness of error in which she attributes the things of God to herself. Finally, the soul by the light of truth enters into death and annihilation. Then the *light of truth* or giving of life appears and draws the soul out of the tomb and Jesus Christ becomes her life. The soul becomes lost in God and she may no longer distinguish her will. As she has lost her will and life, Jesus Christ becomes himself her life, as Paul experienced, this person no longer lives, but Jesus Christ lives within her. He becomes her life of light.

Jesus Christ's light bring three different states of the soul, each with a different effect. First, his light enlightens sinners and draws us from the death of sin to make us live. *The true light, which enlightens everyone, was coming into the world* (John 1:9). This light leads us into the *truth* and by its generosity, causes her to go out and die. Then the light returns to give her life. Then it is the *light of life*.

> Then the Pharisees said to him, "You are testifying on your own behalf; your testimony is not valid." (John 8:13)

It is true that in common rules no one can give testimony to himself or herself. This prohibition, though, hurts and deceives many. Jesus Christ bears witness about himself for the good of others. To keep this rule is to fall into the sin of propriety. The one destined to help others must say for the good of others that the One who lives within him makes him say it.

As long as Jesus Christ was in his hidden and unknown life, he did not speak of faith, but as soon he was part of the apostolic life according to his celestial mission, he spoke out of faith to assist his neighbors. According to the words of scripture, Jesus Christ is an example for human beings and acts only in a way that everyone can imitate.

Secondly, scriptures say that all human beings live in an abyss of vanity. This is true. But the light of God draws the annihilated person out of the darkness of ignorance so that she believes and know that God is everything. God is the origin and essence of all human beings, yet human beings have evil within them. When the light of truth has fully illuminated the person, she cannot have vanity and she feels the misery of her propriety. The light of truth gives to our experience and we no longer doubt what is. Because of this experience, we know our misery and baseness, and no longer dwell in vanity.

> Jesus answered, "Even if I testify on my own behalf, my testimony is valid because I know where I have come from and where I am going, but you do not know where I come from or where I am going." (John 8:14)

Jesus Christ assures us that though he is *testifying to himself* in and for annihilated souls, *his testimony does not fail to be true*. He is truth himself and the testimony is true *because he knows where he is comes from*. The manifestation that he makes to the soul comes from God. We reveal to others what God has done for us. It is not humility to hide what is of God when it comes to glorifying God. It is a sin and propriety to hide this. There are two examples in the Gospel with the ten lepers and the man who had hidden his talent. As Solomon says, there is a time to talk and a time to be quiet. It is evil to speak when we should be quiet, but it is also evil to be quiet when we should speak. We must confess the truth of God and his power when it is necessary for the glory of God, as did the Holy Virgin, the humblest of all creatures, in her Magnificat. There is no vanity in this because Jesus Christ made this *where he came from*. He manifests himself to this soul and makes her see everything in him. Everything must also go back to him. As Jesus Christ is the principle that makes us speak, he is also the end for which we speak. It is not the same for souls in who are still in themselves. They *do not know where Jesus comes from or where he is going*. He comes from his Father; he returns to his Father, where he wants to hide us with him. To be hidden with Jesus Christ in his Father is the principle, end, and purpose of all our works.

> "You judge by human standards; I judge no one." (John 8:15)

Almost all people who are content with the exterior and act as if this brings perfection have many imperfections and even voluntary evil. They *judge* the world and publicly criticize, but they *judge by the flesh* and according to disordered concupiscence and not according to the truth.

Jesus assures us that *he does not condemn us*. All power from heaven and on earth is given to him to judge the world, however he assures us that he does not judge as a human being does. He comes to teach us and not to judge us. The quality of true interior souls is not to judge people and to believe everyone capable of good. Love and simplicity are the two grand virtues that rule all their conduct. Simplicity leads us to not consider the faults of others. As they have no malice, they do not believe that others have malice. Charity makes them cover and hide the faults of their brothers and sisters. Far from publishing them, they excuse them and think well of them. God alone judges human beings, unless their profession is a judge. However, we must continue to oppose evil with all its strength whenever we can prevent it.

> "Yet even if I do judge, my judgment is valid; for it is not I alone who judge, but I and the Father who sent me." (John 8:16)

As both God and man, Jesus Christ assures us, *Even if I do judge, my judgment is just* and true. His judgment is contrary to faulty and unjust human judgment. Jesus Christ as God judges the same way as God the Father, yet Jesus Christ does not judge anyone. Yet there are people who never judge themselves yet judge everyone else.

> "In your law it is written that the testimony of two witnesses is valid. 18 I testify on my own behalf, and the Father who sent me testifies on my behalf." (John 8:17–18)

Jesus Christ assures us that as God, he can judge according to both divine and human law. However, he condemns the judgments that people make. He says, "I do not judge people; however I have the right to do so. How do you justify making the evil judgments that you do? But," continues Jesus, "I am content to judge and to testify to myself. The testimony that I give conforms to that of my *Father who sent me testifies.*" Jesus Christ teaches us that there is a state where we can and must bear witness to glorify God, yet there is none where it is permissible to judge others. The strongest sign of pride is when we make judgments of the actions and words of others and in our heart condemn others.

> Then they said to him, "Where is your Father?" Jesus answered, "You know neither me nor my Father. If you knew me, you would know my Father also." (John 8:19)

Jesus Christ speaks to both Jews and Christians to tell them that only through him can they have true knowledge of the Father. Therefore, we abandon ourselves to Jesus Christ who leads and shows us the way to the Father. As we hide ourselves in Jesus Christ, we are led to the Father.

> He spoke these words while he was teaching in the treasury of the temple, but no one arrested him, because his hour had not yet come. (John 8:20)

As soon as he began to preach, people fought against the truths of Jesus Christ, yet they had no power to *arrest* him or to stop him from preaching, because *his hour had not come*. When we speak the truth, we must expect strange persecution, but the persecution does not stop what we say. Instead it carries us forward with power. It pleases God that the truth causes the death of the one announcing it. Persecutors make people suffer for speaking the truth.

> Again he said to them, "I am going away, and you will search for me, but you will die in your sin. Where I am going, you cannot come." (John 8:21)

Some people when reading this passage take the opportunity to doubt the goodness of God and believe that he is hiding when looking for him. Jesus Christ said to the Jews, that he *goes away*. What he says is true because he withdraws from them when he dies. They will *search for him*, some to persecute his apostles and others to convert to them. Jesus Christ says to them, "*You will seek me* in my apostles to persecute them and to kill me again after having already taken my life. The envy you have for me comes from your pride. You do not want to be healed from this sin of pride because you do not know me. You cover your envy and jealousy with the name of zeal and do not correct yourself." This is why Jesus Christ says, *You will die in your* blindness and *sin*. These types of sin are irremediable because they are refusing grace. Whoever asks God for grace receives this and whoever seeks finds. But those who seek to fight to destroy his kingdom and to establish their own self-love, die in their sins.

Jesus Christ also speaks here of another type of people who do not fight against him, but also do not profit from his presence. He says to them "Look for me while I can be found. Take advantage of what I tell you because there will come a time that *you will seek me* to hear me. I do not say to you that you will *die in your sins* as the others. I only tell you that *you cannot come where I am going*. Because you do not listen to my words, you cannot follow me."

> Then the Jews said, "Is he going to kill himself? Is that what he means by saying, 'Where I am going, you cannot come'?" 23 He said to them, "You are from below, I am from above; you are of this world, I am not of this world." (John 8:22–23)

These people had the habit of accusing others and justifying themselves; hence, they accuse Jesus of doing what they themselves do. They see him as a criminal. *Is he going to kill himself?* How far their pride is hardened! They see Jesus' miracles and they accuse him of crimes! There is no limit to their bad judgments which they do to justify themselves and hide their poisonous hatred that wants to destroy him. We use our words to judge badly, and then we support our evil judgments with more unfortunate judgments. Jesus Christ responds to their words, "*You are from below* and are carnal and flesh. You are filled with malice which is why you do what you do. But as for me, *I am from above*. I am not capable of the crimes you accuse me of, because my thoughts are all celestial and divine, as yours are all terrestrial and criminal. *You are of this world; I am not of this world*. This is why those who want to follow me must abandon and leave the world. My followers will not fear, because I will conquer the world for them."

> "I told you that you would die in your sins, for you will die in your sins unless you believe that I am he." (John 8:24)

Our Lord leaves no doubt that they will die in their sins if they do not believe, yet this does not happen because of a lack of help from him since he tells him he is from above. They will die in their sins, because the world's pride has mastered them. They *do not believe that I am he*. This fault will cause their death, but trust in Jesus Christ will cause their salvation.

> They said to him, "Who are you?" Jesus said to them, "Even what I have told you from the beginning." (John 8:25; RSV translation)

O these wonderful words! "*I am*, says Jesus Christ, the beginning, and everything comes from me. All good comes from me and so everything not from me is evil. It is I who must be the principle of all actions and movements of the will done by human beings. However, they do not receive me and instead reject me! It is I *who speaks with you* and makes you hear my voice. However, you want to be the own principle of your actions and you usurp the honor due to me. Therefore, you abuse me and I am jealous."

This is a strange thing, that everything has been done by the Word, yet this makes the world angry and they do not want to let him do everything.

> "I have much to say about you and much to condemn; but the one who sent me is true, and I declare to the world what I have heard from him." 27 They did not understand that he was speaking to them about the Father. (John 8:26–27)

Jesus Christ says that he has *much to say about* them because of their resistance to him and their usurpation of his rights over them. However, he assured them as an apostle, he has a mission from his Father and does not say anything that does not come from the Father. Yet they did not understand what Jesus Christ was saying to them.

> So Jesus said, "When you have lifted up the Son of Man, then you will realize that I am he, and that I do nothing on my own, but I speak these things as the Father instructed me." (John 8:28)

Jesus speaks here of his elevation on the cross, which is the literal meaning of these words. Yet he also is making known that they would not have a true knowledge of him until after his death. The mystical sense of these words is that we *lift up* and exalt the *Son of Man* by giving him the glory due him as the principle and making him the master of our actions. Oh then we know the truth of his power and how all power has been given to him on heaven and earth! We learn then of the eternal generation of the Word and the ineffable commerce of the Trinity. The Son receives everything from the Father and gives back to the Father everything that he receives. In raising the Son of Man through our annihilation, we receive true knowledge of these things.

> "And the one who sent me is with me; he has not left me alone, for I always do what is pleasing to him." 30 As he was saying these things, many believed in him. (John 8:29–30)

Jesus Christ is always with the Father as Word because of the concomitance that exists between the divine persons. Where the Father is, there is the Son; where the Son is, there is the Father. As the Son is both man and God, the Father *is always with the Son*. Since the Father has sent the Son on his mission, the Father will never leave him, not even for a moment. As man, Jesus Christ regards humanity and was chosen to enter into the human condition. His Father never leaves him, having chosen his humanity to unite with the divinity in hypostatic union. Because of their united wills, Jesus Christ *always does what is pleasing to the Father*. The wills of the Father and the Son are united, hence the will of the man in Jesus Christ is entirely dependent on the divine and has no resistance to the divine. Hence, Jesus says, *I always do what is pleasing to him*. In the same way, when our wills become united with his, he never leaves us for even a moment. The greatest sign that God is present is when we want only what God wants and nothing else. This discourse on the will of God, and the union of Jesus Christ's will with the Father made *many* people *believe in him*. Nothing makes us understand the truth of this state as much as the continual presence of God and submission to his will.

> Then Jesus said to the Jews who had believed in him, "If you continue in my word, you are truly my disciples; 32 and you will know the truth, and the truth will make you free." (John 8:31–32)

Continuing in the word of Jesus Christ, to hear his Word and to accomplish it in all things, O this perseverance is very rare! Sadly, we listen to the Word, when it brings unction and sweetness, but stop when our faith attracts death, destruction, and loss of support. Many people start but few people persevere. This is why there are so *few true disciples of Jesus Christ*.

But those who faithfully receive his Word, and guard and keep his Word in their heart, receive his Spirit and *know the truth*. Therefore, they are disciples of Jesus Christ and he leads them on the way enlightened by truth. There the soul enters God and into *freedom*. The more she is enlightened by God and recognizes her own nothingness, the more the soul is placed in freedom. As she leaves everything behind, God becomes everything to her. Nothing diminishes her annihilation. This freedom is good for spiritual growth and does not turn into profligacy, as some imagine.

> They answered him, "We are descendants of Abraham and have never been slaves to anyone. What do you mean by saying, 'You will be made free'?" (John 8:33)

When we are badly disposed, we take everything wrong and do not want to take in spiritual things. Jesus Christ speaks here of the slavery of the soul, not bodily slavery.

> Jesus replied, "Very truly I tell you, everyone who sins is a slave to sin." (John 8:34)

We are *slaves to sin as long as we sin*. We are slaves to the same magnitude as the enormity of the sin. We stop being slaves when we stop committing the sin. But even though we are freed from sin, we are not entirely free, so long as we can become slaves again. This is the state of a proprietary soul, who is not engaged in crimes or sin, but has received an unfortunate education in slavery and keeps the marks of the irons. Yet, her freedom consists in not resisting God and not opposing the entire possession of the Spirit or fulfillment of God's will.

> "Now a slave has no permanent place in the family, but a son belongs to it forever." (John 8:35)

To become children of God we must persevere and possess a happy powerlessness to be unable to offend God. This powerlessness is moral and not physical. Now the soul only wants to please God by losing the self-will and all propriety which is the foundation of self-will. Her will passes into God and remains forever united to God. Because God cannot want sin, the one whose will unites to God cannot want sin either because he would be separated from God. The person does not use their freedom to commit sin, as some have falsely claimed, because they are united to God and counted as a child. Now they *belong to the family* of God *forever*. This is a very great grace which Paul says, *You, my brothers and sisters, were called to be free* (Galatians 5:13). But this is a happy freedom and not used for profligacy. If we are called to this blessed state, as we cannot doubt, let us strive with all our strength and effort to get there. Jesus would not have spoken about this, if he did not have the means to bring us to this blessed state.

> "So if the Son makes you free, you will be free indeed." (John 8:36)

Only the *Son makes you free* and puts you in this state. We may not arrive here under our own efforts which only makes a faulty freedom. Instead, we must abandon our way to Jesus Christ so that he puts us in this happy freedom. Jesus Christ alone can give power to the Spirit to act in us. As Paul say, *For all who are led by the Spirit of God are children of God* (Romans 8:14). To become a child of God, we need to be led and moved by the Spirit, as a ship is pushed by the wind. We can see that those who wish to drive themselves are far away from the Spirit. They believe that they are doing their will and are free because of this. Instead, they make themselves slaves. The one who always does the will of God is *free* because she is no longer a slave to sin.

> "I know that you are descendants of Abraham; yet you look for an opportunity to kill me, because there is no place in you for my word." (John 8:37)

Jesus Christ says that he is aware that they are *sons of Abraham* in the flesh, but they are not free because they do not live in the Spirit. He says, *You look for an opportunity to kill me.* There are two ways to kill Jesus Christ. The first way is to stop the natural life as was done in the crucifixion. The other way is to stop communication with him and not receive his Word. If we receive the Word, listen to it and let the Word enter our soul, we communicate with Jesus Christ and have his life. But when we do not give a place to his Word, we do not give a place to his life in our soul. His Word knocks without ceasing on the door of our heart. If these people to whom Jesus was speaking had received the Word in their heart, they would not have killed him. Paul gives us this wisdom when he says, *Do not quench the Spirit* (1 Thessalonians 5:19).

> "I declare what I have seen in the Father's presence; as for you, you should do what you have heard from the Father." (John 8:38)

Jesus Christ speaks here of the life of the Word and *declares that he has seen the Father*. He is the Word of his Father and can only speak the words of his Father. He is the image that represents the Father in the natural and he only says what he saw. But instead of listening to his word, which would give us life if we received it, we do not live the life that Jesus Christ has shown us of the Father and instead live the life of the sinner Adam.

> They answered him, "Abraham is our father." Jesus said to them, "If you were Abraham's children, you would be doing what Abraham did. (John 8:39)

Jesus Christ makes them understand that to be a *child of Abraham*, who is the father of interior souls, we must live with abandon and faith as he did. Also, we must sacrifice all things as he did.

> But now you are trying to kill me, a man who has told you the truth that I heard from God. This is not what Abraham did. (John 8:40)

Abraham believed and his faith became justice. We do not believe and this is the cause of all injustices. We listen to the voice of nature which lies. We cannot suffer the voice of Jesus Christ, who only tells us the truth. We *try to kill* this voice and extinguish the Spirit of Jesus Christ. *This is not what Abraham did.* Since he always listened to this voice, he abandoned everything to follow it.

> "You are indeed doing what your father does." They said to him, "We are not illegitimate children; we have one father, God himself." (John 8:41)

In general, all recognize that God is *their father*, however they do not want to obey his voice and act as a child. If there are some who serve him, they serve him as a mercenary and not as a child. This is what obliged Jesus to say this.

> Jesus said to them, "If God were your Father, you would love me, for I came from God and now I am here. I did not come on my own, but he sent me. 43 Why do you not understand what I say? It is because you cannot accept my word." (John 8:42–43)

My God! All these words are great and expressive! The sign of filiation is *we would love Jesus Christ*. It is impossible to be a child of God if we do not desire the kingdom of Jesus Christ and if you heart is not inflamed for this divine person. O whoever will not love Jesus Christ is anathema! Is it possible to love God and not to love the one whom *the Father sends*, who is the only Son who can make a human being a child of God? This is the Son sent by his Father who makes them children of God by the flow of himself in them and who are marked by his Spirit. There are many good things that speak of the glory of God and give testimony to his truth yet are condemned by people and attract their hate.

> "Yet I do not seek my own glory; there is one who seeks it and he is the judge." (John 8:50)

Jesus Christ *does not seek his glory* either in himself or in the people that he lives, but he gives testimony to the truth, which he must support. Some attribute the words of Jesus to pride spoken for his own glory and condemn him. But the consolation of apostolic souls, who the world also condemns, is when they abandon themselves to Jesus Christ and give him all their life, goods, and honor for the glory of God and the goodness of their neighbor. apostolic souls know that one-day God himself will judge all things and give them *justice*. God reestablishes the glory of Jesus Christ which is dishonored by self-interested people who do not want to be humble.

> "Very truly, I tell you, whoever keeps my word will never see death." (John 8:51)

This one passage is enough to convict us of the necessity to listen to God and to hear *his* Word. Those who hear his Word and receive this inside, *conserve* a continual affection, presence of God, and an everlasting love. They will *never die*, either from the death of sin or eternal death. Then if he dies, it is because he has stopped *keeping the Word*. The heart that receives you is careful not to lose you! The heart is so charmed by your sweetness that she would like to lose all things and keep only the Word.

> The Jews said to him, "Now we know that you have a demon. Abraham died, and so did the prophets; yet you say, 'Whoever keeps my word will never taste death.'" (John 8:52)

The blindness of human beings is strange to take everything in such a gross way. We cannot hear, let alone believe, that there are permanent states where God strengthens and confirms souls by a pure effect of his goodness. We regard all of this as reveries and follies. We look at the saints and condemn this understanding of them having Jesus Christ's states of being. We treat this idea as something extraordinary or a new invention. Yet everything that happened in Jesus Christ is still happening today within those who announce his truth. This is why the Jews added:

> "Are you greater than our father Abraham, who died? The prophets also died. Who do you claim to be?" (John 8:53)

The prophets and Abraham had no other greatness than that which they borrowed from Jesus Christ who is the same today as he was yesterday. He is the same in all who receive his Spirit as he was in Abraham.

However, as the people of this century did not cry out for holiness as other centuries had done, so when Jesus Christ appeared, they did not know him. Abraham kept the Word of God and did all God's will and did not have *death*. All those who like Abraham who out of an excessive faith do the will of God and accomplish things that appear impossible, will not die.

> Jesus answered, "If I glorify myself, my glory is nothing. It is my Father who glorifies me, he of whom you say, 'He is our God,' 55 though you do not know him. But I know him; if I would say that I do not know him, I would be a liar like you. But I do know him and I keep his word." (John 8:54–55)

Jesus Christ as a man does not *glorify himself* and he has no other glory than that which the Father gives him. He carried an absolute annihilation. He had no other support except that of divinity, since he receives everything from his Father who communicates to him all his glory. He says that we say, *He is our God, although we do not know him*. We remain in continual ignorance of who God is and who he wants to be in his creatures. That is what makes us live without God's love, totally opposing what he wants to do in us. He created human beings to communicate with them, yet human beings do not want to receive his divine communications given by his Word. John tells us this when he says, *He came to his own home, and his own people received him not* (John 1:11). Jesus Christ was in the world and the world did not know him. He had become a human being but *his own* people did not receive him. The world ignored that he was God and they did not receive his Spirit. No one wanted his communications, which the Father wanted to send by way of his Word.

But, says Jesus Christ who was both man and God, "*I know him*. As the Word, I receive continually a flow of God the Father into me without any hindrance. He flows into me and I lose myself in him. This flow communicates the full and perfect knowledge that I have of God. *I know* all that he is, because I receive all that he is." The reception of God is the knowledge of God. Those who want the knowledge of God will receive the communication from his Spirit. Paul says, *So also no one comprehends the thoughts of God except the Spirit of God* (1 Corinthians 2:11). Jesus as a man also knew God as he received the flow of divinity continually on his holy humanity. His divinity and humanity were united hypostatically in perfection. Also, the knowledge that Jesus Christ has of God is entirely perfect.

Reasoning cannot bring the knowledge of God. We think we know God by the lights of our reason, but they increase our distance from God. The more we think and hope to get to God using our reason, the farther we become. He communicates himself to small, humble, and annihilated souls, empty of themselves. Because our knowledge of him is only communicated through a flow of himself into our soul, he only works in an empty soul. This is why Jesus Christ says, "*If I would say that I do not know him, I would be a liar like you but I do know him* because he is all in me and I am all in him. *And I keep his word* because I am myself his Word. I keep my divinity and my humanity in me by hypostatic union."

> "Your ancestor Abraham rejoiced that he would see my day; he saw it and was glad." 57 Then the Jews said to him, "You are not yet fifty years old, and have you seen Abraham?" 58 Jesus said to them, "Very truly, I tell you, before Abraham was, I am." 59 So they picked up stones to throw at him, but Jesus hid himself and went out of the temple. (John 8:56–59)

Abraham had the knowledge of the eternal day of Jesus Christ through the communication of the Spirit of the Word, and this life-giving knowledge *filled his heart with* joy. Nothing in the world, in heaven or earth, is capable of filling the hearts of human beings with pleasure and joy as much as the reception of the Spirit of the Word and the knowledge of his grandeur and the ineffable communications of the Trinity. Abraham had seen the eternal day of Jesus Christ. Abraham had also experienced *the day of Jesus Christ* in time, because he had been given a very grand knowledge of the mystery of the incarnation. These people to whom Jesus Christ was speaking had only carnal thoughts and understood the temporal birth of Jesus Christ as a lie, thinking only of the body and corporal matters. This is why Jesus Christ speak of his eternal generation, saying, *Before Abraham was, I am*. In the order of predestination, Jesus Christ was, according to Paul, the first of the predestined of many brothers and sisters. When we speak the truth with all simplicity, it attracts the hatred and persecution of people, as it happened to Jesus Christ.

> As he walked along, he saw a man blind from birth. 2 His disciples asked him, "Rabbi, who sinned, this man or his parents, that he was born blind?" 3 Jesus answered, "Neither this man nor his parents sinned; he was born blind so that God's works might be revealed in him." (John 9:1–3)

There are two types of blindness. First, sins cause blindness. Secondly, though, some have blindness because the virtues and favors of God within cause a great brilliance. They believe that they are in the dark, even though they are in the true light. They are happy to approach Jesus Christ, who heals them in a wonderful manner. Their blindness will serve only to make better known the greatness of God and the effects of his goodness toward human beings.

> "We must work the works of him who sent me while it is day; night is coming when no one can work. 5 As long as I am in the world, I am the light of the world." (John 9:4-5)

Jesus Christ is himself the *light* who gives all places the *day* of his presence. Everything is enlightened through him and without him there is no light. Therefore, he acts in the soul *while in the day* of his grace. If the soul allows him to act and operate, then the soul does not fall in the night of sin.

There are two types of *nights* where *no one can work*. There is the night of sin where the soul is dead and has no vital function and does not receive the action which is communicated to her. She is then absolutely in an entire and absolute deprivation of light because she is deprived of all sanctifying light and consequently deprived of the communication of the Word.

There is another night of darkness where the soul may not act but this darkness is different from the first. This is an excess of light that blinds the soul to work inside, but the soul still receives the actions of God. This is a sun covered by clouds and the soul feels deprived, although the soul never had more brilliance or vitality, although the brilliance is hidden. The soul cannot act, for the powers and senses cannot act.

Jesus Christ also speaks of a blindness or night in which the soul out of pride and the love of its own excellence prevents the soul from acting according to the will of God.

> When he had said this, he spat on the ground and made mud with the saliva and spread the mud on the man's eyes, 7 saying to him, "Go, wash in the pool of Siloam" (which means Sent). Then he went and washed and came back able to see. (John 9:6-7)

The blindness of spiritual persons who have a secret love of themselves and support themselves through their own justice is healed by an action of Jesus Christ. He takes from *the earth* of which the human being is made and composed and with *his saliva*, which is a flowing of his wisdom which he sends on the earth, and uniting with it, he makes *the mud*. This mud appears dirty and blind, far from light. However, if God does not enlighten the soul by his own mud, she will always remain blind. God gives the soul an entire knowledge of what she is through mud and blood. The soul feels only this mud, but she is not washed and purified except *in the pool of Siloam,* which is to say, by living water. Jesus Christ is sent to purify the soul, which is to say to purify the person he has made himself. Through Jesus Christ comes pure light.

This mud is made, as it said, from the earth as are human beings. This is an experience of honest baseness, misery, infirmity, and weakness. She feels what she is and God unites with her through a flow of wisdom. This makes her feel what she is even more. She is not purified yet, but she is enlightened forever.

> The neighbors and those who had seen him before as a beggar began to ask, "Is this not the man who used to sit and beg?" 9 Some were saying, "It is he." Others were saying, "No, but it is someone like him." He kept saying, "I am the man." (John 9:8–9)

The change that happens in an enlightened person is great and extraordinary, but difficult to recognize. How do we judge when a person becomes new? Some judge it in one way and others in another. O mud with such a great advantage much more useful than diamonds!

> "How then were your eyes opened?" they asked. 11 He replied, "The man they call Jesus made some mud and put it on my eyes. He told me to go to Siloam and wash. So I went and washed, and then I could see." (John 9:10–11)

When we see such an extraordinary change, we ask the person how this happened. So he gives glory to God and does not hide God's mercy. It is a terrible ingratitude to be quiet. That's why this happy blind man confesses his former blindness openly. In doing so, he declares the mercy God has shown him to which he has done nothing to contribute except by obeying Jesus Christ. Sadly, the people witnessing this were blinded even more and used the light to increase their darkness. It is a strange thing that jealousy prevents their perception of light and their darkness increased. Even this most holy action of God appears to them as evil and they condemn this. Jesus Christ had done nothing wrong, either in his doctrine or in his morals, so they reproach him on a certain circumstance of his conduct, which was healing on the Sabbath, as if time changes whether it is good or not. The Sabbath should be a rest from evil works and works of slavery, but it is not a repose from glorifying God and helping the salvation of our brothers and sisters. However, for this they condemn Jesus Christ. Today we see the same actions against those who desire God with all their heart and who are trying to serve him. The demon raises many persecutions against them from hate-filled and jealous persecutors under the pretext of evil.

> Then the Pharisees also began to ask him how he had received his sight. He said to them, "He put mud on my eyes. Then I washed, and now I see." 16 Some of the Pharisees said, "This man is not from God, for he does not observe the sabbath." But others said, "How can a man who is a sinner perform such signs?" And they were divided. 17 So they said again to the blind man, "What do you say about him? It was your eyes he opened." He said, "He is a prophet." (John 9:15–17)

This interrogation was done by some out of good faith, but by others out of envy who wanted to find an occasion to condemn. Their *division* was based on sentiments. Those of good faith could not condemn a man who had done so great a good and whose charity had to be interpreted favorably. Yet in opposition, others searched for a way to condemn and interpreted the circumstances to disadvantage. They had conceived a condemnation in their heart and wanted to support this before stating it in the light of day.

Today the Catholics do the same thing out of jealousy and division; this causes evil in the church of God. We see them foolishly tear each other apart by criticizing and condemning good things. They are sharp censors condemning the good, while the true enemies of religion and Christianity are left alone. This is a deplorable thing. In doing this, we give heretics a strong place to war against religion and to corrupt Christians. For finally, we condemn the most holy and best things that show the easiest way to go to God. Some say that we cannot be saved without a great love of God. Then they say this love is impossible. Therefore, salvation is impossible. If we cannot be saved without this great love of God, and as God is the sovereign happiness of life, we would be very unhappy to live without love of God and salvation would be impossible. Therefore, there would be no point in hoping for salvation. But what is the difficulty to love an object so aimable, God who wants our happiness, who loved us first, and who has only love, who became a man so that men became gods, and who gave his life for our salvation. After he has done all this for us, can we believe it is impossible to love him? Oh, would it not be more impossible not to love him? Can we believe after so many signs of his love that he wants our loss? My God! This sentiment is insulting to your goodness!

The Jews should have selected people of good faith and understanding to settle their differences they had about Jesus Christ. Today we should do the same to judge the differences we have about the spiritual life by choosing those who are enlightened and have experienced the spiritual life, not those who cannot hear what is being said. This is an astonishing thing that both libertines and nominal Christians are united in condemning interior people. The demon ignites this powerful war, because he knows the terrible losses he suffers when one practices a faith from the heart. If any book on prayer appears, the world cries out against it. No one speaks out against all the many wicked and pernicious books speaking out against Christianity.

> The Jews did not believe that he had been blind and had received his sight until they called the parents of the man who had received his sight 19 and asked them, "Is this your son, who you say was born blind? How then does he now see?" 20 His parents answered, "We know that this is our son, and that he was born blind; 21 but we do not know how it is that now he sees, nor do we know who opened his eyes. Ask him; he is of age. He will speak for himself." 22 His parents said this because they were afraid of the Jews; for the Jews had already agreed that anyone who confessed Jesus to be the Messiah would be put out of the synagogue. (John 9:18–22)

When people do not want to believe the truth, they pretend to be misguided. They want a crowd of witnesses to declare it to them, so they have an opportunity to condemn it and mistreat those who declare it. The malice of these people is great, but it matches the ingratitude of these parents. The parents forget their benefactor out of respect for the crowd of people. Many people are not *afraid* to confess Jesus Christ, yet only some follow the faith as long as there are not obstacles. When they are criticized for their faith, this slightest persecution makes them desist. They then think it prudent to hide their faith. Instead, we must never be embarrassed of the gospel. We confess Jesus Christ and declare we are our true followers of his love and his life's example.

> So for the second time they called the man who had been blind, and they said to him, "Give glory to God! We know that this

> man is a sinner." 25 He answered, "I do not know whether he is a sinner. One thing I do know, that though I was blind, now I see." (John 9:24–25)

They do not want to believe in Jesus Christ and also want to stop others from believing also. They intimidate others. But what is stranger is that they want the poor blind man to believe that his benefactor is a *sinner*. They attribute these most holy things to sin. Some people attribute this to a diabolical spirit. Instead, these are the purest graces of God toward human beings and the movement of his Spirit. We cannot believe how far the malice of people goes. The blind man *answered* with prudence: *I do not know whether he is a sinner* but *I see*. He defends him by showing the miracle done in his favor which is a great sign of his holiness. The greatest miracle is to give sight to the blind.

> They said to him, "What did he do to you? How did he open your eyes?" 27 He answered them, "I have told you already, and you would not listen. Why do you want to hear it again? Do you also want to become his disciples?" (John 9:26–27)

This man perceives well the malice of his interrogators who were trying to use his own words against him. This is what made him indignant and made him answer this way. Nothing displeases more than duplicity. He asks, Do you *want to become his disciples?* It is as if he were saying, Do you want to make yourself better acquainted through the truth of his miracles to find the truth of his doctrine? But if you want to condemn, it is useless to use the holiness of his actions to find who he is.

> Then they reviled him, saying, "You are his disciple, but we are disciples of Moses. 29 We know that God has spoken to Moses, but as for this man, we do not know where he comes from." 30 The man answered, "Here is an astonishing thing! You do not know where he comes from, and yet he opened my eyes." (John 9:28–30)

To put pressure on a witness through insults destroy the reason of the process and no truth will emerge from this. Yet they will not convince this happily enlightened blind man. Because finally, they *do not know where Jesus Christ comes from*. If they see the good he does everywhere, how can they condemn him? It is a strange thing of the world that they condemn what they do not know. It is imprudent to approve and applaud what one ignores, but it is a ridiculous temerity to condemn angrily what they do not know. Frequently we shout out of a self-interested spirit. They are like barking dogs who bark when they hear barking. They should see this person with a holy life, doing the most wonderful things, and know where he is from, particularly among the Jews who are watching for the Messiah. Yet there is no state more crucifying than to work to serve the neighbor because then one is exposed to the censure of all the world.

> "We know that God does not listen to sinners, but he does listen to one who worships him and obeys his will. 32 Never since the world began has it been heard that anyone opened the eyes of a person born blind. 33 If this man were not from God, he could do nothing." (John 9:31–33)

This man, as ignorant as he was, through divine wisdom instructs these learned doctors so ignorant in the spirit of the law that if *this man was a sinner*, as they believed, *this man would not be heard by God*. The great sign of being pleasing to God is to do the will of God because God accomplishes his will through them. *Never since the world began has it been heard that anyone opened the eyes of a person born blind.* Because as this newly enlightened man said, *If this man were not from God, he could do nothing.* Those who are not sent from God yet put themselves in the apostolic state, have many words but no impact. But when we see true and lasting conversions, we believe that the mission is sent from God.

> They answered him, "You were born entirely in sins, and are you trying to teach us?" And they drove him out. (John 9:34)

Now that the blind man is enlightened, he can only confess the truth of Jesus Christ, but this confession will cost him dearly! As soon as we confess ourselves in favor of the truth, we will suffer persecutions for this. The proud Pharisees *accuse him of sin* because the light of truth reveals their own darkness and malice. This man, in whom God had worked wonders, *is shamed* as unworthy to be in their company and as a criminal who must not be received in the company of those who think themselves innocent. True servants of God are frequently shamed by hypocrites and inauthentic devotees. I believe that our Lord does this to remove his servants from those who are not worthy to possess them.

> Jesus heard that they had driven him out, and when he found him, he said, "Do you believe in the Son of Man?" 36 He answered, "And who is he, sir? Tell me, so that I may believe in him." 37 Jesus said to him, "You have seen him, and the one

speaking with you is he." 38 He said, "Lord, I believe." And he worshiped him. (John 9:35–38)

As soon as we confess Jesus Christ, let us declare ourselves for the purity of his doctrine and the holiness of his Word. We want to practice the maxims of the gospel. It is certain, though, that we will be both consoled and persecuted for this. As soon as we find persecutions in the way of God, we find God. But why does Jesus instead of saying some word of sweetness and consolation to the poor blind man, instead asks him, *Do you believe in the Son of Man?* This is mysterious. It is as if he said, "Do you believe that in sharing the Son of God's crosses, persecutions, rejections, and contradictions, you will share in the Son of God and that all who are in him will be persecuted as he is? Do you believe," he tells him, "that the common fate of the Master and his disciples must be the sure mark of their union, and reveals the true servants of God through their persecution?" This poor afflicted man does not understand even half of what Jesus *Christ* was saying so he asks him, "Would you show me who is the Son of Man, *so that I may believe in him* and so I may listen to him?" Jesus responds to him saying, "*You have seen* him. When you have been persecuted, shamed, mistreated, you have seen and known him." Jesus Christ is only known in the cross and persecution. Whoever has been communicated to you through the cross is the *same one who speaks with you*. This signifies that God is shown to the soul in two ways both equally perfect. It is the same God who speaks to the soul in prayer as he who speaks in his cross. The two ways God communicated with us are his cross and Word. This makes us understand the truth first communicated on the cross on Calvary before being communicated to us in the bread. Jesus Christ instructs this man in these two great truths that are imprinted in the foundation of the heart. He says, *Lord, I believe.* And so that his faith does not end in himself and remain locked in his heart, he passes outside of himself in *worship*, that he understands well what has been said. Worship is the sign of submission expressed in annihilation and quiet, which shows that the heart understands. Many people think they worship when they say certain words such as, *God, I love you* when in reality they are not in the state of worship. Worship is the sovereign homage we render to God through which the soul knows God beyond praise and experiences its powerlessness to do this under his own merit but remains in a state of abasement, quiet, and silent tribute to God in his sovereign grandeur. This is why throughout antiquity sacrifice has been united to worship to show that we may honor God not by doing something but by sacrificing for him what we are and what we have.

> Jesus said, "I came into this world for judgment so that those who do not see may see, and those who do see may become blind." (John 9:39)

But it is not the same with those who Jesus Christ truly enlightens. Little by little they lose they lose their own lights without which they will never have the divine light.

> Some of the Pharisees near him heard this and said to him, "Surely we are not blind, are we?" 41 Jesus said to them, "If you were blind, you would not have sin. But now that you say, 'We see,' your sin remains." (John 9:40–41)

The Pharisees were at the same time blind and enlightened. They were blind not to be able to see the truth, but they had voluntarily blinded themselves by extinguishing everything that would help them see the truth. They were only enlightened by reason and science and this is what makes them culpable. They thought that these lights alone could make them discover Jesus Christ. This is why Jesus Christ says to them that if *they had blindness* of ignorance, they would not be guilty. Yet, he states that they are blind out of malice and, because of this, inexcusable. Also, Jesus Christ tells them they have no true light communicated to them from on high, but Jesus Christ as the true light has rapport with heaven. He tells them, *But now that you say, 'We see,' your sin remains* because they are truly blind, but they think they see clearly. Because of this, they do not have recourse to the true light.

> "Very truly, I tell you, anyone who does not enter the sheepfold by the gate but climbs in by another way is a thief and a bandit. 2 The one who enters by the gate is the shepherd of the sheep." (John 10:1–2)

Only God himself *Enters the sheepfold by the gate*. This gate is the heart. Jesus Christ as the Word may enter through the gate. He only has the key to the gate. Exterior objects only enter through the windows. This is why all the creatures that enter by the senses are *thieves* who want to hide what belongs only to God. Only you, O divine Pastor, can enter into the heart by the heart. All the others are usurpers who harm the sheep and do not lead them to their true Pastor. All the mercenary pastors oppose you with all their power because they know that a sheep who is accustomed to follow the true Pastor will not follow another. She distinguishes the voice of her Pastor so well that she cannot be mistaken. She knows not to be diverted from following her true Pastor.

> "The gatekeeper opens the gate for him, and the sheep hear his voice. He calls his own sheep by name and leads them out. 4 When he has brought out all his own, he goes ahead of them, and the sheep follow him because they know his voice." (John 10:3–4)

Jesus Christ himself is the gate and the gatekeeper. He himself says, *I am the door*. I am the gatekeeper since I *open and no one can shut* (Revelation 3:7). If I *close, no one can open*. Therefore, he is the one who *opens the gate* to the true pasture. And who is this Pastor? He is the gatekeeper, the gate, and the Pastor. He has these three qualities that work together. As Way, he opens the gate. As Truth, he is himself the gate through which we must pass into the Father. As Life, he is Pastor but this pastor enters himself into his sheep when he has opened himself to them. He speaks in the heart which he opens to him. He is infinite by his word. *The sheep hear his voice* in the foundation of their heart.

He calls his own sheep by name. He uses his sheep pleasing to his will, and he calls them by a *new name* that he himself gives them. (Revelation 2:17). They do his will which is the divine will. This is why they are called *his own sheep* to distinguish them from those who are only partly his sheep. He says later that he still has other sheep that are not of this sheepfold. But the sheep in this fold he calls his own sheep because they are entirely his sheep.

He also brings out all his own but from where does he get them. Out of themselves, to hide them with *him* in the bosom of his Father. And he adds, *When* the Shepherd who is himself, has *brought out all his own sheep* (I repeat the phrase "own sheep" for he has his own sheep who have left themselves). When they leave themselves, *he* passes the first and *goes ahead of them*, bringing them into his states of being without excluding any. *The sheep follow* him voluntarily, even if the way is filled with thorns because they *hear his voice* in their foundation and his divine voice invites them to follow. They know his voice and sweetness and continually listen for his voice.

> "They will not follow a stranger, but they will run from him because they do not know the voice of strangers." (John 10:4–5)

The Son of God's own sheep have the character of hearing his voice in the foundation of their heart, following, and running away from *strangers*. Other sheep follow strangers easily rather than their legitimate Shepherd because they do not distinguish or know his voice. His own true sheep *run from strangers* and only follow their true and legitimate Shepherd.

> So again Jesus said to them, "Very truly, I tell you, I am the gate for the sheep. 8 All who came before me are thieves and bandits; but the sheep did not listen to them." (John 10:7–8)

Jesus assures us that *he is truly* the gate. If he is the gate, we must pass through him and he introduces us to the Father where the true pastures are. *All who came before him* are *thieves* and his own *sheep do not listen to them*.

> "I am the gate. Whoever enters by me will be saved, and will come in and go out and find pasture." (John 10:9)

All true sheep who enter into God are placed in freedom. They *enter* into God through Jesus Christ. They become lost in God and *find* excellent pastures. God nourishes them with himself.

> "The thief comes only to steal and kill and destroy. I came that they may have life, and have it abundantly." (John 10:10)

The difference between the demon and Jesus Christ is real and immense, yet those who deny these differences call this an illusion and foolishness. They do not want to embrace the way of perfection, yet this is the strongest and most dangerous of all deceptions. Without entering perfection, we always remain in imperfection and in sin and subject to the corruption of nature. When we enter this way, Jesus Christ pulls us out of deception.

I am convinced that there is deception in all things and that nature counterfeits grace making it difficult to distinguish. Moreover, the demon imitates the operations of God and without faith and experience, it is difficult to know the difference. However, there is nothing for the truly humble soul to fear. The devil wishes to deceive her to push past her humbleness, yet the operations of the demon will have the opposite effect that is wanted. Jesus Christ shows us how to distinguish the demon and nature from his grace. The demon is the *thief who only comes to steal*. The demon is the great thief who came at the beginning of the world to seduce humans out of a state of innocence and persuades them that he will place them in a more perfect state. He made human nature participate in his thievery and slipped them his poison. Human nature, which was subject to grace and participated in God, then became subject to and participated in the demon. The human being was then attached to the demon's deceits, usurpations, and stealing. The demon is familiar and subtle, and more difficult to resist than the devil because the demon attacks only with penchants and thoughts. The demon is much to be feared. Very frequently we attribute to the demon what is corrupt nature. Others who are very blind attribute to grace the corruption and depravity of nature, saying that something is grace when it is actually sin.

Therefore, Jesus Christ gives us an infallible way to recognize him from all these thieves. *The thief comes only to steal and kill and destroy* and to take away what is of God *and to lose and kill the sheep*, losing themselves not in God, but in self-love and pride. Jesus Christ *comes* to his own sheep so that *they have* grace which is life that he communicates to them and they have this with *abundance*. What does this mean? Jesus Christ gives the life of grace to those who do not have it. He increases grace to those who have it already. But the true meaning, he does not just give them the life of grace in themselves. Whatever may be the life of grace, it is always bound and limited when it is received in the capacity of the creature. But so the sheep of Jesus Christ have a more abundant life, he comes first to give them life by the communication of his grace, and then even more abundant life by passing into God. No longer do they have their life enhanced by grace, but they live the life of God himself. They will always only live the life of God in himself and for himself. Jesus Christ came to bring this great grace to his chosen sheep who truly recognize him for their own Shepherd.

"I am the good shepherd. The good shepherd lays down his life for the sheep." (John 10:11)

This confirms what has been said. Jesus Christ assures us that he is truly *the good Shepherd*. No one else can have his quality and title of being a good Shepherd because he *lays down his life for the sheep*. He gives his character of being humanly divine and divinely human to make human beings divine. He communicates his more abundant life of the Word to them perfectly, letting them live and work in the Father as he does. In the Father, they have no other life than God which causes them to die and fail in all other lives, however grand and eminent they have been. Then they have a place for the divine life.

> "The hired hand, who is not the shepherd and does not own the sheep, sees the wolf coming and leaves the sheep and runs away—and the wolf snatches them and scatters them." (John 10:12)

Jesus Christ speaks here of the difference between his way and the way of the hired hand. It is he that gives life for his sheep. But the mercenary pastor or director does the contrary. *As soon as he sees the wolf* that brings strong temptations and the sheep are tempted or persecuted, he *leaves the sheep and loses and scatters them.* He lets the wolf take away everything from God in their interior that nourishes them. Mercenaries fear for their reputation if they protect persecuted people. Only a few hold firm. As long as the soul is consoled, they assist them. When the soul is tempted, they abandon them.

> "The hired hand runs away because a hired hand does not care for the sheep. 14 I am the good shepherd. I know my own and my own know me." (John 10:13–14)

Here Jesus Christ assures us that the mercenary will let the sheep perish, because he does not *care for the sheep.* Oh, who is the person who will care for the sheep like Jesus Christ does? Some only have self-centered love? Yet we will trust such a person and follow this person, while we do not trust God and let God lead us. Yet we hear, *I am the good Shepherd, who knows my sheep.* He knows his sheep and *his sheep know him,* because he shows in a particular way through experience who he is.

However, he says well, "I know and love my sheep and I give my life for them. I have continually communicated the life of my Word to them to lead them. I fill them with a thousand goods and give them excellent pastures and utter freedom to graze there. No one wants to be led to me, though I have not lost any of those my Father gave me. I search for those who become lost and carry them on my shoulders! But the mercenary pastors who lose their sheep out of their negligence are the ones trusted by people. O horrible blindness! They do not trust the adorable Pastor, uniquely good, who gives his life for the sheep to nourish them yet trust the one who devours them. We let ourselves be led by the wolf and not the good Pastor!"

> "Just as the Father knows me and I know the Father. And I lay
> down my life for the sheep." (John 10:15)

Jesus Christ tells us about the truth of his death that gives a very real life. This is opposed to the heretics who call his death a fantasy in which he only appears to suffer and die. Therefore, he assures us, *I lay down my life for the sheep*, his life as man and God. It is also real and true that the *Father knows him and he knows the Father*. Here is the truth of his divinity and his eternal generation. Jesus Christ out of his real knowledge of the Father and the Father's knowledge of him engenders him. It is also true that he lays down his life for the sheep.

He *gives his* mortal *life* so he may give salvation to all human beings. But for his own sheep, he communicates his life of the Word in a very real, strong, and abundant manner. He nourishes them himself and finally makes a union in their soul with the life of his Word and of his humanity. He alone can communicate this to his sheep through grace. He made himself bread to institute the adorable Sacrament on our altars, to be able to communicate to his sheep his divinely human life, that he had only for them. O charity! O infinite goodness of the Pastor, who really gives his life for the sheep and who really is God! O terrible ingratitude of the sheep, that they do not want to be led and animated by the divine Pastor. Instead, they want their own life, which is only an apparent life and yet a true death. Instead, the life of the Word hides under the appearance of death, a very real and eminent life.

We have trouble letting ourselves be led to Jesus Christ who communicates life to us through his death. This is what makes the pain and repugnance that we feel about receiving his life, because we only receive it through death. However, his death becomes our life. The spiritual life always includes some lights, graces, and favors, which are very small things. But true surrender always includes strange deaths. No, poor sheep, your pastor has given his life for you and communicated life to you through his death. You will never receive true life except by his death. If you only have shadows of death, you will only have shadows of life.

> "I have other sheep that do not belong to this fold. I must bring
> them also, and they will listen to my voice. So there will be one
> flock, one shepherd." (John 15:16)

Remember, O divine Savior, this promise: O that this is understood! Jesus Christ speaks here not only of the preachers of the gospel sent to the Gentiles or Jews. He speaks of the reunion they will have at the end of the world under one Pastor, where all people of the earth recognize the true God. All people will be interior and will be led by their true and legitimate Pastor, because he only may lead and the people will be led if they hear his voice. But how will they understand if they do not listen? We must listen to the divine voice, as David said, *I will hear what the Lord God will speak in me* (Psalm 84:9). Oh if all the human beings would listen, all human beings would be holy. For they would know in their exterior to flee the evil and do good. In their interior, they would know to listen to God speak in the soul, yet he does not speak in a distinct way as we imagine. He speaks in this way by his angels in an immediate and muted word. This is not heard like noise but by a peaceful and tranquil infusion. The most intimate part of the soul hears this substantial word. Very frequently the soul discovers nothing other than tranquility, peace, and mortification of desires through faith, with a certain ravishment that cannot otherwise be explained.

> "For this reason the Father loves me, because I lay down my life in order to take it up again." (John 10:17)

In this passage we hear Jesus Christ as man and God, who *lays down his life in order to take it up again* in the resurrection, and also as Word. It is the ineffable communication of the Trinity. The Word communicates with his Father, letting the Word return to the Father to take it back again in the communication of himself in himself, the love of the Father for the Son and the Son for the Father. The Father and the Son love each other by the return and flowing of the Word in the Father and listening to the Father in the Son. In this way, to the measure that the Father sends his life to the Word makes their love. To the measure that the Son flows into the Father, he takes new life, as it is said, being newly and continuously engendered. This eternal and continual generation of the Word, this continual return of the Word, makes the love of the Father and the Son. Continually, this well-beloved Son gives his life and also continually he takes it again. And to show that he speaks of the eternal generation, he speaks in the present tense. He does not say, I will lay down my life but *I lay down my life in order to take it up again*. I leave my life and receive my life. The same moment that I return to my Father makes my Father live in me. Voila! Here is the eternal and continual generation of the Word on the earth. Jesus Christ is the *beloved of his Father*, because he is willing to leave his glory for a temporal and new life on earth.

"No one takes it from me, but I lay it down of my own accord. I have power to lay it down, and I have power to take it up again. I have received this command from my Father. For this reason the Father loves me, because I lay down my life in order to take it up again." (John 10:18)

Jesus Christ lived as a man in his divine life. *No one takes it from me*. We must see the equality of God the Father and God the Son. Jesus Christ receives his life from the Father and returns his life generously to the Father. The Son acts externally on what he receives from the Father. The Son and the Father and the Holy Spirit are united essentially and act as one unit. Their power and force are one and equal, without distinction between the three persons. However in the communication of the persons, the first interior action comes from the Father, although this does not have a moment of priority. There is no moment that the Father has not engendered the Word who has given this back to the Father. The Trinity has different and distinct actions, but they do not have priority over each other. Although the first action of the eternal generation of the Word is attributed to the Father, this action does not have priority. They are united in one and indivisible principle; therefore their productions are equal and infinite without distinction of persons. Although the persons are equal, the Father is not the Son and the Son is not the Father and the Holy Spirit is not the Father or the Son. The Father and the Son and the Holy Spirit are one God united in essence without division or distinction.

Therefore, the Son leaves *his life* to *take it up again* in a new life. He loses his old life and moves into new life. As God he says, "*I have power to lay it down, and I have power to take it up again.* As both man and God, I am freely and voluntarily incarnate. No person can take this from me. Becoming a human being, I am always living without being subject to death, because my hypostatic union makes me free of the law of death, because my body was pure of Adam's corruption, I do not participate in Adam's death. I am therefore, both human and God, but I voluntarily accept death, finally to *take again* a new life. I am immortal in nature so that *I have received this command from my Father,* having made me man to obey him, to leave my life, and to take it again new." Jesus Christ leaves his life to take the new life and teaches all people to leave their old life of Adam. To have a new life, we must let the tomb become our cradle, as it was for Jesus Christ. Without death, no life. Also, without life, there would be no death. This is why St Paul had known this and understood when he said, *If Christ has not been raised, your faith is futile and you are still in your sins* (1 Corinthians 15:17).

> Again the Jews were divided because of these words. 20 Many of them were saying, "He has a demon and is out of his mind. Why listen to him?" 21 Others were saying, "These are not the words of one who has a demon. Can a demon open the eyes of the blind?" (John 10:19–21)

As soon as we hear his words on *death*, we suffer *division* and pain. When we talk about gifts, graces, and marvelous things, we admire and esteem them. But when we talk about death, and the ways God uses for the death of souls, O then we accuse others of mistakes and *demonic* operations. Unjust people attribute to demons the strongest operations of grace but others say, *Can a demon open the eyes of the blind?* Which is to say, Could it be that demonic operations could enlighten the soul with such great truths, and put it in the true light, which makes known to the human what he is and what God is?

> At that time the festival of the Dedication took place in Jerusalem. It was winter, 23 and Jesus was walking in the temple, in the portico of Solomon. 24 So the Jews gathered around him and said to him, "How long will you keep us in suspense? If you are the Messiah, tell us plainly." (John 10:22–24)

It seems that these circumstances that the Evangelist reports are entirely useless but they are admirable. *The festival of the Dedication* is no other thing than the consecration that we make of ourselves. The *winter* is no other than the time of tediousness, drought, and aridity. The soul in this state does not leave herself to celebrate the festival of the Dedication or Consecration. Jesus Christ is in the middle of her but she does not know this. She often tells him with simplicity, "O my divine Savior, if I find myself in a state where I do not know you, or I only see coldness, make me know by a sign. *How long will you keep me in suspense?* This state is one of pain and uncertainty." But Jesus Christ responds:

> Jesus answered, "I have told you, and you do not believe. The works that I do in my Father's name testify to me." (John 10:25)

Jesus Christ says this because the soul has nothing to assure herself of the truth of the state. Jesus Christ *answered* in the foundation of the soul but the soul does not know or believe that it is he. Nothing can assure or strengthen the soul, but she should not stop at what is said. *The works I do in my Father's name* in him, by him, and through him.

> "But you do not believe, because you do not belong to my sheep. 27 My sheep hear my voice. I know them, and they follow me." (John 10:26-27)

Jesus Christ shows us that *faith* is the sign of belonging to him. *But you do not believe* said Jesus Christ. "That is to say, you do not have faith and trust in me but I am not surprised *because you do not belong to sheep*. Faith, abandon, and trust are the only characteristics that distinguish my sheep from others. *My sheep* allow themselves to be led and why do they let themselves be led? They listen to me and, listening to me, they have the advantage of *hearing my voice and following me*." O, if we want to listen to the divine voice, after a little perseverance, it becomes impossible to listen without following. Listening to God's voice and following him brings the happy advantage of the fortunate sheep, who belong to so good and worthy a shepherd.

> "I give them eternal life, and they will never perish. No one will snatch them out of my hand." (John 10:28)

The advantage of being one of Jesus Christ's sheep with its gifts, graces, and favors does not end in this life. This admirable Pastor also says *I give them eternal life*. The way that the sheep are nourished in this interior life by the Word is a taste of eternal life. He assures them, *They will never perish*. Yet some say the opposite by asserting that the interior life is only loss, and that the demon uses it to tear souls away from Jesus Christ. However, Jesus Christ assures his sheep that he leads them as their true and legitimate Pastor, that the sheep will never perish, and that *no one will snatch them out of his hand*. Oh, it is good to abandon ourselves to God to leave us in his hands in all things! We will never perish. The word of Jesus Christ is true. If we perish, it is because we were not led by him. Because once we have given ourselves to him, we do not perish. It is true that this good Pastor, in order to save us, makes all that is of Adam perish within us and all that is of ourselves. We then believe that everything perishes, but this loss is a great gain. St Paul, who had lived this say, *I regard everything as loss because of the surpassing value of knowing Christ Jesus my Lord*. We have to lose everything to be his without reserve.

> "What my Father has given me is greater than all else, and no one can snatch it out of the Father's hand. 30 The Father and I are one." (John 10:29–30)

Jesus Christ speaks of what his *Father has given* him either in his own person or in other people. In his own person, he has been given hypostatic union, the life of the Word for both eternal and temporal generation. He has also been given souls so he may dispose of them. Sadly some by malice and evil use their freedom and take it away from Jesus Christ. If the human being gives herself to Jesus Christ, this is right because he has authority over humanity and creation and through the Word everything is done. Creation is attributed to the Father, yet it is made through the Word and without him nothing is made. Through his blood, he acquired the gift of redemption.

When the human being is in harmony with Jesus Christ, she returns to him what she owes him because of his titles of power and authority. Jesus Christ possesses this domain, which he renders to his Father as he goes there continually, losing himself and all his souls in the unity of God alone.

It is in this way, as St Paul says, our life is hidden with Jesus Christ in God in the unity of the principle in whom they dwell (Colossians 3:3). It is then that *Jesus Christ and the Father are one.* Having come out in distinction from that same Father, she finds himself united in the unity of principle without distinction or division, in separating and reuniting again continually. The soul flows and is lost in this way, but she remains hidden with Jesus Christ in God, until it pleases Jesus Christ to reproduce himself in her, putting herself in the apostolic life. There she remains indistinguishable in her union, with the disproportions that must always be assumed, and multiplied and distinct in outside things. The soul that comes here cannot fear anything, although it seems that she has more reason to fear. Because as Jesus Christ has said that nothing may be taken away from him that his Father has given, it says here that after he returned to his Father what he had received from him, *no one can snatch it out of the Father's hand.* And as his Father and he are one and the same, souls that are given to him will never perish.

> The Jews took up stones again to stone him. 32 Jesus replied, "I have shown you many good works from the Father. For which of these are you going to stone me?" (John 10:31–32)

Human beings love their own way of life. As soon as someone talks of a state taken away from him in order to allow himself to be led to God and surrender to God without reservation, they cannot suffer him. This is why they *take up stones to stone Jesus Christ* as soon as he taught them this doctrine, although it is full of sweetness and goodness and advantageous for them. Jesus Christ though with admirable skill, without complaining of the injustice they were doing, only asks them, *For which of these good works are you stoning me?* This is as if to say, "When a doctrine so pure is accompanied by holy works that are done, they must not be suspicious. If you have any difficulty in believing what I teach you, then the works that I do will be sure proofs of the truth that I announce to you."

> The Jews answered, "It is not for a good work that we are going to stone you, but for blasphemy, because you, though only a human being, are making yourself God." 34 Jesus answered, "Is it not written in your law, 'I said, you are gods'? 35 If those to whom the word of God came were called 'gods'—and the scripture cannot be annulled— 36 can you say that the one whom the Father has sanctified and sent into the world is blaspheming because I said, 'I am God's Son'?" (John 10:33–36)

They would not acknowledge the *good works* of Jesus Christ in order to have a good reason to condemn him. *It is not for a good work that we are going to stone you, but for blasphemy.* When we cannot find fault with the actions of God, or condemn them, we try to surprise the interior souls of prayer in their words because they use unconventional terms among people who do not know them. They take for blasphemies and impieties the truest expressions of divine things. Jesus Christ uses scripture himself to support what he says, *You are gods to those who receive the word.* O these words have strength! To receive these words is to receive the Word. To receive the Word is to receive God. Receive God in faith, live God, and be infused with God. We may not doubt the strength and truth of these words that are well-applied to interior souls who live truly in God and are transformed in God.

Finally, so that we do not doubt the truth in these souls, Jesus Christ assures that *scriptures cannot be annulled* in these souls who listen and receive the word, in whom Jesus Christ is manifested. These words of Jesus Christ are beautiful, when he assures us that scripture will not lose its strength. Scriptures have a force in themselves that infinitely passes the words themselves and this is the admirable difference that is between holy scriptures and the works of human beings. Scriptures written under weak and simple words contains a force entirely divine. The writing of human beings is entirely different because they use strong and elegant terms in an attempt to hide that they express very weak things. They only have strength from their expressions.

As scripture assures us, all who have received the Word within them are changed into him and carried into the Father and become *gods*. Do we find this strange that we use the word *deification*, which is no other than transformation?[3] *The soul transformed is a deified soul but to avoid misunderstandings, it is probably good to use the word transformation which expresses all that the mystics say in the word deification.* Jesus Christ is God by his divine nature and has been sanctified as human by the Father to be in a hypostatic union as Word and to be sent into the world to bring holiness. How do they say that he with all these qualities blasphemes because he says he is the Son of God?

> "If I am not doing the works of my Father, then do not believe me. 38 But if I do them, even though you do not believe me, believe the works, so that you may know and understand that the Father is in me and I am in the Father." (John 10:37–38)

Jesus Christ's task is to make known to them the truth of who he is. This way, as St Paul says, they are without excuse.

These words of Jesus Christ can still be very well-heard when he comes into souls and works there. Those who fight against the interior life without believing in or submitting to the kingdom of Jesus Christ in souls, it is for them that Jesus Christ speaks when he says, *"If I am not doing* in souls *the works of my Father, then do not believe me. But before condemning me, judge the truth of my dwelling in the soul by the works that I do. If I do not do the works of my Father, if I do not operate in them, you do not have to believe. But if I operate, why do you say anything? Should you not believe the truth of the state? If you do not believe, you have no excuse for this error. Believe the works, so that you may know and understand that the Father is in me and I am in the Father* and that I live and dwell in righteous souls. I am in them and they are in

---

3. Guyon's footnote. This word and other equivalents are used many times in St Macaire, Basil, Chrysostom, Athanasius, Cyril, and many other holy fathers; also in St Bernard and many mystics who experienced this such as St Lawrence, Justinian, Bonaventure, Rusbrochius, Tauler, Harphius, Blosius, Denis the Carthusian, and Gelenius. The word transformation is from St Paul himself in Romans 12:2 and 2 Corinthians 3:8.

me. Everything is consumed in the unity. Believe because of the works, the virtues, and all the grand things that I operate in souls."

> Then they tried to arrest him again, but he escaped from their hands. (John 10:39)

The interior of Jesus Christ with its living truth was persecuted. Do not be astonished that today the same thing happens to those who love and defend him. Persecution is the best sign and the most assured testimony of the truth of the interior.

> He went away again across the Jordan to the place where John had been baptizing earlier, and he remained there. 41 Many came to him, and they were saying, "John performed no sign, but everything that John said about this man was true." 42 And many believed in him there. (John 10:40–42)

After repentance has worked in the soul, Jesus Christ does not fail to come to live in the soul, but he will not come unless the repentance is sincere and true. There comes a state where you can no longer do repentance by one's self. God then stops this useless self-repentance and the soul suffers many other things. It is therefore foolishness to believe that they are interior without passing through very strong mortifications of the senses. This mortification, though, must be accompanied and supported by prayer. As has been said many times, prayer is a good mortification. When it is time, Jesus Christ himself comes to take his place. O then he works and operates everything! After the first state of penitence, in the purgative state, Jesus Christ truly comes to live in the soul. As it says, he stayed with John, the figure of repentance, *where* John had once lived.

Then the soul enters into the illuminative life where everything seems divine and consumed. Scripture says, *many came to Jesus* because of the *miracles* he had done. Such a soul is admired, applauded, followed, esteemed by all the world, because of the grand things God does in her and all the world takes this for the consummation of holiness. It is seen that this soul is elevated above that of penitence. In the purgative state, God does not *do miracles* in this soul. The people saw that *John performed no signs*. Not that John was not very holy, and more holy than the others were, but he was the figure of penitence. As the precursor of Jesus Christ, penitence always precedes Jesus Christ in the soul. Miracles appear in the illuminative life where are the extraordinary things. In the apostolic states, God does miracles for only his reasons.

> Now a certain man was ill, Lazarus of Bethany, the village of Mary and her sister Martha. 2 Mary was the one who anointed the Lord with perfume and wiped his feet with her hair; her brother Lazarus was ill. (John 11:1–2)

Why does the Evangelist tell all of these circumstances? They are necessary to understand penitence and the illuminative way that follows. We may see here the way that God leads souls. *Mary* is and will always be the figure for the contemplative life and *Martha* the active. The illuminative way is a mixture of activity and passivity. Though lights and extraordinary things are received passively into the soul, this state is not properly called passive because the soul has the power of love and strength in her interior and in action externally in order to see the glory of God. In the interior, the soul is Magdalen, all burning with love. She burns with soft and strong fire. This state would consume the life of the soul in a way both delicious and holy, if God by an infinite goodness, who does not want his lover to remain there, did not make *Lazarus sick*. This malady is a malady that is the beginning of truth but will be followed by death. The *brother Lazarus* is the foundation and center of the soul, or rather, it is interpreted in this place as the power and vigor of the soul which supports in its love the external by an animating heat, a facility to remain in love, and to do nothing but love. In the exterior, Lazarus has an admirable agility for all that is the glory of God and his will. But alas! This brother falls sick; a certain languor takes hold of everything in himself. We feel little by little this interior fire slow down. At the same time, we lose the facility for external good works that we do with pleasure. The greatest and most continuous pleasure was to remain in prayer. We do not allow ourselves to adore external good works because they are not the main thing but the accessory to prayer. When we did these works, it was with an admirable satisfaction because the interior vigor is spread on all things. But as soon as this good brother of the two sisters who supported him becomes sick, the sisters do not know what to do. What will they be in this state? From the Evangelist we will learn.

> So the sisters sent a message to Jesus, "Lord, he whom you love is ill." (John 11:3)

The poor *sisters* afflicted with this malady and languor *sent a message to Jesus Christ*, as to the only one who can bring some remedy to their evil. *Lord*, they say, *he whom you love is sick*, the one whom you approved. Nothing pleases you more that this animating and fiery love, which makes the soul do with great pleasure all your will. She then has no desire but to remain with you, to love and please you. Lazarus whom you had chosen and given all your affection is sick.

> But when Jesus heard it, he said, "This illness does not lead to death; rather it is for God's glory, so that the Son of God may be glorified through it." (John 11:4)

O my divine Savior, what do you mean? You say, *This illness does not lead to death; rather it is for God's glory*. However, Lazarus dies. Can you say, O infallible oracle of the truth, that Lazarus will not die, since he dies indeed. Lazarus really dies. Yet his illness was not a death, because death is only death when it separates us from God. It required a real death, however, because it was the figure of a mystical state where truly the death was real. This was not a death that deprived the soul of God, a death of sin. But here the soul dies mystically, but she does not die from sin. This is why Jesus Christ did not say, Lazarus will not die, because he died as a man but *this illness does not lead to death*, that is to say, although this dear brother is losing his vigor that leads to life, he will not be separated from God, but always be bound by grace. This illness is necessary *for the glory of God* and for the *glory of the Son of Man*. In a definition, this means the glory that Jesus Christ had to draw from this to give back to his Father. But according to the mystical sense, this means that this death operates the death of the sinning and animal human being mixed with his loving vigor. This sickness also glorifies this man by taking away all that is corrupted in him in Adam, to leave him only what is of Jesus Christ and in Jesus Christ. God is glorified, because he only remains in the soul and his enemy is destroyed.

> Accordingly, though Jesus loved Martha and her sister and Lazarus, 6 after having heard that Lazarus was ill, he stayed two days longer in the place where he was. (John 11:5–6)

The expression of the Evangelist is admirable. He says, that *Jesus loved Martha and her sister and Lazarus* and yet *after having heard that Lazarus*, far from helping him as he could, as he could, *he stayed two days longer*. Is it a sign of his love to do this? Should he not rather go to help him? Oh no, this is the greatest sign of his love, that he does not give in to this state and prevent death. This is why the Evangelist says that *Jesus loved* this holy family, because he remained without going and without being shown. If Jesus Christ had gone to see sick Lazarus, he would not have died. The absence and distance from Jesus Christ caused his death. It is the same with the soul. In whatever languor and weakness that she falls, if Jesus Christ did not go away, she would not die. Or if after his absence, he appears for a moment, this moment of his presence will restore life, and prevent death.

> Then after this he said to the disciples, "Let us go to Judea again." 8 The disciples said to him, "Rabbi, the Jews were just now trying to stone you, and are you going there again?" 9 Jesus answered, "Are there not twelve hours of daylight? Those who walk during the day do not stumble, because they see the light of this world. (John 11:7–9)

Most souls do not want to go to places where they have already suffered. But the true servants of Jesus Christ in imitation of their dear Master do not look at persecution. It is enough that it brings glory to God so they suffer all sorts of things. Jesus Christ makes a beautiful response, *Are there not twelve hours of daylight,* that is to say, there are many times for conversion. Whoever was a persecutor can in the same day become a disciple. So let's not look at things by what they were , but what they are. Jesus Christ says, *Those who walk in the day*, who only act with a clear knowledge of the will of God, cannot be mistaken, because they walk in the true *light*. Jesus Christ says in these words to follow the movements of the Spirit of God and not to follow others. When we have once known these movements, we must let ourselves be led, and not stop at the counsels that would be contrary to this, unless it was given by a person to whom we must obey, like a king, indispensable superiors, or in direction. Some people know and do God's will absolutely.

> "But those who walk at night stumble, because the light is not in them." (John 11:10)

Jesus Christ affirms that when people are in the divine light, they must follow all the divine interior movements because they are in God. Then they will not make mistakes because they are in the full light. It is not the same for those who dwell in their self-light of darkness and ignorance. As they *walk at night,* they *stumble,* and have faults and make mistakes. Most souls without the light walk in darkness, even as they believe they have the light. Believing that they follow the movements of grace, they only follow their corrupt nature. Most souls lose out by wanting too much to happen before the divinely ordained time. This causes all the errors and mistakes in the spiritual life.

> After saying this, he told them, "Our friend Lazarus has fallen asleep, but I am going there to awaken him." 12 The disciples said to him, "Lord, if he has fallen asleep, he will be all right." 13 Jesus, however, had been speaking about his death, but they thought that he was referring merely to sleep. 14 Then Jesus told them plainly, "Lazarus is dead." (John 11:11–14)

To be *Jesus' friend and to be dead*, how can that happen? Jesus Christ does not say *Our friend Lazarus* is dead, but *Lazarus is dead*. He shows that this is not death from sin, but a sleep and a mystical death that deprived much of the apparent life but not that of grace. That is why the man who died in this way is the friend of Jesus Christ. This is asleep and not a death from which will release a new man. In his sleep Adam without his knowledge gave life to Eve, who was the mother of the living. She was named Eve to show that such a sleep could only produce life. Lazarus sleeps in the tomb and will come out alive. He dies because he is the figure for Jesus Christ, who was asleep in the tomb to destroy death and to give birth to life, but a life that cannot become lost. It is necessary that all people who aspire to this resurrection experience this death or sleep, which draws the soul out of the corpse and leaves a seed of immortality. It can be said again that Jesus Christ did not contradict himself when he spoke of sleep and death. This was sleep because it was not a death to be followed by eternal life and that Lazarus had to die again. However, this was a death because anything that deprives us of life is a death in some regard to the life that we have lost. But the true death can only be called such when the person is reduced to ashes and there remains nothing alive. What follows would be a resurrection from the dead. In this way Lazarus was in both asleep and a death.

> "For your sake I am glad I was not there, so that you may believe. But let us go to him." (John 11:15)

Jesus Christ shows his disciples that the death of Lazarus was more useful to them than to Lazarus himself because he was the figure of the mystical death that all of them would suffer. He made them understand that this must be the object of their faith, so that they understand that these kinds of diseases were not for death but only for his glory. He adds that if he healed Lazarus before he died, he would have prevented the second miracle which was advantageous to the whole church.

> Thomas, who was called the Twin, said to his fellow disciples, "Let us also go, that we may die with him." (John 11:16)

Why does the Evangelist notice so exactly this place of Thomas' faith? Why did Jesus Christ allow this apostle to have on this occasion more zeal and ardor than all the other apostles? O this is mysterious! Our Lord allowed him to have more eagerness than on other occasions to show the means of death which God wished to use for Thomas.

This is for two reasons. First, usually the places in which we had more strength and perfection are the ones where we are most destroyed. The faith of St Thomas appears grand in this occasion yet his faith still lacks. St Peter's faith failed in the very place where he had shown the most ardor and the most love. St Thomas saw and understood at this moment the mystery of the resurrection, knowing that Jesus could raise him too. However, to show that all his own light and advantages were useless, when he fell into the nets of death, St Thomas fell in the place where he had had the most certitude. The second reason is that because St Thomas of all the apostles was to have the most famous testimony of the resurrection of Jesus Christ, his weaknesses and faults served to establish the faith of the resurrection. He had to be first in this present action of Jesus Christ resurrecting Lazarus, who was a figure of Jesus Christ. O adorable invention of love, which leaves no refuge, excuse, or means of escape for the souls he wants to entirely destroy!

> When Jesus arrived, he found that Lazarus had already been in the tomb four days. (John 11:17)

The historian writes this as if Jesus Christ ignored the time of Lazarus' death. Jesus Christ knew the time of Lazarus' death, because he caused it and designed these circumstances to establish the faith in both the real resurrection and the mystical resurrection. The more death consumed, the more faith was needed. This is why Jesus Christ wanted these circumstances to find Lazarus in death.

> Now Bethany was near Jerusalem, some two miles away, 19 and many of the Jews had come to Martha and Mary to console them about their brother. (John 11:18-19)

Jesus Christ wanted this miracle to be famous as a testimony to his resurrection. He was teaching the world about death and the resurrection and how this operates.

> When Martha heard that Jesus was coming, she went and met him, while Mary stayed at home. (John 11:20)

Who would be able to judge the process these two sisters went through? See *Martha go to meet Jesus*. Will we not take her for the most faithful and passionate of lovers? And see *Mary stay in the house*, would we not accuse her of indifference? O that humans judge badly! You alone, O God, know how to judge! You gave the prize of love to Mary who was accused of staying behind in idleness? Luke describes her this way, *Mary has chosen the better part, which will not be taken away from her* (Luke 10:42). Even her idleness was excusable, because she had abandoned all things to remain with you. But now that she stays and does not think to come meet you, what will we think? O love of Mary, so strong and vigorous! Mary was so advanced and had made so much progress in love that she enjoyed him in her heart without going to meet him. She had a bond of continual love that was not interrupted by bodily absence or increased by his presence. Her repose made all her happiness. She was so taken and abandoned to her love, that she waited for him to come to her. She did not think of going to find him, but she was waiting for the moment of his will. Jesus Christ allowed this absence of Mary, in order to have more place to prove to St Martha the truth of the resurrection and to leave to the church the authentic marks of his faith and of the one we must have. Mary was so consumed in her love that she could not have said a word.

> Martha said to Jesus, "Lord, if you had been here, my brother would not have died." (John 11:21)

Martha's complaint is the most fair and true in the world because it is certain that if Jesus had been present this brother so dear and it seems needed by these two sisters would not have died. Oh this death of her brother was advantageous to Martha! She has learned from experience that everything depends on God, and that only he can prevent death. It is in vain that we work to guarantee living, if God does not do it himself!

> "But even now I know that God will give you whatever you ask of him." (John 11:22)

From her admirable faith, she draws strength from her weakness. When all hope is lost in the creature, then we learn to hope only in God. And when we hope all the more in God, we despair in all the rest.

> Jesus said to her, "Your brother will rise again." 24 Martha said to him, "I know that he will rise again in the resurrection on the last day." (John 11:23–24)

When faith is not yet firm and immutable, it has little moments of hesitation. Martha had just protested that everything was possible for Jesus Christ. However, when he says that her brother will *resurrect on the last day*, she takes this for the general resurrection and not for the one Jesus Christ speaks about. She knows that God can do this if he wants. She does not doubt that God can do this. However, there is no hope that this will ever be.

> Jesus said to her, "I am the resurrection and the life. Those who believe in me, even though they die, will live." (John 11:25)

My God! What wonderful words! How can we read these without being filled with admiration and charm? Jesus Christ says, *I am the resurrection and the life*. Yes, to you only, O divine Word, you *resurrect* a soul lying in its sepulcher but you are not content to only do this but you also give *life*. She no longer lives by herself, but in him. This is the life of the Word that vivifies and animates her after losing the life of Adam. Then Jesus Christ himself becomes her life, as St Paul experienced and said, *It is no longer I who live, but it is Christ who lives in me*. Paul also explained the mystical death in this way, *For you have died, and your life is hidden with Christ in God*. At the time of death, the soul discovers that she has no life because all her life is not in her but in God. Her life is hidden with Jesus Christ in the bosom of his Father, that is to say, the new life she must take is there. It is already her life but she is not yet vivified. She does not know this, because it is hidden from her. She is truly dead and her life is passed and hidden in God with Jesus Christ. This life is Jesus Christ. But in the time of resurrection, this hidden life is manifested and Jesus Christ after being *resurrected* becomes the *life* of the soul. That whoever is dead and has lost all life, yet retains *faith* and *trust* in God, lives in God, *even though he dies* in himself.

> "And everyone who lives and believes in me will never die. Do you believe this?" (John 11:26)

Jesus Christ speaks here of another state of life that precedes death when they live in him. But whoever *believe in me will never die*. This applies to the death of sin or the mystical death. She who has faith, whenever she sins, is promptly raised. If she dies the mystical death, she is infallibly resurrected, provided she abandon herself and trust in God. Jesus Christ wants to assure the faith of St Martha, most particularly in this place and in others, because he was for her. This is why he says, *Do you believe this?*

> When she had said this, she went back and called her sister Mary, and told her privately, "The Teacher is here and is calling for you." 29 And when she heard it, she got up quickly and went to him. (John 11:28-29)

Mary who appears unhurried when Jesus does not order her to come to him yet moves quickly to do his will when he calls to her. Her passive love is not idle. It remains tranquil until God calls to her because he desires to possess her. She works to do his will when he *calls*. Then nothing in the world may stop her. With what eagerness she runs to do what pleases Jesus! Martha says, *The Teacher is here and is calling for you*. This is truly her Master because he was the Master of Mary's heart. O how few hearts are yours, O divine Jesus!

> Now Jesus had not yet come to the village, but was still at the place where Martha had met him. 31 The Jews who were with her in the house, consoling her, saw Mary get up quickly and go out. They followed her because they thought that she was going to the tomb to weep there. (John 11:30-31)

Now Jesus had not yet come to the village but was still at the place. Why did he not come into Mary's house? Oh this is mysterious! It was necessary that the resurrection be done first and that Lazarus, who signifies the foundation and center of the soul, was the first revived. The difference is that there is a resurrection of the first life. The first life between the powers and senses passes into the foundation. But the second life of resurrection begins in the center and moves into the powers and senses. The sisters signify the senses and powers who witness a true resurrection.

The Jews who were with her in the house, consoling her over the death of her brother thought she was going to the tomb. They believed Mary *wept* over her brother's carnal death. Ah! She weeps not over the loss of Lazarus, but the general deprivation and loss of support for interior vigor. This most passionate lover thinks she has lost love. This is a strange desolation. Oh, that humans judge things badly! No one can judge the sorrow of Mary and what causes this.

> When Mary came where Jesus was and saw him, she knelt at his feet and said to him, "Lord, if you had been here, my brother would not have died." (John 11:32)

Mary says to Jesus the same words as Martha but as their loss was different, their sorrow was also differed. They both knew that the loss of their brother meant the loss of support because of the absence of Jesus Christ. Martha only lost her pleasant and agreeable exterior but this was not necessary. Mary lost vigor of her love and she believed that she lost her love. This is why she says to Jesus: *If you had been here, my brother would not have died.* O divine Jesus! You drew me from the horrible death of sin and gave me life through your presence; the first moment in which you approach makes me happy, Alas! Your absence causes the death of this same life, so that I only want you. This dear brother has been taken away, O divine Savior! You give to the soul this life of love as soon as you make her a part of your divine presence. You by your absence make her lose the life that you have given. Be consoled, O afflicted soul. He only takes away to give with more advantage. Have a little patience, and you will see the gain made by this loss.

> When Jesus saw her weeping, and the Jews who came with her also weeping, he was greatly disturbed in spirit and deeply moved. (John 11:33)

Where does this sadness of Mary come from? The Evangelist tells us about Mary whose desolation and sadness were much more profound than Martha who had exterior sorrow, the loss of her ability to do good in activities. Mary, though, had the loss of active love and nothing is worse than this loss. In activities the soul is distinct and seen, but in the vigor of love, the soul tastes peace in this same love which entirely occupies it and made strong in the love. The loss of interior love is the loss of all exterior support.

But why was *Jesus greatly disturbed in spirit and deeply moved* and *wept*, as it says below? He saw then how little faith that these souls would have to let him be killed and destroyed, and how few would have the courage to pass through this death. But he saw at the same time the great pitfall of this death and the reactions of people full of fear and pride. O the meaning of this passage is delicate! Where are the souls who have through grace let themselves be killed and destroyed and annihilated, without having interfered with it or defended against it or precipitated themselves into it too early and without vocation? Frequently, as St Paul says, after having begun with the spirit, one ends with the flesh because one follows the movements of nature and not of grace.

> He said, "Where have you laid him?" They said to him, "Lord, come and see." 35 Jesus began to weep. 36 So the Jews said, "See how he loved him!" 37 But some of them said, "Could not he

who opened the eyes of the blind man have kept this man from dying?" (John 11:34–37)

Jesus did not know the place where Lazarus was but he wanted his resurrection to be made in all forms. Even those who had placed him in the earth and covered him from human eyes contributed to the resurrection. God usually uses the same things that give death to bring life. For the exterior, the same people who have tarnished the reputation are frequently the ones to reestablish it.

Jesus began to weep, as we already noted. He mourned our cowardice and how few souls willing to given themselves up to death, after he had already done this. So *the Jews said, "See how he loved him!"* O souls, if you knew the love that your God has for you, you would be perfectly ravished and astonished! You would die a thousand deaths to know a love so excessive! But the love of Jesus does not consist, as many people imagine, in preventing this death. O God! *"Could not he who opened the eyes of the blind man have kept this man from dying?"* Without doubt you are able but it was infinitely more glorious and more advantageous for him to be resurrected after his death, than to prevent his death. You give sight to the blind but you do not do this before they are blind. You give a view a thousand times more perfect than nature has given. They do not comprehend the happiness of the view, if they have not experienced blindness. The same is true that we do not understand the advantage of the possession of life, if we have not tasted death. O fortunate death, that produces such a happy life! This is the sign of the great love that Jesus may give a soul, to procure such a death. But he does not know it, as long as this operation lasts because he cannot think of the good that will follow this death. He only thinks of the present sadness. If he could envision a future good and resurrection, he would never die and his life and hope would prevent this death. Those who see this as a defect of God are mistaken for God only does this out of an excessive love. This death is a sad ecstasy, which brings the soul out of itself to pass into God.

> Then Jesus, again greatly disturbed, came to the tomb. It was a cave, and a stone was lying against it. (John 11:38)

See with what care the Evangelist reports how Jesus Christ cried over Lazarus, that he had not done over others. He *cried* two times. This shows the pain that Jesus Christ had over three things. First, that Lazarus was in a state that figured a sinner, though this was not the reason he was there. Secondly, Jesus Christ saw that this death was only a half-death and a sleep. That is why the resurrection was not sustainable and Lazarus must again die. If total annihilation does not always follow death, one can always die and resurrect many times. They are sleeping and waking, rather than death and resurrection. But when annihilation follows death, the soul resurrects permanently. O then this is the perfect pleasure and contentment of Jesus Christ. But when he resurrects before total destruction, he does so as regret. The second cause of the tears is over the pain that he suffers from compassion over what the soul feels in this state of death.

> Jesus said, "Take away the stone." Martha, the sister of the dead man, said to him, "Lord, already there is a stench because he has been dead four days." 40 Jesus said to her, "Did I not tell you that if you believed, you would see the glory of God?" (John 11:39–40)

One has faith for moments but this is not a permanent and lasting faith until the soul is consumed in the same faith. Martha said yes to what Jesus Christ said about the resurrection, but when it comes to the effect, she does not believe. The reason that she gives is, *There is a stench*. But when circumstances appear desperate to the eyes of humans, the easier they are to God. However, people do not understand and do not want to attempt anything. This is why Jesus says sweetly, *"Did I not tell you that if you believed, you would see the glory of God?"* What does this mean? Only faith can render to God the glory that is due to him. The more she trusts in God, the less she trusts in creatures.

> So they took away the stone. And Jesus looked upward and said, "Father, I thank you for having heard me." (John 11:41)

To take away the stone is to take away the obstacles that stop the soul from resurrection. This is a certain shrinking or tightening that holds the soul captive and stops the soul from entering into true freedom.

This stone or obstacle is what Jesus Christ says in this admirable prayer with its well-hidden meaning, *"Father, I thank you for having heard me."* How should this be heard? We need to know that God created humans free, but that Adam through his sin had made human nature captive to the demon and that reason itself became subject to concupiscence and a corrupt nature. Jesus Christ entered the world to glorify his Father and to free human beings through his death and resurrection. Only Jesus Christ may give this freedom, as he himself says, *So if the*

Son makes you free, you will be free indeed (John 8:36). Jesus Christ sees already in this death of Lazarus, the destruction of nature. In this future resurrection, the human will be put in freedom. Jesus Christ desires this for all humans, as he says, "*Father, I thank you for having heard me.* I see already the fruits appear from my being made man in the incarnation." He also adds:

> "I knew that you always hear me, but I have said this for the sake of the crowd standing here, so that they may believe that you sent me." (John 11:42)

"For me," says Jesus Christ, "*I knew that you always hear me* because you cannot refuse what I ask as both man and God." But, O divine Savior, if your Father hears you always, and if you desire nothing but to see human beings in freedom, and you come to bring freedom, why are not all of them free? Oh, this is the secret of malice and the unhappy freedom of humans, that they use their freedom for evil and do not enter into the death of Jesus Christ, so they do not have freedom. For these reasons, Jesus Christ cried, to see that he could not put human beings into freedom that he had merited for them because they did not want to be his captives and enter into the slavery of death. This is why when Jesus Christ was resurrected and all the patriarchs with him, scripture says, "*When he ascended on high, he made captivity itself a captive*" (Ephesians 4:8). He captivated the captivity that held human beings under the heel of death to allow them to enter into true freedom. They cannot be free until Jesus Christ captivates captivity; in his new life he causes the death of death. In another place it says that the light has risen on those who sit in the darkness and in the shadow of death (Luke 1:79). We must pass through death, suffering, and enter into captivity to be enlightened with the divine light Jesus Christ to make us free. This is also what the divine Savior says, *I knew that you always hear me* because I ask for life for those willing to become my captives and submit to death: *I have said this* so that people who know and *believe that you sent me*, follow me and be my captive, so that one day I will make captivity itself captive.

> When he had said this, he cried with a loud voice, "Lazarus, come out!" 44 The dead man came out, his hands and feet bound with strips of cloth, and his face wrapped in a cloth. Jesus said to them, "Unbind him, and let him go." (John 11:43–44)

Jesus Christ uses the word for resurrection because he is the active Word of the Father. He gives this divine life by his word and makes the resurrection. The soul dead to all other life truly receives this life of the Word, who says this: *Lazarus, come out!* This is to say, finish getting out of yourself, where you remain dead in a sepulcher to pass into me. *Come out* of your captivity to enter into my freedom. This word is efficacious and *the dead man came out*. He came out of death to enter into life. But it must be noted that after Lazarus was resurrected and he became truly alive, he remained with *his hands and feet bound with strips of cloth, and his face wrapped in a cloth*. This means that the soul is indeed sometime in life and new life without distinguishing it and cannot act like a resurrected person. As a newborn infant who lives but does not know his life, this soul lives. Not feel the pains and horrors of death anymore, she begins to perceive that she lives. Finally, little-by-little, with *unbound* feet and hands, she may walk in resurrected life and perfection. When she is *unbound*, she is given freedom to act. Those who believe that after resurrection they have the same powerlessness to act externally as they had at the time of death and annihilation are mistaken. This place in the scripture tells us this. If they cannot act, they have not had a total death and resurrection, or they are in a voluntary powerlessness. True freedom consists in being able to do everything without having to do anything. This is why Jesus ate after his resurrection.

> Many of the Jews therefore, who had come with Mary and had seen what Jesus did, believed in him. (John 11:45)

Miracles and extraordinary things create some belief in curious minds. But this belief lasts only while the impression is alive in the mind. As soon as the idea passes, they lose their faith because it is only an idea and words, and not based in the interior. The interior faith (called a nude faith) believes in God without distinction or reason. This faith is strong, though the strength is not known to the one who possesses it. Because the faith is completely nude, the foundation is not based in the human being or in works of the human being but in God.

A second type of faith is based in works and subject to change. But being based on the works, gifts, and miracles alone, the faith remains external subject to perishing. A belief in Jesus Christ based in miracles continually vacillates. After having believed at one time, they do not believe in another time. They change from being admirers of Jesus Christ to persecuting him. Because the object of their faith is not Jesus Christ, their faith lacks also. But the others who believe in Jesus Christ for himself go from strength to strength.

Nude faith is always certain. This faith is in God and for God, not for herself. The faith is supported in God alone. There are two degrees of nude faith. This is a distinct and expressible faith based on God is still distinct and expressible. They are consecrated in the goodness and power of God and faithfully says, "I consecrate myself to God who is all powerful."

In the second degree of nude faith, the power of God is contemplated directly, This faith has a nudity without discerning any substance. We are not talking here of faith and theological virtues, or ordinary faith that believes everything that needs to be believed and everything that the church commands. We speak of a prayer of faith or a state of faith.

> But some of them went to the Pharisees and told them what he had done. 47 So the chief priests and the Pharisees called a meeting of the council, and said, "What are we to do? This man is performing many signs. 48 If we let him go on like this, everyone will believe in him, and the Romans will come and destroy both our holy place and our nation." (John 11:46–48)

The strange monster of self-love stops all good and makes all evil by making herself her own object and the end of all things. She rules her faith based on her convenience. If she believes something is advantageous, she will never believe that this causes harm. If the Pharisees had not been possessed by this passion of self-love, they would have admired the miracles of Jesus Christ and tasted his doctrine. But far from this, they arm themselves with defenses so they are not caught. They think that if he is given credit, they will have less. Their self-love that makes them want much good, actually deprives them of the greatest of all goods. We should actually call self-love, self-hate, because it certainly deprives the person of all true goods. We need to listen and follow Jesus Christ and not prevent him from acting. In our world today, interior people are persecuted in the same way that Jesus Christ was persecuted. Instead of seeing and listening to interior people, if they see some good they do, they want to prevent it, so that they do not get the credit.

> But one of them, Caiphas, who was high priest that year, said to them, "You know nothing at all! 50 You do not understand that it is better for you to have one man die for the people than to have the whole nation destroyed." 51 He did not say this on his

> own, but being high priest that year he prophesied that Jesus was about to die for the nation. (John 11:49–51)

If Jesus Christ *was about to die* to save *the nation*, he should be seen as the Savior of the nation. The blindness of human beings is terrible! They know a great truth and they do not accept it. They did not admire the Savior's miracles and doctrine and death would save the nation. However, he dies as a malefactor. We see here the prophesy of Caiphas that is not a prophecy of the saints. God may give knowledge of the future to the greatest of sinners. The demon understands this and makes them known.

> And not for the nation only, but to gather into one the dispersed children of God. (John 11:52)

O great words! O passage that gives us a sense of the infinite and may not be understood! The Evangelist assures us that Jesus Christ did not die only for the nation, but for all human beings, so they would not perish. But he also died *to gather into one the dispersed* and multiplied *children of God*. O my love! One of the ends that Jesus Christ had in his death was to bring all his children into the unity of God alone. This is why the demon through false pretexts fights with all his power to stop human beings from entering into this union. The demon wants them in multiplicity. However, Jesus Christ dies not only to save us but to call us into union. Yet we try to make his death useless in us! The demon knows these two ends that Jesus Christ has in dying for human beings, which are to save us and unite with us. So the demon understands that he cannot entirely stop believers, so he stops the union so they do not fully participate in the death of Jesus Christ. It was Jesus Christ's intense desire for the union of all his children that had him make this prayer, *As you, Father, are in me and I am in you, may they also be in us* gathered and consumed in unity. It was as if he said, "This is my most pressing desire, and I die to achieve its fulfillment." We do not fully participate in the death of Jesus Christ, if we are not gathered in union. O admirable union that gathers all the true children of God in union with God alone. There they are united and reunited in their principle. There they are returned by virtue of the death of Jesus Christ to their origin, never to come out again. O Jesus! If you had not let us know from your well-beloved disciple that you had died to join us in unity, who would have dared to believe in and hope for this? Will we say after this that we are not called to union? We are called to both union and salvation, as St John says in this passage.

> So from that day one they planned to put him to death. 54 Jesus therefore no longer walked openly among the Jews, but went from there to a town called Ephraim in the region near the wilderness; and he remained there with his disciples. 55 Now the Passover of the Jews was near, and many went up from the country to Jerusalem before the Passover to purify themselves. 56 They were looking for Jesus and were asking one another as they stood in the temple, "What do you think? Surely he will not come to the festival, will he?" (John 11:53-56)

The leaders thought only of killing Jesus Christ who had given them life. Jesus Christ *was hidden* not to prevent death, but because his hour had not yet come. There is a time when Jesus Christ wants us to flee persecution. There is another when he wants persecution to happen, as he did in the next passage.

> Six days before the Passover Jesus came to Bethany, the home of Lazarus, whom he had raised from the dead. 2 There they gave a dinner for him. Martha served, and Lazarus was one of those at the table with him. (John 12:1-2)

We easily see that Lazarus after his resurrection freely functions as he did before. Martha according to her ordinary ways also serves Jesus at the table, that is to say, she occupied herself with works of charity.

> Mary took a pound of costly perfume made of pure nard, anointed Jesus' feet, and wiped them with her hair. The house was filled with the fragrance of the perfume. (John 12:3)

Mary is always generous with her love. She will spare no costs to give Jesus proofs of her love. *The perfume that she spread* is a figure of her continual prayer rises continually before God. Lazarus participates in the feast, while Martha actively serves but Mary was neither eating nor serving. Love holds her so closely, that it allows her only one application.

> But Judas Iscariot, one of his disciples, (the one who was about to betray him), said, 5 "Why was this perfume not sold for three hundred denarii and the money given to the poor?" 6 (He said this not because he cared about the poor, but because he was a thief; he kept the common purse and used to steal what was put into it.) (John 12:4-6)

Self-love makes jealousy, avarice, envy, and all the other evils. It is strange but it covers the evil with the appearance of good. O God! There will be a day that reveals foolish people! All that appeared as great virtues will be seen as a day of terrible faults! The proprietary soul has no virtue. But, O God! The true and solid state is annihilation because it holds the creature in its place by giving God all that is due to him.

> Jesus said, "Leave her alone. She bought it so that she might keep it for the day of my burial. 8 You always have the poor with you, but you do not always have me." (John 12:7–8)

What do these words of Jesus Christ mean? *Leave her alone. She bought it so that she might keep it for the day of my burial.* If she spreads it, how does she keep it? To the letter, this is what she did for his burial and what she would have liked to do then. This perfume was the only one spread for the burial of Jesus Christ, because the perfume Mary Magdalen carried was useless because she found Jesus Christ resurrected. Mystically Mary had to keep both interior and exterior balm for the burial of Jesus Christ. The anointing and holy balm she had inside preserved the heart of Mary at the time of the burial of Jesus Christ. Otherwise, she would have been killed with grief without this divine interior anointing. So truly, she kept the perfume for the day of his burial. Jesus Christ gave her this interior balm to strengthen her and to protect her at the moments of his death and burial.

Jesus Christ adds, *You always have the poor with you, but you do not always have me.* This adorable Savior communicates with the soul to say that at this time all the exterior acts of charity must cease so we apply ourselves to him alone and have joy in his presence. Because we always have the poor, we may at all times apply ourselves to them, but we will not always have him. "Peace be with you and treasure what I communicate to you." There will always be time for external works. He also says, *Let the dead bury their dead; but for you, follow me.* When Jesus Christ calls, and allows us in his presence, we leave behind all the rest.

> When the great crowd of the Jews learned that he was there, they came not only because of Jesus but also to see Lazarus, whom he had raised from the dead. 10 So the chief priests planned to put Lazarus to death as well, 11 since it was on account of him that many of the Jews were deserting and were believing in Jesus. (John 12:9–11)

To see a man dead and corrupting in the sepulcher walk with all the functions of life would attract astonishment and curiosity from others. How rare is it to see a man resurrected? Simple people are more credulous and docile. They could not help but *believe in Jesus Christ* after a miracle so surprising. But the Pharisees with their horrific pride blind themselves so they do not see the truth. Their malice prevents them from seeing this. They even *planned to put Lazarus to death*, as if they feared that Jesus Christ who had resurrected one man would do so to many others.

> The next day the great crowd that had come to the festival heard that Jesus was coming to Jerusalem. 13 So they took branches of palm trees and went out to meet him, shouting, "Hosanna! Blessed is the one who comes in the name of the Lord—the King of Israel!" 14 Jesus found a young donkey and sat on it; as it is written: 15 "Do not be afraid, daughter of Zion. Look, your king is coming, sitting on a donkey's colt!" (John 12:12-15)

Here people honor Jesus Christ in the same place where he will triumph over the enemies of humanity through his cross and death. In this way God wonderfully leads souls destined to be faithful imitators of his Son by making them triumph in certain ways and places. The place of triumph is usually also the place of ignominy. This still shows the inconstancy of people who applaud and condemn at another time. Oh, servants of God, do not be surprised to see yourself deceived and persecuted in the same places and by the same persons who applauded you the most strongly.

O truly you are the good *King of Israel*, since you deliver Israel out of its captivity. You are the conquering King. But why did Jesus Christ come *seated on a donkey's colt*? To show that he comes to deliver human nature from its slavery. It was placed in slavery by its sin and he comes out of his mercy to give freedom. This is why he took the *donkey's colt, the one who is under a yoke*, as another Evangelist said. Our human nature is under a yoke, but Jesus Christ took human nature and put it in liberty. He rides on this colt as a sign of his royalty, as divinity surmount humanity, and by this surmounts the slavery of all human nature. This same human nature had withdrawn from the divine in order to be raised by the demon and to become a slave of the demon. Jesus Christ must overcome the same nature and take it out of slavery. O *daughter of Zion*, interior soul! Look, *your king is* always *coming, sitting on a donkey's colt*, that is to say, we bring our human nature to him so he surmounts and tames it at the same time.

> His disciples did not understand these things at first; but when Jesus was glorified, then they remembered that these things had been written of him and had been done to him. (John 12:16)

This passage confirms that we know the truth of Jesus Christ's dominion over nature when he is in his glory.

Why does the Evangelist say the apostles *remembered that these things had been written of him and had been done to him*? The apostles did everything they could on their part so that Jesus Christ reigned in them. First, they brought themselves to Jesus Christ. This is no other thing than making a gift of themselves and their nature, so that he surmounts them and becomes their master. The second thing is they were stripped of their habits and covered by Jesus Christ to show that they have put off all self-righteousness so he is their master.

> So the crowd that had been with him when he called Lazarus out of the tomb and raised him from the dead continued to testify. 18 It was also because they heard that he had performed this sign that the crowd went to meet him. 19 The Pharisees then said to one another, "You see, you can do nothing. Look, the world has gone after him!" (John 12:17–19)

The Evangelist notes well that the miracle brought *the crowd to meet him*. Because without the hope of a new life, no one would subject himself to his kingdom because of the persecutions and deaths they would suffer. The anxiety and jealousy of the Pharisees cannot, however, prevent Jesus Christ from reigning when he wants and from the people following him. The Pharisees *can do nothing*.

> Now among those who went up to worship at the festival were some Greeks. 21 They came to Philip, who was from Bethsaida in Galilee, and said to him, "Sir, we wish to see Jesus." 22 Philip went and told Andrew; then Andrew and Philip went and told Jesus. (John 12:20–22)

When we desire to *see* Jesus and his knowledge, we are sure to be rewarded. All the evils of this life come when we do not know Jesus. Oh, if Jesus were known, he would be tasted! Oh, if he were tasted, he would be loved! This is an astonishing thing that the *Greeks* who never speak of God are often more rewarded than stubborn devotees irritated and distracted by everything.

> Jesus answered them, "The hour has come for the Son of Man to be glorified." (John 12:23)

Jesus Christ saw that *the hour has come for the Son of Man to be* truly *glorified* among the Gentiles by the loss of his life. To those capable of receiving, he gave true impressions of his lights. He inspires the Greek *to want to see* and know, but not out of curiosity. This is the first step which happens to introduce people into his kingdom. Oh the great *glory* that Jesus Christ receives on the earth is to reign in hearts. But alas! There is little of this now! And those who give themselves to him, do they sometimes withdraw later from his kingdom?

> "Very truly, I tell you, unless a grain of wheat falls into the earth
> and dies, it remains just a single grain; but if it dies, it bears
> much fruit." (John 12:24)

After Jesus says it is his time for glorification, he shows in this parable of the *grain of wheat* the way of glorification. O God! If a soul, which by your care is a *grain of wheat* that you have cultivated in your field, being fallen in the earth of your human nature, does not truly die, *it remains just a single grain*. Staying alone, hidden, and driven into himself, it bears no fruit, does not glorify you, and is not useful to other human beings. Without dying, he does not take from him a germ of life and remains always alone as nothing. To be fit for something, it must be united to others. But *if it dies, it bears much fruit*. Death in the same soul is needed for great works for others.

> "Those who love their life lose it, and those who hate their life in
> this world will keep it for eternal life." (John 12:25)

Jesus Christ teaches us that he must die and the way he must die. *Those who love their life* and conserve their self-life, will lose their life. Yet for *Those who hate their life in this world*, the hatred becomes a door to leave this world and lose themselves in God. Through this aversion we have for self-life, the life of Adam, we preserve everlasting life where in place of a perishable life, we are given eternal life. Jesus Christ also speaks here of what all the newly converted Gentiles will have to lose for him.

> Whoever serves me must follow me, and where I am, there will
> my servant be also. Whoever serves me, the Father will honor.
> (John 12:26)

Through these words of Jesus Christ, we learn that it is impossible to *serve* others unless we *follow Jesus* which means walking in his steps and going to places where he has been. What good service can we give him? We do everything with the assistance of grace. Jesus Christ shows us his plan in becoming man, which is to have us follow and imitate him.

This is why he takes an entirely common life, so that all can imitate. To redeem human beings, he only needed to become a man and this act of submission and humiliation was sufficient. His design in living a long time on the earth was to be imitated. St Paul told his brethren to imitate him, if they could not imitate Christ because he was no longer present. St Paul wrote, *Be imitators of me, as I am of Christ* (1 Corinthians 1:11). It was as if he said, "I try to be a faithful copy of this excellent original, so if you can imitate me, you will imitate him."

But what does it mean to imitate Jesus Christ? Everyone prides themselves on serving Jesus Christ yet no one imitates. Do we imitate Jesus poor, suffering, contemplating, abased, and infinitely humiliated, the shame of the people and the contempt of the people? Or are we barely occupied with God, love riches and pleasure, and never contemplate? However, we pretend to be a servant of Jesus Christ and do not follow him. If we *follow Jesus Christ* we are *where he is*. And where is he? In the bosom of the Father. We can happily be lost in God, living with Jesus Christ in the bosom of the Father, as St Paul says. But before this, we must share in the sufferings of Christ in order to share in his glory. This is why Jesus Christ adds, *Whoever serves me, the Father will honor.*

> "Now my soul is troubled. And what should I say—'Father, save me from this hour'? No, it is for this reason that I have come to this hour." (John 12:27)

If even Jesus *is troubled* in his inferior part, advanced souls must not be astonished when they sometimes experience *troubles*, though they are rare in advanced souls. The difference advanced souls have is that if heaven and the earth were turned upside down they would not be troubled because of their faith.

Two reasons cause trouble in Jesus Christ by the abandonment that was made in the lower part. The first reason was the suffering that was represented in this moment because Jesus Christ does not see things as a man but by the impression of divinity. Human reflection with its limited range of comprehension is imperfect, and Jesus Christ did not do this. Jesus Christ could see nothing but God in his direct gaze. He did not look at human things in themselves outside of God. Divinity represented things to him as they are. The feeling of suffering was only given to the inferior part when the superior part wanted it. All this was done by divinity. In this moment two things were impressed on Jesus Christ that caused trouble, one was the suffering, as we have just said. The other is that few people would want to follow him. Therefore, after having said that those who serve him follow him and that they will be where he is, he sees how few will follow him by the terrible way of the cross and will have the advantage of being with him in God. This is why he says to himself as a form of interrogation, *And what should I say?* If I ask to be delivered from this evil, that I only endure in order to find imitators, *It is for this reason only that I have come to this hour.* It is necessary to note that Jesus Christ did not say, "It is for this reason that I came into the world." He had come into this world to repair the glory of the Father and to give the world the sight of God in his submission to God. But he said, *It is for this reason that I have come to this hour* and that I embrace this hour of suffering. Is was as if he said, "However, I hardly find anyone who wants to enter the way of imitation of my life. Those who are considered to be the best, are content to consider me in my sufferings. But no one imitates me."

Jesus Christ must be imitated both in his interior and his exterior. He cannot be imitated in his exterior unless he is imitated in his interior. The reason for this is that we meditate in the beginning. It is very good to meditate on the states of Jesus Christ with his continual contemplation, so he can be imitated. A painter looks at a potential painting. When he has the idea and becomes familiar with it, the more he will paint with growing perfection. He will no longer need to consider every detail. While we once learned by books or by consideration, now we have God become man to imitate, in both interior and exterior. We must mold ourselves on this original. The divine Savior was in continual union. We too must devote ourselves to contemplation and take the shortest way to reach this union. After this, we must enter into him as small, annihilated, dead, with a love of abjection into a hidden and crucified life.

> "Father, glorify your name." Then a voice came from heaven: "I have glorified it, and I will glorify it again." (John 12:28)

This *glory* that Jesus asks for *the name of his Father* was that he extended his kingdom in all the earth. This is why the Father responds, "*I have glorified it* in you in the effable mystery of incarnation, where the Father has received in Jesus Christ the greatest glory that his name may receive. *I will glorify it again* in the sacrifice that you will make on the cross. I will glorify it in human beings by your death. So my name will be glorified throughout the earth."

> The crowd that stood there and heard it said that it had thundered. Others said, "An angel has spoken to him." 30 Jesus

answered, "This voice has come for your sake, not mine." (John 12:29–30)

Jesus Christ says that *this voice has not come for his sake*. Like the prayer that he made for human beings, this response was also in favor of humans. Jesus Christ asked that the name of his Father be glorified, and that there be some people who would glorify the Father's name. Give to God the glory of his name and do not usurp God's rights. Take nothing away from God. Almost all people boast in themselves and do not seek to glorify God. Those who are the holiest among people *glorify God in himself and in themselves* by losing all their self-glory through a total annihilation. This is why Jesus Christ says, "O my Father, since human beings are so ungrateful that they do not want to let you glorify your name in themselves, at least take glory from your Son. Your glory is great because it is infinite. However, my Father, let there be some humans who glorify your name, if they do not glorify it in an infinite way, at least let them glorify your name by the loss of all things." This is why the sacrifice of the martyrs was so agreeable to God because they honored him by the loss of their life. At the present time, the sacrifice of interior souls is the sacrifice of annihilation, which is the most glorious sacrifice to God that a creature may render.

Jesus Christ therefore says, "*This voice has come for your sake, not mine* because I have given him the greatest glory that I can. This is for you that you give to him the glory also great that I desire you give. The way in which I give glory to my Father is the most perfect that can be chosen; you also must follow and annihilate yourself following my example so that God alone glorifies, honors, acts, and operates in me and in you."

To be truly annihilated must include both the person and actions. As the free action of the human is her noblest production and the only one that belongs to her, this must be the most annihilated. We are annihilated in our honor and goods, and in all things external to us. We must glorify God by this active annihilation. Even if we annihilate our honor and our goods, even our life, we may not lose the desire to conserve ourselves. There is a way to lose this voluntarily by losing our sluggish human reason and taking on the quality of pure intelligences. When the human loses her own action, reason, and reflection, she takes the action of God within her. In place of reflection, she acquires her fixed and immovable gaze in God. Her intelligence becomes simple and purified. There is the loss of all that she was, and then she lives and exists to honor God in God.

It will be said to me, that if it is necessary to honor God in this way through annihilation, the angels do not honor God. Yet the angels honor God without actions free or self-centered, by resting in total annihilation, receiving simply God's action as the pure and clean ice receive the action of the sun. This ice is of two types with one receiving the rays of the same sun by reflection. The others are penetrated by light and the rays pass over and enflame what is behind the mirror by refraction. It is the same with the angels who receive and send glory back to God which may penetrate into other hierarchies. Human beings can render to God an even greater glory because they can act freely. They voluntarily destroy their own actions that prevent the actions of God and by doing so, give God a place to work in her by refraction or reflection. Oh, if human beings were so faithful to stand in this way before God, all would be well and in a very short time they would be inflamed and penetrated by God's love.

> "Now is the judgment of this world; now the ruler of this world will be driven out. 32 And I, when I am lifted up from the earth, will draw all people to myself." (John 12:31–32)

The judgment to be done *in the world* by Jesus Christ is to return to heaven what is of heaven and let earth remain with what is left. True judgement consists in taking back what is usurped. The usurpations of the prince of the world, the demon, took away from God what was not theirs. It is necessary that the judgement is made against the three things in three ways. First, with regard to the usurpation of the demon, who had dominated the world by pretending to be God, making oracles like God, it is necessary that he *will be driven out* and God be known and adored. The demon would render justice to God by returning to the abyss.

Secondly, the sinners have sought the delights of heaven on earth and give themselves all sorts of licenses. As David reports, *Fools say in their heart, "There is no God."* (Psalm 14:1). Judgement will be made against sinners and they will feel the weight of the fury of those they have misled.

Third, the righteous have made usurpations when they wanted to make heaven on earth by attracting the Messiah to the earth. They want on the earth the holiness of God, as the sinners want to attract their idols. Yet judgement is given, and the Messiah is returned to heaven. Virtue, greatness, and possession is for heaven and for the earth poverty, simplicity, and that the virtuous human remain annihilated. With judgment, virtue, holiness, and justice are restored to God, while the human remains in simplicity.

And after judgement has been executed by the death of Jesus Christ, *When I am lifted up from the earth, I will draw all people to myself.* The love he had for human beings made him a man who descended on the earth. The love he still has for them leads him to make them gods and draw them to him. Yet he must be elevated in two ways. He must be elevated on the earth on the cross and in his glory. He also must elevate human beings by drawing them to the cross and through the cross to glory.

God's friends have the cross in both their external and in their interior lives. But they also have in this life the advantage of essential beatitude which perfect joy in God in the intimacy of the soul. Yet God draws this inferior part from the cross to crucify it with him but he calls the superior part to be lost with him in his Father's bosom. This is again a favorable *judgment* that he exercises for his servants. Some humans in their external life want pleasures, glory, and honor, yet in the interior they neglect the possession of God, which is the sovereign good. For their growth, God takes away honors and pleasures from the outside, changing them to the cross and ignominies and in the interior, he calls them to possession of God. But what am I saying? God possesses them and God possesses himself in them. O admirable judgment, that takes away all usurpations, the demon, and all sinners!

> He said this to indicate the kind of death he was to die. 34 The crowd answered him, "We have heard from the law that the Messiah remains forever. How can you say that the Son of Man must be lifted up? Who is this Son of Man?" (John 12:33–34)

This place shows as the Jews wait from the Messiah, they wait in a human and earthly way, as if they believe that *the Messiah remains forever* on the earth. The law, however, does not say this but only that his eternal reign will have no end. Being God, he must eternally remain God. Being man, he must die to save human beings and he must resurrect to end death. Therefore, he remains eternally in heaven and in the letter of the Law. Jesus Christ also dwells on the earth until the consummation of the centuries through means of the Holy Eucharist. He cannot remain in another way. What he says himself, he will remain with us until the consummation of the centuries means the Holy Eucharist. His glory though will never end and never be consummated.

> Jesus said to them, "The light is with you for a little longer. Walk while you have the light, so that the darkness may not overtake you. If you walk in the darkness, you do not know where you are going." (John 12:35)

Here Jesus speaks to the Jews of the benefit they have of his presence while he is there. Because he only is the *light* of the world, he enlightens people by coming into the world, but those who walk without him *walk in darkness*. These words may be justly applied to souls of grace who must strive with all their might to advance when *the light is with you* and present. This light is given to them to advance in favor to God, as a flame is given to a traveler to help her advance in the way. If she neglects the light, she destroys herself and the darkness will overwhelm her and she cannot walk. The divine light is given to a soul beginning her journey to God. It is then she must run to God with all her might. If she does not run to God with indefatigable effort by the loss of all the rest, she will never advance because a time of darkness will come when she can no longer walk. She has then only what she acquired in the light. If the light has been strong, if her faithfulness is great enough to bring her to God, the darkness serves to make her pass into God. But if she did not make use of the light and instead amused herself, the darkness stays in her, depending on how much she has tried to amuse herself.

When I speak of following the light and walking in its favor, I am not speaking of extraordinary lights, which will stop the soul in itself. I am speaking here of lights that reveal faults, to continually combat the evil of the senses, while loving everything that crucifies her.

All lights, whether ordinary and simple or extraordinary with distinct things, are given for two effects: to make God known and to make us known to ourselves. The soul to be faithful to the light should receive these two effects, surpassing all others, and should not stop at the superficial externals of the light or at the manner in which it is given. The superficialities must remain in an eternal forgetfulness. In regard to knowing God, it is not a question of distinguishing anything in God but to know that he merits all our love and to follow him. Knowledge of ourselves does not consist in seeing whether we have one disposition or another, a favor or a grace, if we advance or in what manner God communicates to us, but it consists in making us comprehend that there is nothing good in us except for God. Our propriety is sin and all good is in God. This knowledge, which is frequently very simple and without reason, makes us flee from ourselves and run to God who is sovereign good. Once we distance ourselves from ourselves, and follow God, we will finally pass into God. This can only be done by continually stretching and forgetting one's self, to want no good such as spirituality, gifts, graces, power, wisdom, or anything else. But all for God; the more we leave everything, the more we are content. This is our goal: to stop at God alone. All for God and nothing for ourselves.

> "While you have the light, believe in the light, so that you may become children of light." After Jesus had said this, he departed and hid from them. 37 Although he had performed so many signs in their presence, they did not believe in him. (John 12:36–37)

Jesus Christ continues, *Believe in the light while you have the light.* When I am with you, believe in me that I am the light. So that you may follow and *become children of the light.* The light of the interior is present in all the world, but few follow it. We will not allow ourselves to be led by this light. We want to follow our own self lights and never leave these to follow Jesus Christ, so we remain in natural lights. Wise sages follow lights of reason and their reasoning is fertile. However, these are very small lights. Jesus Christ has the real darkness of eternal light. Who follows self-light does not want to receive divine light. What happens to those who do not want to receive this light? Then that the light withdraws. Jesus Christ *hides* first and sees if they look for him but they do not, because they do *not believe in him*, even though as soon as he appears, there are miracles and wonders. This is why they harden their hearts and bully him, so they do not have to understand him.

> This was to fulfill the word spoken by the prophet Isaiah: "Lord, who has believed our message, and to whom has the arm of the Lord been revealed?" (John 12:38)

Not only do these people not want to receive the light, but they *do not believe his message* and his message is light. In our interior, we experience a certain touch in the soul's most profound foundation as a message to follow. But they search outside for the light externally when they feel the touch inside. Instead of looking at the light within at the place it is manifested, they turn their back, and look for light in another place.

It is also added, *To whom has the arm of the Lord been revealed?* His arms are no other than his entire power. They make mistakes because they do not know the divine power and the dominion he has over human beings. If they knew the divine power over the human soul, and that this power is revealed, they would see the necessity of submitting. Then they would want nothing for themselves and realize that there is no power in human beings. They would abandon themselves to God without reserving anything and follow the admirable light without resistance.

> And so they could not believe, because Isaiah also said, 40 "He has blinded their eyes and hardened their heart, so that they might not look with their eyes, and understand with their heart and turn and I would heal them." (John 12:39-40)

The first reasons that they do not believe are the love of self, esteem of their own actions and operations, and ignorance of the divine power. The second reason is that *He has blinded their eyes and hardened their heart*. How should this passage be heard? We must not believe that the goodness of God, which is great, obscures the eyes of souls. No, it does not happen in this way. But how does this happen? The person believes that the light is mistaken and withdraws from the light. God does it in this way. When he places the light in an ungrateful heart who refuses the light, he withdraws the light and the heart enters into hardness and blindness. In the same way, an ice is half formed, like congealed water, and hardens as soon as the sun withdraws.

And why does it happen in this way with God in his goodness? He says this with clarity, *So they might not look with their eyes* of reason, since they refused the light of grace. Because they do not receive this, they receive nothing at all and do not *understand with their heart*. In what manner do we understand? They do not want to receive this grace, meant to melt and dilate his heart. They are then in a state of not understanding or containing any good or any morality. Then the souls who refuse the light enter into a state of brutalization. But why is it added, *That they not turn and be healed*? This brutalization makes the soul powerless to turn and receive healing so they could be converted. Blindness and hardness of heart only come because of the absence of light, because they turn their backs. To be healed, they need to turn to the light. This is conversion, to be turned to the light from which they have turned away. But they are in a state that they may not turn by themselves because no person can do this without grace. This does not exclude coming to a time of God by a pure effect of his mercy, without any merit on his part, by being lifted by the divine light. But there is nothing that offends God so much as rejected grace.

> Isaiah said this because he saw his glory and spoke about him. (John 12:41)

Isaiah said this because he saw the glory of God and in what it consists. All the glory of Jesus Christ is received in the Father and communicated to human beings. The desire and passion that Isaiah has for this glory is deplored by blind human beings who do not want his glory and do not want to receive the spirit of Jesus Christ, the divine light, who only asks that this be communicated. Having understood the ingratitude of both Jews and Christians, Isaiah said these things in speaking of Jesus Christ, because the glory of Jesus Christ was revealed to him and he loved that glory.

> Nevertheless many, even of the authorities, believed in him. But because of the Pharisees they did not confess it, for fear that they would be put out of the synagogue; 43 for they loved human glory more than the glory that comes from God. (John 12:42–43)

There are still many people of this caliber in this century who *love human glory more than the glory that comes from God*. Alas for this choice! How do people know and are convinced of the truth, yet refuse to follow because of a small point of honor and because they fear the consequences? If they have some good, they use it for their own sake, and not for the love of God. They do not want to declare that they know the truth, because the *Pharisees*, who have strong spirits of human pride, do not approve and they love their friendship and esteem. The love of their own glory is that which holds and stops almost everything in the world, which is deplorable. Only Jesus Christ may say truthfully that he is not seeking his own glory, but the glory of the one who sent him, because all human beings look for their own glory. Ah! Where are the people who do not search for their own temporal or eternal glory, but only for the glory of God without relation to the creature? We love God's glory in the things of the world, but when we understand, we should seek God's glory in virtue, goodness, holiness, and in God himself.

> Then Jesus cried aloud: "Whoever believes in me believes not in me but in him who sent me." (John 12:44)

Jesus Christ says that the one who *believes in me, believes not* only *in me, but in him who sent me* because it is impossible to believe in Jesus Christ and not believe in God. The other way of understanding these words is that Jesus Christ was so annihilated, that he did not want his own glory, but only wanted the interests of God alone. If we listen mystically, the soul by faith in Jesus Christ passes through faith into God alone and all are reduced into unity, without distinction, whoever she is because the Father is in the Son and the Son in the Father. This is why he adds:

> "And whoever sees me sees him who sent me." (John 12:45)

Our knowledge of God in Jesus Christ shows us both the Son and the Father because of the indivisibility between the Father and the Son, being the same as to the Father as to the unity, though different in person.

> "I have come as light into the world, so that everyone who believes in me should not remain in the darkness." (John 12:46)

Jesus Christ is truly the *light*. He is the splendor of the saints and as Word, being the term of the Father's knowledge, he is also the term of light. He is also light of the word and the word of light. He is *come into the world* as light and word to declare to people and destroy the *darkness* of ignorance and to instruct. But no one can have the true effect of light without *faith*. This light is only received through faith, as the word is only received through love.

> "I do not judge anyone who hears my words and does not keep them, for I came not to judge the world, but to save the world." (John 12:47)

To show us that the light and word cannot be separated from Jesus Christ, he says that his word comes to enlighten human beings. First, he says he *came not to judge*. Secondly, we must *keep his word*. He does not say we must keep his light, but only to receive this, but we must keep his *word*. His light is like lightning that precedes the thunder. The light precedes the word. If we believe in the light, then we open to the word and we receive the word. But there is a difference between the light and the word. The light only requires faith and holds nothing back. She believes and in believing she sends everything back to the one who sends it. But the Word must be kept in the heart. The Word influences by this word. Faith makes it come and love keeps it.

He says, *I came not to judge the world, but to save the world*. He is *Christ, Savior, and Mediator*. He does not want to lose and condemn sinners. He has come to break the wrath of God. But how does this passage agree with the article of faith that *He comes to judge the living and the dead*? As redeemer, Jesus Christ is the pledge and bail for all people. As long as they live, he is interested in them. He does not come to condemn but to redeem and to save. But after death and the end of the world, he will judge for the interest and glory of his Father against the malice of human beings, just as he opposed his Father's wrath against human beings. Then measuring his anger against his love that he has for human beings, which is infinitely grander than they merit, he will be filled with infinite indignation against sinners. He will cease being Mediator to be Judge. Jesus Christ is filled with such great justice to condemn in these ungrateful sinners who by extreme malice do not profit from his goodness, grace, and blood; who reject his love; even after Jesus Christ has left the bosom of his Father to become man. These miserable sinners prefer themselves to God and did not want the glory he acquired by his blood.

> "The one who rejects me and does not receive my word has a judge; on the last day the word that I have spoken will serve as judge." (John 12:48)

The one who *rejects Jesus Christ* and *does not receive my word* does so because his word may and must operate in the soul. But this *same word*, as he has said, will be the word that *judges us on the last day* because it has been rejected and not received. It is not a muted word but it will be thunder which will crush these unfortunates. It will not be a weak word, but a powerful and strong word that punishes. It will not be a short and abrupt word but a word extended into infinity.

> "For I did not speak on my own, but the Father who sent me commanded me to say all that I have spoken. 50 I know that his command leads to eternal life. So whatever I say is just what the Father has told me to say." (John 12:49–50)

Jesus Christ as a human being was hypostatically united as Word of the Father and as such what comes out of his mouth are only what the Father has spoken and ordained. Jesus Christ suffers the divine action and works for this action, and has no support except for divinity, which at the same time is the principle for all actions. This is why he adds that this *word commanded* and sent on the earth *is life eternal* because the Word is eternal life in him. It is also the Word, as was said on high, that was given to communicate permanent life to human beings which will never perish, because the participation of life in the Word causes immortality in the soul. And this is why Jesus Christ continues to say, *Whatever I say is just what the Father has told me to say* is a prophecy that the words of Jesus

Christ are an expression of the Father, and he may not speak any other thing that is. This makes the advantage and to hear his words inside, because through the Word he expresses himself in exterior practice.

> Now before the festival of the Passover, Jesus knew that his hour had come to depart from this world and go to the Father. Having loved his own who were in the world, he loved them to the end. (John 13:1)

These words of St John mark the excessive generosity of Jesus Christ's love. Therefore he gives proof of his love in the end of his life in the institution of the Holy Eucharist and in his death. In the perseverance of his love he becomes even stronger, far from weakening. We do a great insult to the goodness of God when we say that it is not good to enter the way of piety or abandon one's self to God, because we will not persevere and that God will allow the souls to be deceived. They say some live like angels yet die as demons. O injustice of human beings and the secret adorable judgements of God! The death, that appears like that of a demon, is frequently, that of a saint, who is paying right now what is due to God so that he does not need to pay it in the next life.[4] Or some who have had a bad life but kept this hidden with pride hiding the deregulation in their heart will reveal in death what was hidden.

St. John believes he has said everything about the institution of the Eucharist, when he speaks of the excess of Jesus Christ's love in his end. After the other Evangelists have written of the action, John writes of the cause; that is to say, he says, *Having loved his own who were in the world, he loved them* even more strongly *to the end*, giving them an immortal pledge of his love, remaining always with them until the consummation of the centuries. And to prove this was a mark of his love, St John says in his gospel what was not said in other gospels. The cause of Jesus Christ's death was his love for Christians who remain in the world. John also said this at the beginning of his gospel. Other gospels began with the temporal generation of Jesus Christ; St John speaks of the eternal generation, which is the source and origin of the temporal.

> The devil had already put it into the heart of Judas son of Simon Iscariot to betray him. (John 13:2)

Judas had resolved for a long time to *betray* Jesus Christ but did not admit it at the table. There are also many bad Christians who are allowed

---

4 Guyon's footnote says "See for example Taulere in his life."

to approach his table. But alas! This is to their condemnation. Because why do they go there? They bear the design to betray Jesus Christ with hatred in the heart, or impure love, sin and the inclination to sin in the body.

> Jesus, knowing that the Father had given all things into his hands, and that he had come from God and was going to God. (John 13:3)

O love, *knowing that the Father had given all things into his hands*, salvation for all humans and the power to rule humans. The Father had made you the ruler and sovereign. You also knew the love you had for humans and the desire to possess them entirely and to be yourself their portion and heritage, you *had come from God*. That is why St John says these admirable words and has no terms to explain them. *Jesus Christ knows that the Father had given all things into his hands*, the interests of his glory and those of the salvation of humans, and knowing at the same time, *that he had come from God and was going to God*. This coming from God is an ecstasy of love, which brought the God of love outside of himself to bring himself to humans so they can imitate him. God came to human beings by a transport of love, so that human comes out of human by the same love to become God. And in order to teach humans by a new ecstasy *he returns to God*, he opens the bosom of his Father and opens heaven, so that humans may be received there. He opens up all eternity in the bosom of his Father where he goes and he is lost in the same by an infinite and immense love. Jesus Christ does the same in time, with love for the glory of his Father, he came to human beings and with love returned the human beings to God. O human, you left God but you came out only to return to God who is your principle. But by an inconceivable evil, sin closed all the avenues so it was impossible to return to God. So the eternal Word, the God of love opened the way into the bosom of the Father with a new passage that sin had forever closed. Only Jesus Christ could make this. This is why he said, *No one comes to the Father except through me* (John 14:6). As Word, he opens the bosom of the Father. As Triumphant Savior, he brings with him into the same bosom those who please him.

The Word is the way of full knowledge of God and the infinite love of God coming from the Father. God's love is grand because it is the one and unique love between the Father to the Son and the Son to the Father. This love operates by the Holy Spirit which communicates in the Trinity.

For this reason, the Son of God became incarnate by the operation of the Holy Spirit because anything external to God is done by the Holy Spirit and his principle. Only Jesus Christ as Word is the principle of the Father but the Holy Spirit is the principle of human formation and hypostatic union done by his operation. The Holy Spirit joined the Word with human nature. If there is anything here contrary to the faith, I submit it like the rest.

> He got up from the table, took off his outer robe, and tied a towel around himself. 5 Then he poured water into a basin and began to wash the disciples' feet and to wipe them with the towel that was tied around him. (John 13:4–5)

This ceremony of Jesus Christ, along with the circumstances and words that precede it, is a wonderful model. First, after the Evangelist notes that Jesus Christ knows he has come from God and is returning to God, before his return which will open the way, he shows to his apostles the ways to keep and the purification he must do to souls. Otherwise, they will not pass into his Father. As he says to St Peter, he would have no part in him unless he allows himself to be purified in this way. Jesus Christ *took off his outer robe* for us to understand that we will not participate in his glory if we are not stripped of humanity. This is necessary to purify us. It also shows we are to be stripped of ourselves and the true purification is done in this stripping. After which, he *tied a towel around himself* to show the measure to which the soul is stripped of herself, she is clothed in the robe of innocence. This shows that he was stripped of the vestment of his glory for our purification. At the same time, he was clothed in our weak nature signified by the white towel to show the purity of his nature. *He poured water into a basin*, showing how when the body is formed, the Word like water spreads making the two natures of divine and human united. This shows how all of human nature is purified by the attachment of the Word to human nature. The divine Savior applies himself to each of us particularly. He washes our souls and purifies us by the water of his divinity and cleans us by the towel of his humanity.

> He came to Simon Peter, who said to him, "Lord, are you going to wash my feet?" 7 Jesus answered, "You do not know now what I am doing, but later you will understand." 8 Peter said to him, "You will never wash my feet." Jesus answered, "Unless I wash you, you have no share with me." (John 13:6–8)

If a human is not purified by Jesus Christ, he will never be pure. Perfect and passive purgation is only achieved by essential union which purifies from all stains. The Word alone purifies. It is strange that some people do not want this purification. Those with malice become indignant and the others out of false humility refuse. They attend to themselves with their own efforts. Peter refused Jesus' washing out of an ignorant humility. This is why Jesus says to him, *You do not know* the mystery of washing my feet and the necessity of passive purgation but one day *you will understand.* St Peter still did not want to suffer because he was not enlightened about this great mystery, but he did hear that it was entirely impossible to have a share in Jesus Christ without suffering this purification. What share was Jesus Christ talking about? He was not speaking only of his glory but of his intimate union and his suffering. It is impossible to participate in an intimate union with God by any other way. This is why as we see in the next verse, after this purification, Jesus Christ makes this admirable prayer. *As you, Father, are in me and I am in you, may they also be in us* (John 17:21).

One might say that this is only a figure of speech and that if the apostles and the ancient fathers had known this state of union they would have preached or written about this. This is easy to respond to. First, we have very few writings of the apostles. St Paul however writes frequently about this in his letters. We must note that the apostles were not preaching to devoted Christians about the secrets of the interior. Instead, they were trying to persuade sinners and idolaters of the truth of Jesus Christ. They worked to convince human beings that they killed God like a malefactor. Jesus Christ provided in all times for the needs of his church. The fathers were writing about the needs of the church and the heresies raised against it, so their work was to destroy error and combat heresy. They did not leave this work to sow things about the interior in their works because this was not the present need of the church. Those who were truly Christian did not doubt that the interior was essential because the love of the interior buried holy saints in the sepulchers of the dead.[5] What could have happened in these frightful deserts, if they had known the interior and had not tasted the happy commerce of the human with God? Jesus Christ in his gospel speaks to us almost only from his interior. In the present, the church has little repose, because all the evils of the church

---

5   Guyon's footnote. "The homilies of St Macaire are full of all these works."

come from the fact that there is no interior. In this century God speaks and writes more than in the others.

We must not be amazed if the interior is persecuted more in this century than in the others. Truth is solid and the Christian religion is only established by persecution and opposition. Never has the truth of Jesus Christ been better established than by persecution. All the most fundamental truths of the church are established because there were people who persecuted them. The church examined and eternalized them by strong and incontestable decrees. To the level that these heresies are raised, God has taken learned humans to fight by their pen and to combat strong and invincible arguments for the Christians who were following. If Cerinte and Ebion had not denied the divine nature in Jesus Christ, we would have been deprived of the admirable *In Principio* and all the rest. St John was the first to combat the error and in combatting this, established this solid truth so it did not suffer more contesting. This is why Jesus Christ said it was expedient that scandals were coming. But woe to those by whom the scandals arrive! God establishes the greatest good on the greatest evils. There is every reason that the truth of the interior will be established throughout the church of God, since at the present it is now combatted.

> Simon Peter said to him, "Lord, not my feet only but also my hands and my head!" (John 13:9)

As soon as Peter understood what Jesus Christ wanted him to say, he wanted Jesus Christ to completely and radically purify him. But Jesus Christ responds:

> Jesus said to him, "One who has bathed does not need to wash, except for the feet, but is entirely clean. And you are clean, though not all of you." (John 13:10)

This is to say, "The ones I have washed and purified myself, and who I must purify by the effusion of my blood, have no other need of purification." Jesus Christ then speaks of efficacy of salvation and the redemption through which he carries upon himself and purifies our strongest defilements as well as our languor. The only thing left to purify on us is our *feet* that is to say the malignity of corrupt nature in Adam which excluded us from salvation. Jesus Christ repaired all that was due to his Father. He adds, *And you are clean* because there is in you no obstacle to receiving the application of my merits. But you are *not all* clean because Judas was in mortal sin and consequently incapable of receiving the application of the merits of grace for redemption. Jesus Christ died for him as well as the rest of humanity, but the efficacious application of redemption cannot be applied to a soul in mortal sin, because it has an absolute impediment to receiving the flow of grace, because all the avenues are blocked. Although blood and grace flow in such abundance that they would inundate a hundred million people, it cannot enter this blocked soul. Like water seeking an entry but finding none, the grace runs over her without a place to receive it. Yet grace is abundant and would overwhelm anything if it found a place to enter in. But alas! Grace cannot find a place so flows in abundance on other hearts disposed to receive grace.

> After he had washed their feet, had put on his robe, and had returned to the table, he said to them, "Do you know what I have done to you? 13 You call me Teacher and Lord—and you are right, for that is what I am. 14 So if I, your Lord and Teacher, have washed your feet, you also ought to wash one another's feet." (John 13:12–14)

Jesus Christ explains the external ceremony and what it signifies for them to do according to their present capacity. He gives them a method for humility that all virtuous communities can do: to take pleasure in serving each other in humility. The true sense is that he gives power to purify and cleanse the sins of others in confession. However, as not all the apostles were annihilated, Jesus Christ gives them an example of external humility to show them the interior that they must have, which consists in them preferring always others to themselves, to put one's heart under their feet, to be always ready to show to all the world that their mastery is not a tyrannical domination but true service to the neighbor.

> "For I have set you an example, that you also should do as I have done to you." (John 13:15)

Jesus Christ adds that he has given *an example* that we must *do* to others either in regard to purification or to humiliation.

> "Very truly, I tell you, servants are not greater than their master, nor are messengers greater than the one who sent them." (John 13:16)

Truly, Jesus Christ speaks here of his annihilation. This is why he says, *Messengers are not greater than the one who sent them*. If it took many annihilations and pains for me to enter into glory, you also will never get glory in another way. If Christ had to suffer to enter into glory, how can we presume to enter into his glory acquired with the price of his blood, without suffering like him and with him?

> "If you know these things, you are blessed if you do them."
> (John 13:17)

Jesus Christ assures his apostles that if they understand the secret of annihilation and suffering, *they are blessed if you do the* suffering and annihilation. There is a difference between knowledge of the advantage of suffering and suffering well. Many know that suffering is necessary. Speculating about suffering is a beautiful thing, but no one wants to suffer or let themselves be annihilated. When it happens, we defend ourselves against it as the greatest of all evils, although in speculation it has been considered as the greatest of all goods.

> "I am not speaking of all of you; I know whom I have chosen. But it is to fulfill the scripture, 'The one who ate my bread has lifted his heel against me.'" (John 13:18)

Jesus Christ speaks of Judas and also because of Catholics who after having been at the table with him turn against him and offend in so many ways. There is no greater malcontent or malice more dangerous that a person who having been with God leaves and offends. Everything irritates her. Should not Jesus' remonstrances have touched Judas? However, he continues in his pernicious design.

> "I tell you this now, before it occurs, so that when it does occur, you may believe that I am he. Very truly, I tell you, whoever receives one whom I send receives me; and whoever receives me receives him who sent me." (John 13:19-20)

Jesus Christ gives us this knowledge to support our faith. This is why he says, *I tell you this before it occurs so you may believe in me* because you know that I predicted this and to show you the love I have for this man who must betray me. I myself passed into you by my life of the Word. The one who receives me, receives the one who sent me because everything that passes into me is imprinted as Word, because we are only one and indivisible essence.

> After saying this Jesus was troubled in spirit, and declared, "Very truly, I tell you, one of you will betray me." (John 13:21)

There are two things to note about the trouble of Jesus and this circumstance in time. For his *trouble*, we must note the strange ingratitude that Judas has after having been rewarded with so many good deeds and experiences with others. But the most amazing thing is that Jesus Christ, who did not ignore this betrayal from the first moment of his incarnation, is troubled now. And how can God be troubled? The Son of God because of beatitude was impassive as God and man through his hypostatic union. Jesus Christ was not able to be troubled but could only suffer what divinity imprinted on him and what he wanted to suffer. He had in him two parts to suffer, according to his choice of suffering, the soul and the body. Bodies may feel torments and sorrows that humans have, but the soul could not be altered. Nothing external could make this blessed soul suffer. But the hand of God who made an impression on him made him suffer and troubled. This is why after having known from the beginning what would happen, he did not suffer because the impression of suffering had not been known on his holy soul. But now in this moment, he truly suffers only in the inferior part of his soul all the punishments that God impressed there. The superior part of the soul had essential blessedness and did not suffer. As God, Jesus Christ had to carry the impression of these pains, yet there was no exterior cause to this. It is not surprising that advanced souls can do the same. It is true that interior souls who have achieved perfect immobility have no more trouble in the foundation or for things that happen externally in the soul's inferior part. Yet God in his design imprints on them the impressions of suffering which they do not deserve. They could not give these impressions to themselves and they cannot remove them from themselves. But it must be noted that finally the pain is from God and his impression. No external event or thought or imagination gives rise to this pain. In contrast, devouring sorrows are profound and deep within the senses because they are the pain of purification. In this, the inferior part is abandoned without help from the superior part so there is no support but an entire division which is always known to those who experience this.

Jesus Christ wants to carry all our weakness in order to clothe us with divine strength.

> The disciples looked at one another, uncertain of whom he was speaking. (John 13:22)

The hardness and cruelty of Judas is strange; even after all the goodness and admonitions of his good Master, he does not let go of his evil design. The apostles each wondered who was guilty of this and who would be capable of committing such an immense crime.

> One of his disciples—the one whom Jesus loved—was reclining next to him; 24 Simon Peter therefore motioned to him to ask Jesus of whom he was speaking. (John 13:23–24)

As St Peter had an extremely affectionate heart, he was the one of all the apostles who pressed the most to know who was the guilty one and to make sure he was not the one. The amazing thing is that when Jesus speaks in general, Peter wonders if he is the one. But when Jesus Christ speaks to Peter directly about this, Peter denies this. There are two reasons for this. First, when Jesus speaks in general, human nature does not feel directly attacked or complained about. Secondly, as long as we have virtue and humility, we can support easily any reproaches about mistakes that we did not make. But when we touch an actual problem, human nature arms itself with all its power for its justification. When we see a person defending herself, it is a sign that the person committed this fault and presumes punishment for it.

St. Peter and St John act in different ways and it should be noted. We cannot doubt that they both love him. However, St John when hearing of Jesus Christ's prediction of this dark betrayal does not defend himself or try to know who will do this evil. St Peter, though, fears, asks, and wants to know. Will it be said that St John did not love his Master or that his love is presumptuous? No, we cannot say that about either one. John desired God to whom he had abandoned himself without reservation. As he had passed into the *bosom* of Jesus and reposed within him, he was in Jesus and Jesus was in him. That is why they did not call him the disciple who loved Jesus, but the *disciple who Jesus loved* because he loved Jesus by Jesus' love of himself. John loved Jesus by the very love of Jesus toward him.

> So while reclining next to Jesus, he asked him, "Lord, who is it?" (John 13:25)

O Disciple very blessed, very fortunate friend! Why are you lying on the chest of your very dear Master? What do you think about in this admirable position? O John, lying on the bosom of Jesus makes you ecstatic. You leave yourself and pass into Jesus and Jesus in return passes into you. This is why Jesus told you on the cross you are the son of Mary, because you are entirely filled with the life of Jesus. You then learn the ineffable communication of interior silence which is felt by those whom God favors.

There is a communication of silence between God and the soul. This communication also happens among creatures that are almost equal in degree of interior prayer but for this it is necessary to be very advanced. Remaining in prayer together, an interior language is made, where the interior communication is not spoken, provided the interiors are in harmony, like two lutes playing together. When the master touches one, the other sounds the same tone. Jesus had a double conversation of silence with John. Jesus as Word communicates to John in the secrecy of silence. It is there that he gave him an abundant flow of the life of his Word, that made him hear the secrets of eternal generation. He did not then understand that this life of the Word was to be communicated to all other Christians coming into the world. No one can be enlightened except by this divine light. He understood with what profusion this life is communicated to the heart that makes no resistance. It is not necessary to be lying on Jesus' bosom as both God and man to support the superabundance of graces communicated to St John. This is why this dear disciple follows him in this communication so extraordinary. If he had died a thousand times, he would not have found support and life more abundant. Jesus supported this disciple so that he could carry the immense weight of his love and graces. So that John losing his being and life mystically, and in a perfect way, he recovers the life and being of the Word. There was no longer John in John, but all was Jesus Christ who lived in him. St Paul himself assures us of this. This was a transfusion of the soul of Jesus into John and the soul of John into Jesus. This must be understood mystically. Jesus Christ as friend made an admirable communication to John by revealing his most hidden secrets. A friend hides nothing from his friend. He reveals all things. Jesus Christ hides nothing from John that regarded him. Jesus revealed to John his sufferings, which would have made him die of pain and love if he had not been clothed with divine power.

Simon Peter therefore motioned to him to ask Jesus of whom he was speaking who would betray him. St Peter believed that this friendship would infallibly be accompanied by this communication and he was not mistaken.

> Jesus answered, "It is the one to whom I give this piece of bread when I have dipped it in the dish." So when he had dipped the piece of bread, he gave it to Judas son of Simon Iscariot. (John 13:26)

Out of love, Jesus did not want to name the traitor. However, because of his goodness he did not want to keep his disciples for a long time in suspense and in pain. He revealed the betrayer by a blessing and with courtesy. He gives us an admirable example of the way we conduct ourselves towards our greatest enemies. His charity was not changed. As soon as we are wronged, we want to justify ourselves with invectives and cry out against those who offend us. It is permissible to say the truth and justify ourselves on those occasions but we must do so in charity. We do not wrong those as we do this. This rule of charity is good for us to follow as Jesus Christ gave us this example.

> After he received the piece of bread, Satan entered into him. Jesus said to him, "Do quickly what you are going to do." (John 13:27)

This is a strange thing that the favors and blessings of God that charm the good ones and makes them holy, have the opposite effect on evil ones and cause their bad disposition and corrupt choices. Scripture says, *After he received the bread, Satan entered into him.* Was Satan not already there by the plan which he had formed to betray his good master? Yes, without doubt, but consent is not entirely given, but the blessing of Jesus Christ, which should make him die of regret, increases Judas' malice. This is customary. A good thing placed in a sour stomach easily corrupts.

But why does Jesus say, *Do quickly what you are going to do.* Is this commanding him to do evil? No, not at all. Two things oblige Jesus Christ to speak in this way. First, to let Judas know that Jesus is aware of this crime and Judas should convert. Secondly, Jesus' ardent love that he has for the glory of his Father and for the salvation of human beings makes him press Judas. It is necessary to note what he does not say. Jesus does not say, "Do quickly what you want to do" but says "Do quickly what you are going to do." Because the evil was conceived and formed in his heart, it actually existed. He says, *Do quickly what you are going to do.* This was as if he said, "Consummate quickly your malice, so that I can consummate the effects of the most violent of all loves."

> Now no one at the table knew why he said this to him. 29 Some thought that, because Judas had the common purse, Jesus was telling him, "Buy what we need for the festival"; or, that he should give something to the poor. (John 13:28-29)

It seems that this passage is contrary to what has proceeded it, where Jesus gives Judas a morsel of bread to show he is the traitor, yet here it seems that the disciples do not know it is Judas and did not understand these words. (It is supposed that Jesus Christ did not speak these words softly.) The charity of the disciples causes then this blindness. Charity stops their judgement to believe that a sinner is capable of these crimes. They were also defiant in not accepting Judas' guilt, for God cannot be the author of sins and does not command them. They do not understand the love of Jesus Christ asking for a prompt consummation of his sacrifice.

> So, after receiving the piece of bread, he immediately went out. And it was night. (John 13:30)

All of these circumstances are necessary for the consummation of sin. It would be little that the devil had entered Judas's body, if Judas had not *immediately gone out*. The devil would have had no power over him if Judas had stayed in the company of his dear Master. But what is he doing? He leaves the house and withdraws from Jesus Christ. *And it was night*. This means that away from the true light of Jesus Christ, he enters into night and the darkness of error and sin, after having lost the lights of grace.

> When he had gone out, Jesus said, "Now the Son of Man has been glorified, and God has been glorified in him. 32 If God has been glorified in him, God will also glorify him in himself and will glorify him at once." (John 13:31–32)

How do you hear this, O divine Master? What glory will you now receive? A betrayer will deliver you into the hands of your enemies. You say that now you are *glorified*. But where does your glory come from? It is that *God is glorified in himself* by this grandest of all sacrifices that ever was. God will not receive greater glory outside of himself than this sacrifice of Jesus Christ.

Jesus Christ is *glorified* in the glory *of his Father*. God is also glorified *in him* because the greatest glory that he may have is to give God dignity worthy of God, which no one other can give him. The Son of God took a mortal body so he could suffer and die. There is nothing greater for human nature than what Jesus Christ did by going to this end of suffering and dying for the *glory of his Father* to save human beings that the Word had in this hypostatic union. This is why he says that the Christ must suffer and there enter into his glory.

The second way that Jesus Christ had just been glorified and the Father in him was the institution of the Sacrament, which perpetuates his glorious sacrifice to his Father and his ministry to human beings. As he was made man to give himself entirely to human beings and God, so he finds a way of giving himself in the most particular way possible. No union equals that of food, which becomes the substance and sustenance of the person who takes it. And what better way to make human beings God than to have them live as God? All human beings could not have hypostatic union, so he married human nature by his same union. To do this he made a real and sacramental union, so that each human being may be united with him in a way which closely approaches hypostatic union.

Jesus Christ continues, *If God has been glorified in him* in a perfect way, he cannot draw glory equal to that. *God will also glorify him in himself* in a consummation of glory that will surpass everything that has been said, absorbing in him, where he remains hidden, according to St Paul, annihilated and lost. If the Father is glorified in this way in the Son, the Son is also glorified in the Father. He adds, the Father *will glorify him at once*. Because the double glory of the Father in the Son, and the Son in the Father, has happened. He speaks also of the *glory* of his resurrection that happened after the sacrifice of his death.

> "Little children, I am with you only a little longer. You will look for me; and as I said to the Jews so now I say to you, 'Where I am going, you cannot come.'" (John 13:33)

O sweet and tender words! It appears that Jesus Christ is the most tender when he is on the point of leaving! O my Savior! I must call you cruel. Does your testimony so full of love make your loss harder and more unbearable? You speak words of sweetness and you add the hardest word of the world. You call them *your little children* expressed in tenderness. I love them because they are little and have an extreme need of their Father because they are little children who will have this loss. You, my little children, I cherish and love you but I am leaving you. Alas! In your pain you say you will seek me as a little child looks for her nurse, and you will be desolate because you cannot find me where you look. *Where I am going, you cannot come.*

But, Lord, how do you mean this? You say in all places to follow you yet here you say, that we may not go where you are going? It is here that you say that we may not go through his suffering and death. As Jesus

Christ speaks of his glory, he says to his disciples that they may not follow *now* because he must suffer first. Jesus Christ preserves this way for all interior souls. He gives them a thousand caresses that melts them in love and gratitude; they have experienced his excessive goodness, which delights and ravishes them. When he leaves, the heart is as full of pain as it was full of sweetness. They search for him, but in vain. They may not go where he is going into death and sadness.

> "I give you a new commandment, that you love one another. Just as I have loved you, you also should love one another." (John 13:34)

The *commandment* of Jesus Christ to mutual love is a *new* commandment. Although it is the testament commandment of Jesus Christ, it is the one most badly followed with some loving one's self in disorder while another hates one's self with excess. However, Jesus Christ wants us to *love* others *as he has loved us*. Out of love, he has given his life for us. He wants us to love our brothers and sisters, and to love our enemies until we give our lives for them.

> "By this everyone will know that you are my disciples, if you have love for one another." (John 13:35)

Love for the neighbor hides faults and bad things they have done. This is the true characteristic of true disciples of Jesus Christ and true interior souls from others who are not. No matter how egregious the faults, the true disciple continues to love.

> Simon Peter said to him, "Lord, where are you going?" Jesus answered, "Where I am going, you cannot follow me now; but you will follow afterward." 37 Peter said to him, "Lord, why can I not follow you now? I will lay down my life for you." (John 13:36–37)

Jesus Christ confirms here what has been said earlier: St Peter cannot follow in to suffering and death at this time because he must work for the church. But Jesus assures him that at another time, Peter will have the advantage of following him into the same torture. Sensible love believes that all is possible. Peter who experiences the sentiment of love and understands what his good Master is saying, says to him in a transport of love, "What is there to stop me from following you now, since I will lay down my life for you?"

> Jesus answered, "Will you lay down your life for me? Very truly, I tell you, before the cock crows, you will have denied me three times." (John 13:38)

There is a difference between sensible love and nude love. Sensible love judges based on ardor, believes all things possible, because it measures its power based on sentiment. However in the occasions when this warm love slows down, we only experience the weakness and it becomes less than we thought. Nude love is the opposite. She presumes nothing and does not advance. Even in her foundation, she thinks herself weak, and fears opportunities in case she lacks the courage because she feels a cold death. However, she has a concentrated fire inside and in a strong and violent occasion, she makes a generous effort and shows what was hidden. The first love is only weak sentimental love. That is why those in this state are ready to do anything, they judge from their superficial foundation and make mistakes because in the occasion they do not have the strength. Yet nude love feels only a cool love externally but within is a burning fire. Their love is like a fever and the fire is concentrated within yet chills without. The outside is cold and weak, yet the interior is red and enflamed.

> "Do not let your hearts be troubled. Believe in God, believe also in me." (John 14:1)

After Jesus Christ reveals the betrayal of Judas, strange predictions, testimonies of love and goodness, and *trouble*, astonishment and disorder within the apostles, then Jesus Christ says, *Do not let your hearts be troubled*. Trouble may not prevent sin or heal the one who has committed sin. To the contrary, trouble places us in discouragement. This is why Jesus Christ adds, *Believe in God* as Creator, in his sovereign power and infinite justice. *Believe also in me*. That is to say, trust in me as your Redeemer, who can prevent you from falling and deliver you from sins that you have committed. Do not be troubled with an apprehension over an evil future and have sadness about passing through evil. Instead, abandon yourself to me and trust in my goodness.

> "In my Father's house there are many dwelling places. If it were not so, would I have told you that I go to prepare a place for you?" (John 4:2)

In heaven there are many degrees of glory. *There are* in God *many dwelling places*. Because God is infinite, there are within him infinite spaces. There are places for penitent sinners and places for those who have preserved their innocence, and frequently they are in the same dwelling. But if there are many dwellings, there is only one way to lead to these dwellings. This way is Jesus Christ himself. Many want to interpret this place in scripture, *There are many dwelling places*. Some conclude that is it acceptable to stay in an imperfect way. Others want to stop at the entry, to hide their fear and lack of courage; they say that God does not expect perfection from them and there are *many dwelling places*. I am convinced with them that *there are many dwelling places* but these places are *in the house*. To have a dwelling place in the house, small or grand, you cannot remain in the entrance to the way which is far away from the dwelling place. We must enter the house and leave it to the Father of the family to give us a place that pleases him. We must not fail to do this out of a bad disposition or lack of courage.

Jesus Christ is the door and the way who leads us into this house. None may go except through him. This is a fundamental truth to which we must agree, but most just want to look at Jesus Christ. I admit that a simple sight of Jesus Christ is very consoling when we follow him. But all depends on following him, abandoning ourselves to him, and letting him conduct us blindly by following by our renunciation in all things, following him in all states by the impression he gives to us, which is very different than the way we would take. He assures us about these things saying, *If it were not so, would I have told you?* As our guide, he himself *prepares the place*. But to leave us no doubt that he will lead us to the same place where he lives, he adds:

> "And if I go and prepare a place for you, I will come again and will take you to myself, so that where I am, there you may be also." (John 14:3)

I am leaving, Jesus Christ said, to prepare the place and to open the entrance to my Father's bosom. Then *I will come again and take you to myself*. Oh, what admirable words! Will Jesus Christ be incarnated once again and have we seen him come to seek his apostles? However, these words are true! It is true that Jesus Christ goes first as an example and model to prepare the place. We need to follow Jesus Christ and bear his states until we are crucified with him. O then he truly becomes incarnate in the soul in a mystical way. Then that he takes the soul with him. After hiding the soul within him, he is formed within her, born there, and believes until to the perfect day of eternal glory. Then he then leads her to himself and she remains with him eternally where he is himself and not in another place.

> "And you know the way to the place where I am going." (John 14:4)

There is a great difference between knowing the way and following the way. Many may know Jesus Christ but few walk in the way. The apostles had walked with Jesus Christ and had followed his examples. This is why they truly know the way not only by light, but by experience. But however they were not in a state to go where he was going because Jesus Christ was not yet formed in them.

> Thomas said to him, "Lord, we do not know where you are going. How can we know the way?" (John 14:5)

St. Thomas is ignorant about how Jesus Christ leads the apostles in their own state. Sometimes spiritual directors need to have their ones in direction ignore their state, especially if they are called to a great grace and have much courage. If they have little courage, we cannot expect a high degree of perfection of them. We have to tell them that they are fine, so as to encourage them to continue to follow. But for the others, they must be left in absolute ignorance of their way. There are two types of souls. Some know too well that they are fine with goodness and certainty in their state. They know too well that they are fine and are full. These are souls of light, led by gifts and extraordinary things. Spiritual directors need to pursue them a lot because with lights and certainty they hide many faults. They must be pursued closely and annihilated to expose hidden faults. This serve as an antidote to lights. Yet, the others are very ignorant. They are led by a strong darkness and cannot believe that this way is good. For those, we must encourage and support them gently without pleasing them too much but letting them know that this way honors God more than the way of lights. St Thomas therefore thinks that he does not know the path that must lead the soul to Jesus Christ to remain eternally with him. He did not know it, although he was in the way, being under the guidance of Jesus Christ. This is why:

> Jesus answered, "I am the way and the truth and the life. No one comes to the Father except through me." (John 14:6)

"It is I," says Jesus Christ, "who *am the way*, coming to you so I do not lose you. The world should follow my way, which can only be followed by living as I lived. When we walk in the way, we enter into the *truth* where the way leads us. I am the *way who you follow*. *I am* myself this *truth*. As Word I am *the truth* who teaches those who listens so she becomes lost in my truth. And how can I not be true because I am the faithful expression of my Father? I lead others into full knowledge of the Father because I am the light and the truth."

Therefore, in following the human life of Jesus Christ, we enter into the truth of the Word. But how do we enter? In listening, as the Father taught us: *This is my beloved Son*, that I engendered, *Listen to him*. He is the Truth, who speaks for God. Oh, how advantageous it is to listen to him! The heart of the human being receives the truth of the Word, which is no other than the movement of the Spirit. First, we listen to the Word. The function of the human heart is to only listen to the Word which is given to it.

After the soul walks in the *way* of the human Jesus Christ, she enters into the *truth* of Jesus Christ as Word and she receives a new movement of *life*. Oh, then the life of Jesus Christ is formed within her and brings the state of human being as God, giving the human being divinity within the soul in whom Jesus lives. All of this must be understood mystically, as has been said many times. However, it is impossible to come to the Father except through the Son. Without following him, we cannot be saved.

> "If you know me, you will know my Father also. From now on you do know him and have seen him." (John 14:7)

Jesus Christ is the perfect image of his Father, but the image has nothing less than the original. In his quality of a divine person, he is the principle of the same in his union with divine essence so that the Father has nothing more than him. Everything is imprinted in the Son and he is equal to the Father. *Who know the Son, knows the Father* and who knows the Father knows the Son.

How does Jesus say this, *From now on you do know him and have seen him*. Having seen the Son, they have really seen the Father, but they did not understand this because they did not comprehend God's united essence.

> Philip said to him, "Lord, show us the Father, and we will be satisfied." (John 14:8)

The apostles did not understand well the unity of essence in the persons of the Trinity as seen in Philip's question. The soul is at times occupied in the union with Jesus Christ and in conformity with his life. It is also absorbed in the divine union, without knowing and distinguishing this. Jesus Christ's response is wonderful.

> Jesus said to him, "Have I been with you all this time, Philip, and you still do not know me? Whoever has seen me has seen the Father. How can you say, 'Show us the Father'?" (John 14:9)

Here Jesus Christ teaches about the Trinity as three persons united in essence and how to see the Son is to see the Father. The Son is not the image representing him in the natural but they are indeed the same thing.

> "Do you not believe that I am in the Father and the Father is in me? The words that I say to you I do not speak on my own; but the Father who dwells in me does his works." (John 14:10)

Jesus Christ describes the wonderful commerce and union of essence between the three persons of the Trinity. *Do you not believe that I am in the Father* where I am lost continually in his being. *The Father is in me* because he communicates entirely within me. *I am in him* since he is continually engendering me. *He is in me* and flows into me in a unitive and grand love. *The words that I say to you I do not speak on my own* refers to eternal generation which makes the Father's word. *The Father who dwells in me does his works* because there can be no division with a perfect union. The Father and Holy Spirit are always with Jesus Christ. When God calls a soul into union with him, the interior maintains a perfect union while the exterior multiplies in many different ways.

> "Believe me that I am in the Father and the Father is in me; but if you do not, then believe me because of the works themselves. 12 Very truly, I tell you, the one who believes in me will also do the works that I do and, in fact, will do greater works than these, because I am going to the Father. 13 I will do whatever you ask in my name, so that the Father may be glorified in the Son." (John 14:11–13)

After he taught them such great truths, he asks if we believe, because these truths are not understood, but believed. Through faith comes the communications.

Jesus Christ speaks of two types of faith, a pure and nude faith, and a supported faith. If, he says, you don't *believe* in my word, and your faith is not simple enough now, then *believe me because of the works* themselves and the marvels *that I am* who supports your faith.

Then he adds, *Very truly I tell you, the one who believes in me* with a pure faith *will also do the works that I do and, in fact, will do greater works than these.* It seems that the apostles made works more extraordinary than Jesus who took care to persuade others of the effectiveness of his remaining in souls. During his life his presence was known, and they searched for him. His words had a special appeal. And even more, Jesus Christ who wanted to be imitated had a very common life. The miracles he did were more to assure the faith of the apostles than the others, because his infamous death lessened in appearance the good that his preaching had done. It was however a germ of life, a seed which would bear fruit and whose apostles one day would reap the fruit. Jesus Christ says, *I sent you to reap that for which you did not labor.* But to make these works it is necessary to have a pure faith. Jesus Christ lives in the Father while at the same time working in the soul and accomplishing fruit through her. There are souls in whom their pure and simple faith continually works miracles and they do not perceive this. All these souls ask for, they receive because Jesus Christ works in them and grants the request the *Father may be glorified in the Son.*

"If in my name you ask me for anything, I will do it." (John 14:14)

This is a continuation of what Jesus Christ says, that he does what is *asked in my name*, that is, by the movement of his Spirit.

"If you love me, you will keep my commandments." (John 14:15)

The true mark of love is to do the will of God and *keep his commandments.* Many believe that they love God because they feel a certain warmth in their prayers, but this is not enough if they do not do the will of God and keep his commandments.

We know in scriptures both a declared and a hidden will. In our exterior we must follow the declared will and in our interior we abandon ourselves to his hidden will. There are people who believe that they follow certain instincts, that give them freedom to violate the commandments of God. God does not contradict himself so we cannot go on a path against the commandments of God. This is the grand rule that everyone must follow. God has an essential will with his absolute authority which the soul cannot remove, defend itself against it, and prevail against it. The soul should hold on to this declared will and offer a testimony to God by staying there.

> "And I will ask the Father, and he will give you another Advocate, to be with you forever. 17 This is the Spirit of truth, whom the world cannot receive, because it neither sees him nor knows him. You know him, because he abides with you, and he will be in you." (John 14:16–17)

We do not lose the distinct and perceptive presence of Jesus Christ (when it is by grace and not by the sin) when the *Advocate* is given. The Comforter is *an* infused *spirit*, filling and absorbing the soul with a general and tranquil love which is only distinguished by the peace operating in the soul. This Spirit fills the soul with *Spirit of Truth* and reduces it into unity with God through annihilation and losing everything in God. The Comforter does not leave her anymore, except by the person's dark and horrible infidelity.

The Spirit of truth *is not received in the* sinning and criminal *world*. And how could this Spirit be received because the world does not *know him*. It also does not *see* or taste him because the world is directly opposed to him. The world is full of tumult and trouble, while the Holy Spirit lives in peace. The world is full of lies and multiplicity, and the Spirit is truth and simplicity. *But for you*, continues the divine Savior to his disciples and to all souls devoted to him, he will come one day that you *know*. It will not be by lights and illustration, but it will be in your experience and *he will abide with you* in a permanent way. And so that you will be possessed, *he will be in you*. Oh, if we were well persuaded of God living in us, we would be content and we would stay with the One who lives within us with a charity as infinite as he is!

> "I will not leave you orphaned; I am coming to you. 19 In a little while the world will no longer see me, but you will see me; because I live, you also will live." (John 14:18–19)

When our Lord seems to abandon us the most, it is then he shares with us in a particular manner. He says, *I will not leave you orphaned*, though you lost me in a perceptible and sensitive way. *I am coming to you* in a more perfect way that will be more intimate. Although its profound depth does not allow you to discover it in a distinct way, its effects will be so grand, that it will be impossible not to believe.

The world will not see Jesus Christ, because it is entirely opposed to him. *But you will see me* who are my disciples and being led to me, *you will live* because you know me and have experienced my work in your soul. But to the world, I am a stranger and they do not know me.

> "On that day you will know that I am in my Father, and you in me, and I in you." (John 14:20)

There comes a time when the soul knows so clearly that God dwells within her and that nothing more is needed. She knows how the Father engenders his Word in the soul and how the Father is in the Son and the Son in the Father. The soul is also aware of the procession of the divine persons within her. After knowing the Word in this way, can we doubt the intimate union between the Creator and his weak creature, as he assures us himself that *he is in her and she is in him* as he is in his Father? Oh, ineffable happiness, to which the creature can and must aspire, being created for this! She accepts this. Some look at this as impossible and as foolish. However, this is the goal of Christianity. Jesus Christ came into the world to merit for us this favor: to be in us and for us to be in him.

> "They who have my commandments and keep them are those who love me; and those who love me will be loved by my Father, and I will love them and reveal myself to them." (John 14:21)

We cannot show our love more to God than by faithfully *keeping his commandments*. It is not those who say *Lord, Lord*, who enter into the kingdom of heaven, but those who do the will of God and obey his commandments (Matthew 7:21). How can we say we love God and yet violate his law? All the commandments of God are echelons that lead the soul to the premier and unique commandment *To love God with all our heart* with unlimited love and charity. The commandments of God show the degrees of growth as the soul ascends into the purest charity and also show the fruits and the effects of this same charity. It is like Jacob's ladder. God's charity is the support for this ladder and on this ladder, we go to God to become lost and annihilated in him. Then the whole law is surpassed by an excessive love and pure charity, which is no other than God himself. The law, though, is overridden but not violated.

Some abuse all the best and most holy things because they have not understood that love is the consummation of the law. There is no law for the just, but we do not violate the law and claim a false liberty from it (1 Timothy 1:9). It is strange, but others want to hang on to the letter of the law without entering into the spirit of the law. St Paul describes this so well: *The law was our tutor until Jesus Christ came* (Galatians 3:24). But when we arrive in Jesus Christ, we do not need the tutor. He speaks here of the ancient law which in its rigor leads us to God and pure charity. But when the soul arrives in perfect charity, we surpass the law with our excessive love but we do not violate the law. St Paul says this very well, *For you were called to freedom, brothers and sisters; only do not use your freedom as an opportunity for self-indulgence of the flesh.* So there is a great difference between surpassing the law and violation of the law. Jesus Christ puts an order of charity in this passage, *They who have my commandments.* The beginning is when we receive the commandments of God with pleasure and joy. These are the ones who love God and show signs of this with a more perfect charity. *Those who love me will be loved by my Father* which is a reciprocated love between the soul and the Father. The Father makes a law for all his servants and this law regards the respect that is due to him, that he wants us to render him. The Son is above the law, however, far from violating the law, he keeps it with more perfection. His love made him accomplish the law more perfectly and crowns the law by his love and fidelity. Jesus adds about this *I will love them and reveal myself to them.* The Father reveals and manifests himself to the Son and makes known his secrets to him. Oh, then is the ineffable commerce between God and the soul! God makes the soul know a pure manner of service that she had ignored before then. If she releases all her own self-interests, she delights as the same angels do.

> Judas (not Iscariot) said to him, "Lord, how is it that you will manifest yourself to us, and not to the world?" 23 Jesus answered him, "If anyone loves me, he will keep my word, and my Father will love him, and we will come to him and make our home with him." (John 14:22-23)

The response of Jesus Christ to the question of St Judas is admirable. Jesus Christ says, I will reveal myself to the apostles and to all those who love me. *If anyone loves me, he will keep my word.* Those who love me receive and keep my word with fidelity and obey all the will of God. We hear the Word in two ways, both interior and exterior, and in each way, it must be heard, received, and kept.

The soul who hears God speaking within her *receives* the interior word. She hears by continual attention. As David said, *I will listen to what the Lord God says speaking within me* (Psalm 85:8). After having heard and received his word, it is necessary to *keep* it. Love like this is the grace of all graces, giving an intimate, durable, and permanent union. Jesus Christ speaks here of a permanent and durable *dwelling* which is no longer transient.

> "Whoever does not love me does not keep my words; and the word that you hear is not mine, but is from the Father who sent me."

If we do not love him, we do not discover the word. The sign that we love him is to *keep his word*. Jesus Christ promises, The word that you hear is not mine, but the *Father who sent me*. I am the one who speaks, but it is not me who speaks.

> "I have said these things to you while I am still with you. 26 But the Advocate, the Holy Spirit, whom the Father will send in my name, will teach you everything, and remind you of all that I have said to you." (John 14:25-26)

When these words are said to the soul, she does not understand them. This word is a loving touch that animates, delights, and inundates the soul in such a way that it discovers nothing but a profound peace. But when the consummation of charity came, the Comforter comes into the soul, the light and ardor of the Spirit, Oh! he reveals and manifests what was previously secret and hidden. Then the soul knows and understands all that was spoken to her in profound words, that she could not previously discover.

> "Peace I leave with you; my peace I give to you. I do not give to you as the world gives. Do not let your hearts be troubled, and do not let them be afraid." (John 14:27)

After Jesus Christ speaks of his word, he says, *Peace I leave with you*. Because his word is a word of peace, the word never enters a soul without bringing peace and can only be distinguished by peace.

Jesus Christ gives to his disciples a permanent and durable peace that they will not lose. This is why he says, *My peace I give it to you*, that is to say, a generous and permanent peace. *I do not give to you as the world gives* because the world can only give a superficial peace, a peace that does not last and depends on the circumstances of life. Jesus says, It is not the same with my profound and intimate peace as it does not depend on any created thing. This peace subsists in me only and it is immutable like me. *Do not let your hearts be troubled* for there will be no trouble for us after being confirmed by the Holy Spirit. There is no fear either, because you will be clothed with perfect love which banishes all fear.

> "You heard me say to you, 'I am going away, and I am coming to you.' If you loved me, you would rejoice that I am going to the Father, because the Father is greater than I." (John 14:28)

Jesus Christ here teaches his apostles about pure and disinterested love, and the character that distinguishes advanced souls from those who are not. *If you loved me*, says Jesus Christ, more than you love yourself, and if self-interest is forever banished from you, *you would rejoice that I am going to the Father. I am coming to you* in another way. My humanity attracts you most now, but I must return to my Father. *The Father is greater than I* and this is my advantage and only goal that I must strive for. If you love me, he said, you must prefer my glory to all your advantages.

> "And now I have told you this before it occurs, so that when it does occur, you may believe. 30 I will no longer talk much with you, for the ruler of this world is coming. He has no power over me; 31 but I do as the Father has commanded me, so that the world may know that I love the Father. Rise, let us be on our way." (John 14:29–31)

We see the truth of a thing when it is predicted and happens and conforms to the words that were spoken. This is why prophecy is the most assured sign. However, the demon can counterfeit the signs and announces many falsehoods. The demon mixes falsehoods and something real together to make people believe. So we do not stop at extraordinary things, but we look only at what supports religion. Then we are delighted to see the conformity in all things that Jesus Christ says to his apostles. He speaks according to scripture and to establish his church. His words had their effects. When he speaks now to souls, he uses scripture and the thinking of the church. If words and prophecies are contrary to the Spirit or the words of the church, they are not his words. Jesus Christ says again to his disciples, *I will no longer talk much with you, for the ruler of this world is coming. He has no power over me.* Jesus Christ subjected his body to the ruler's malice. He did this for the love he has for the Father and immolated himself for God's glory. *I do as the Father has commanded me* because it is God the Father who wants the sacrifice of me, as much as I want it myself. Finally to give the world the signs of his love's generosity and ardor, he says, *Rise, let us be on our way.* Let's go to torture and death.

> "I am the true vine, and my Father is the vine-grower. 2 He removes every branch in me that bears no fruit. Every branch that bears fruit he prunes to make it bear more fruit." (John 15:1–2)

Jesus Christ is *the true vine* to whom we are connected and his *Father is the vine-grower* who cultivates his vines. But a strange thing, all the fruit that is not borne in Jesus Christ is *removed*. O human beings, you are so foolish to bear fruit only in appearance! This is fruit born in themselves and is frequently the product of pride and love of self-glory. But true fruit is borne in Jesus Christ, and therefore Jesus Christ is the author. Oh, it is rare to find someone who only looks at the glory of Jesus Christ! We are in the church of God like so many branches united to this beautiful vine. But it is not enough to say as children of the church, we believe what it says, if our fruit is not born in Jesus Christ and has Jesus Christ as its principle and goal. This is why in useful prayer, we let the Spirit of God act so that we have fruit in him. This comparison of Jesus Christ is so beautiful. Branches do not receive anything within if they do not receive it from the parent vine. Anything they receive from a foreign source will be superficial. In the same way, we only receive the Spirit of life and the animating spirit communicated to us through Jesus Christ. All that we get through our own effort is strange. It is like a rain that wets and seems to make green, but the plant rots because the water is not communicated within. We note that the vine's nurture to the branch is imperceptible and we only know it is happening because the branch is green. If the branch stops communicating, the branch dries up. It is the same with the animating operation of the Word within the soul. These simple and natural operations are only distinguished by a certain secret vigor communicated to the soul. In contrast, operations of the self are external and accomplish only superficial things without any advantage.

Every branch in Jesus Christ that bears no fruit is absolutely *removed* and thrown out. But *those that bear fruit in* Jesus Christ, what does this admirable wine-maker do to them? He prunes them constantly by crosses, afflictions, and frightful slanders. This is the way the father of the vineyard treats his branches. What does this branch do thus cut? She cries and feels lost. Finally, though, she receives in superabundance from the vine. Oh, wonderful comparison! It is the way to make her fruit more abundant. But what is this fruit from the vine? It is a fruit that is only to crushed under the press and lives only in loss. There the true fruit is born in Jesus Christ, which is all the more useful, because it is promptly crushed, broken, and destroyed. The difference between the raisin and other fruits is that the goodness of the raisin comes from its destruction: its health in its loss, its immortality in its death, and by changing its nature. Losing its own being, it acquires an infinite being more noble than it had than being an insipid fruit. It comes out of its annihilation an exquisite liquor and guarded from corruption. It is the same with us. This comparison is so clear, that nothing more can be said.

> "You have already been cleansed by the word that I have spoken to you." (John 14:3)

The *word of Jesus Christ speaks* in the foundation of the soul and truly *cleanses* the *soul*. It is a teaching, consoling, and purifying word.

> "Abide in me as I abide in you. Just as the branch cannot bear fruit by itself unless it abides in the vine, neither can you unless you abide in me." (John 15:4)

You are pure, says Jesus Christ, by my purifying word. But to be consummated in this purity, it is necessary to *abide in me as I abide in you*. My God these are beautiful words, so well-destined and understood! *Abide in God!* What is the abode of the soul in God? It is when the soul has left so much of herself that she passes into God. But to pass into God, we must leave the self. Oh, what is no longer the self? All the world works to establish the self and no one wants to pass into God, although God himself invites them there; *Pass into me, all that desire me* (Ecclesiasticus 24:26). Abide in God; we should never leave God to look at self or any other creature. And what is the dwelling of God in the soul? Oh, it is the height of happiness! God abides in the soul and the soul abides in God. He acts and governs as sovereign, and he frequently visits the soul before remaining permanently there. But when he abides there, the soul passes into God and remains there to be lost and submerged in God, as an empty vase that is full of the sea and in the sea. The soul is surrounded by God, full of God, and included in God, but does not understand God.

But what does this soul do while lost in God? Does it seem like she does nothing? Oh, it is then that she *bears the true fruit!* Following this wonderful comparison of Jesus Christ, *Just as the branch cannot bear fruit by itself unless it abides in the vine, neither can you unless you abide in me*. But what is this attachment between the vine and the branch? It is an intimate union that makes the vine and the branch one thing. O wonderful union! The soul who experiences this will understand it. It is in this holy union where the branch has no movement or life of its own, and bears fruit, but fruit so exquisite and abundant, that it delights all those who taste it.

> "I am the vine, you are the branches. Those who abide in me and
> I in them bear much fruit, because apart from me you can do
> nothing." (John 15:5)

Jesus Christ repeats these words to better imprint them on the soul. Therefore, he says again that *he is the vine* and *we are the branches*. Those who abide him in this way, *bear much fruit*, a very abundant fruit, because *apart from me you can do nothing*. However, even the best people work as if everything depends on them, even with Jesus Christ telling us we can do nothing.

> "Whoever does not abide in me is thrown away like a branch
> and withers; such branches are gathered, thrown into the fire,
> and burned." (John 15:6)

There are two ways to abide in God. The common one is to abide through ordinary grace, with being united to Jesus Christ as a member of his church. There is another way, which is as been said, by the way of faith and abiding in God.

There are also two types of fire and those in the fire will burn according to their state and degree. If we are separated from Jesus Christ and deprived of the first union which is that of grace, they will burn in the fire of hell. If they are deprived of the second union, they will burn in purgatory.

> "If you abide in me, and my words abide in you, ask for whatever
> you wish, and it will be done for you. (John 15:7)

If we abide in this way in God, and we do his will, which is to keep his word, he himself gives you everything that is *asked*. Because there is no other movement than his and no other will than his, we may ask only what he wants to give. This happens provided one remains in God and does not act only for one's self.

> "My Father is glorified by this, that you bear much fruit and
> become my disciples." (John 15:8)

This is the glory of God that *you bear much fruit* in this way, only fruit that is produced in Jesus Christ that will glorify him. We become *disciples* of Jesus Christ, that is to say, we obey his words and follow his examples.

> "As the Father has loved me, so I have loved you; abide in my
> love." (John 15:9)

Jesus Christ compares the *love* he has for his disciples to the love his Father has for him. This grand and infinite love so excessive, he died for human beings. He only asks that the human being recognize his infinite love, and that we remain in his love. Yet that is what the human being does not want to do. O horrible ingratitude! When he asks and recognize his love, we are blessed. This is his mercy and the graces of graces that he grants us.

> "If you keep my commandments, you will abide in my love, just as I have kept my Father's commandments and abide in his love." (John 15:10)

Jesus Christ gives an example for us to follow in both our exterior and interior. For the exterior, he asks to *keep his commandments* and all the will of *his Father* by doing as he did. For the interior, we have no other thing to do than to *abide in his love*. What does it mean to abide in his love? In our interior, we abide in his grace and charity, and receive the operations of love within and nothing else. In our exterior, we love, and imitate Jesus Christ, and do what is our duty. In the interior, love; in the exterior, act according to the will of God.

> "I have told you this so that my joy may be in you and that your joy may be complete." (John 15:11)

Jesus Christ assures his disciples that *his joy will be in them*, not a worldly joy, but his joy. Those who abide in the pure love of God are in the ineffable joy of God. Therefore, the love gives the joy of God. But why does he add *that your joy may be complete*? It shows that our fulfillment is to have the joy of God. What makes all our sorrows often comes from the sight and knowledge of our helplessness to love or to act. Jesus Christ says that when we abide in his love, that is sufficient. If we cannot act, let us content ourselves in abiding in his love, which the noblest and more perfect of all actions. In this way the joy of God abides in us, and all joy will be completed, consummated, and surpassed by divine joy.

> "This is my commandment, that you love one another as I have loved you." (John 15:12)

Mutual and reciprocated love is Jesus Christ's commandment. In *his commandment* he wants us to *love one another as I have loved you*. He does not say to love only those who are lovable. This would be a small thing. But we are to love *as he loved us* which extends the law. This is not advice, but it is a *commandment*. Jesus Christ loved us when we had no charm or merit that would attract his love; when we were his greatest enemies and full of faults and miseries; when we offended him by our arrogance; when we had contempt for his goodness. He wants us to love others, the way he loved us with such a sincere friendship that we are ready to give our lives for our greatest enemies.

> "No one has greater love than this, to lay down one's life for one's friends." (John 15:13)

Jesus after having made it known that he wants our charity to be based on his own shows that excessive charity means *to lay down our life for our friends*. But, O God! You have exceeded in charity. Not only have you given your life for your friends but you have given your life for your enemies and sinners. Alas! How do you give your life for your enemies and yet we reject even our friends with insult after insult? For if our friend even makes a mistake about us through not thinking about it, we make him our enemy.

> "You are my friends if you do what I command you." (John 15:14)

O ineffable happiness! To be raised to be a friend of God and have all the advantages of his true friendship! But we do not receive this kindness without doing the will of God and observing not only the commandments of the law, but even his counsels.

> "I do not call you servants any longer, because the servant does not know what the master is doing; but I have called you friends, because I have made known to you everything that I have heard from my Father." (John 15:15)

The true character of friendship is the opening of the heart, when we hide nothing from our friend and our hearts join together. O wonderful friendship between God and humans! God makes known to the person all his will, revealing to him his secrets, spreading his heart within hers. The human may not discover God without losing herself within God! O friendly commerce of God and his beloved! Who can comprehend this without experiencing this? This is what makes the difference between the true friend and his servants. As our great friend has proven, *God gives the Spirit without measure* (John 3:34). What happens in the heart of God is only known by the Spirit of God. As the Spirit of God is given without measure, the secrets of God are revealed without measure.

> "You did not choose me but I chose you. And I appointed you to go and bear fruit, fruit that will last, so that the Father will give you whatever you ask him in my name." (John 15:16)

But so that we do not believe that our happiness signals that we deserve being friends with Jesus Christ through our merits or that we are all about him through our efforts, he adds, *You did not choose me* by the sight and consideration of my kindness, goodness, and who I am. You did not choose me by your choice and power. *But I* by a good impossible to merit *chose you*. And not only did I choose you for myself, but *I appointed you to go* to others *and bear fruit* in all hearts, making them know and love me. But let this fruit come from me, so that it *lasts* despite strange persecutions. *My Father will give you* in favor for all those you have won for him *whatever you ask in his name*. Oh, we cannot believe the good that will come from all people united to God and how many hearts they will win for God! And because of this great fruit, the demon persecutes with all his power people who teach others about the interior way.

> "I am giving you these commands so that you may love one another. 18 If the world hates you, be aware that it hated me before it hated you." (John 15:17–18)

Jesus Christ repeats again his *commandment* of brotherly charity and *mutual love*. This commandment is closest to his heart; however it is less practiced. All the souls who want to be with Jesus Christ will suffer the strangest persecutions that the world does. *The world hates you* and persecutes interior souls and they get even good people to condemn and blame them. O Jesus! You are just and holy, however, you support the contradiction, outrage, and blame of the creatures. *The world hated me before it hated you* and Jesus Christ was put to death as a criminal on a cross. If you had been treated like this, should your friends be astonished at being treated like this? O the greatest sign that we are following the way of God is the persecution raised against those who follow Jesus. They are slandered with a thousand lies and treated with the cruelest persecutions.

> "If you belonged to the world, the world would love you as its own. Because you do not belong to the world, but I have chosen you out of the world—therefore the world hates you." (John 15:19)

In the world, debauched and criminal people are not persecuted but they pass for honest people. Everyone tries to please them. Why? Because they belong to the world, and the world loves and approves them. To the contrary though, a person who practices virtues and lives in the gospel spirit will suffer the strangest persecutions. People attribute crimes to them, as if they were libertines. The virtuous person is condemned, while the libertine is applauded, justified, and excused. There are many kinds of persecutions that happen to the servants of God. The world makes peace with the enemies of the servants yet retains outrage against the servants. What makes the persecutions even stranger is that the persecutors frequently have a good reputation. This makes the persecutions even worse. For if the persecutors have a good reputation, Oh, this makes the persecution appear as justice. No one doubts the truth of the accusations, and the persecutors believe that they are giving a service to God. All of this happens because *God has chosen* these souls in a particular manner and drew them *out of the world*.

> "Remember the word that I said to you, 'Servants are not greater than their master.' If they persecuted me, they will persecute you; if they kept my word, they will keep yours also." (John 15:20)

But finally so the saints are not astonished at the strange persecutions they will have, Jesus Christ himself wants them to be treated in this way. *Servants are not greater than their master* and his servants will also be persecuted. *They will persecute you*, says Jesus Christ, because I am your master and I am holiness and justice. Would you complain about being treated like me? *If they persecuted me, they will persecute also.* There is no doubt that Jesus Christ was truly persecuted. So do not expect any other thing than persecution. However, those who *keep the word of Jesus Christ, will keep the word of the disciples also.* But those who reject and despise his word, despise and reject his disciples also. There are three types of disciples to whom the word is announced. The first receive and do not keep it. The second do not want to receive the word and despise this. Yet the third type receive the word with joy and keep it faithfully.

> "But they will do all these things to you on account of my name, because they do not know him who sent me." (John 15:21)

What must console the servants of God in their afflictions is that they suffer *on account of the name of God*. Those who persecute them in this way, ignore that they are *sent by God* for their sanctification and to teach them the way they must follow.

> "If I had not come and spoken to them, they would not have sin; but now they have no excuse for their sin." (John 15:22)

Jesus Christ showed them with words and examples his purest principles. Because of this, they *have no excuse for their sin*. They did not listen and follow the ways that he taught. Their blindness makes them fight arrogantly against things as clear as day and mistreat the purest love that ever was.

> "Whoever hates me hates my Father also. 24 If I had not done among them the works that no one else did, they would not have sin. But now they have seen and hated both me and my Father." (John 15:23–24)

It is impossible to love God and not love Jesus Christ. We can only love Jesus Christ when we also love all his principles, counsel, and example. But those who hate the gospel and who cannot suffer his severity, do not love Jesus Christ. However, when he asks something more particular from souls, it is accompanied by miracles. If something out of the ordinary is asked from a soul, he fills it with grace. If the person refuses to do what he asks, she is not filled with grace. That's what makes people without excuses and makes them *criminals*. For they have tasted the goodness and sweetness of God, yet they avoided doing what God asked of them. They love the pleasures of consolation yet hate the cross and bitterness that comes from knowing Jesus Christ. They *hate* Jesus Christ and hate to do what he likes; they *hate his Father*. They will say, we love him. He is not the one we hate, but the cross and pain. They love the friendly parts of God but hate the suffering. This is abuse.

> "It was to fulfill the word that is written in their law, 'They hated me without a cause.'" (John 15:25)

Oh, it is without *cause* that bad Christians *hate* Jesus Christ! They hate him excessively, and would destroy him if they could, so they would have more freedom to sin. They cannot stand his justice. They know well that he punishes, but the love they have for crimes makes them despise his goodness and hate his justice. They *hate God* but it is *without cause*, since they hate him when he does the most good.

> "When the Advocate comes, whom I will send to you from the Father, the Spirit of truth who comes from the Father, he will testify on my behalf. 27 You also are to testify because you have been with me from the beginning." (John 15:26–27)

When the divine *consolation*, the *Spirit* of grace and love, *comes* into a soul, O *he will testify to Jesus Christ*. This is a *Spirit of truth* who dissipates the darkness of error from souls. It is then that the cross, bitterness, chagrins, persecutions, misfortunes, maxims preached about mortification, renunciations, all which we hate, appear to be kind and divine. The soul then loves these same things that it once feared. This is the sign that the *Spirit of Truth has come* in a soul. She loves what she previously hated, she seeks what she fled, she wants what she feared. Then this Spirit *testifies* in the foundation of the soul to the truth of Jesus Christ, and this soul dies of love and pain that she has come to know this love so late. She feels her love even the more ardently because she sees clearly her error and folly. She says like St Augustine, "O beauty ancient and new, beauty that I have known so late, goodness that I have loved too late!" (*Confessions*)

But why does Jesus Christ says to his apostles that they *are to testify because you have been with me from the beginning*? This truth is understood not only for the apostolate but also accompanies those anointed by the Holy Spirit. Because when God wants to convert a person, he sends *a testimony* to a person who announces this externally. At the same time, grace flows internally, which is the double testimony of the apostolate. Besides this, there is yet another testimony that happens when we see the effects of grace in the hearts who convert. We cannot help but testify once we have tasted and felt this. We see new life in others who have experienced this, so we take the opportunity to testify to the reign of Jesus Christ within souls. Those who have long experienced this state are in a better position to announce this. Jesus Christ says to them, *You have been with me from the beginning*, you have known, tasted, and experienced my goodness, have been companions of all my actions, witness to my miracles, on whom my graces flow abundantly, who have followed me in my afflictions, who have been strengthened so long by my presence, it is up to you to *testify about me* to others.

> "I have said these things to you to keep you from stumbling. 2 They will put you out of the synagogues. Indeed, an hour is coming when those who kill you will think that by doing so they are offering worship to God." (John 16:1–2)

Jesus Christ warns his apostles of all that will happen *to keep them from stumbling*. He wants his followers to believe in the goodness of the way where God meets and holds the soul, so that he, sustained by testimony, may preach with success. But when holy people are mistreated and condemned by those who should support them, who hold the keys to science, O then they frequently believe that this is foolishness. We fear a doctrine that is condemned and fought against around the world. It is then that others are scandalized by the truths that had edified them. In adversity, they leave the way of God that had supported them in prosperity. This is why Jesus Christ predicts to his disciples what they will do and all they must suffer, so that when this happens, they will see clearly his prediction. What is even more harsh in the persecution done against the saint is that the persecutors believe *they are offering a sacrifice to God* and this makes them more fervent. They convince themselves to increase their zeal in persecutions.

> "And they will do this because they have not known the Father or me. 4 But I have said these things to you so that when their hour comes you may remember that I told you about them. (John 16:3-4)

The reason for the maltreatment comes from ignorance within them. Jesus Christ preaches that those who will suffer will be consoled and will know Jesus Christ *told us about them.*

> "I did not say these things to you from the beginning, because I was with you. But now I am going to him who sent me; yet none of you asks me, 'Where are you going?'" (John 16:5)

As long as Jesus Christ *was with them* in a sensible and perceptible way, *he did not say these things* about what they would suffer. This was a time of joy and sweetness with nothing to suffer in his company. The greatest crosses suffered with him would be pleasures. But as soon as he withdraws, alas! There is only sadness and bitterness, both inside and out. Before he leaves, he tells us of the crosses to be suffered for him. He warns the soul of the crosses and she accepts willingly with all her heart, because Jesus Christ is present. To suffer with him is a blessing. But suffering does not come until he leaves. Then the soul feels her loss but there is no remedy. When Jesus Christ leaves the soul in a perceptible manner, he prepares her for this loss. So she abandons and resigns herself to this. But she does not think to ask where *he is going* or if it is for a long time.

O soul, if you knew what this absence would cost you, you would not sacrifice yourself to it voluntarily. However God asks for the soul to be contented, which she gives without paying much attention to what she is asked or where she must follow.

> "But because I have said these things to you, sorrow has filled your hearts." (John 16:6)

Even though she is not thinking about anything, she does not fail to be *filled with sorrow*. The heart feels some degree of pain, which plunges her into a deep wonder. She does not distinguish anything, except that her strong pain is still a peaceful pain. If we asked such a soul what she has or what she wants, she cannot say.

> "Nevertheless I tell you the truth: it is to your advantage that I go away, for if I do not go away, the Advocate will not come to you; but if I go, I will send him to you." (John 16:7)

Yet though this deprivation of Jesus Christ is distressing and desolate, she still finds it useful. Because without this state of desolation, the soul will not pass into another state which is to her advantage. It is necessary that the deprivation of Jesus Christ gives death, so that the Holy Spirit comes to vivify the soul and fill her with abundant and durable grace. However, most do not receive the divine *Comforter* because they do not want to be deprived of the sensible presence of Jesus Christ. We always want to hold on the first way we knew Jesus Christ, yet we should never do this. We are to remain content as long as we are left in deprivation. We must go through this because without it *the Advocate will not come to you*. If we do not leave meditation, we will not pass into contemplation. Most souls want to advance and arrive at final degrees, yet they would not want to leave the first degree. We want to grow yet lose nothing. This is why we do not gain anything.

> "And when he comes, he will prove the world wrong about sin and righteousness and judgment: 9 about sin, because they do not believe in me; 10 about righteousness, because I am going to the Father and you will see me no longer." (John 16:8–10)

When the Holy Spirit begins his divine infusion into the soul, he produces three different effects, which he produced when he came upon the apostles. *He will prove the world wrong about sin, because they do not believe in Jesus Christ.* In the same way, he convinces the soul in whom he comes *of sin* because she has not believed in the divine operations in the soul when she has had them. She is then convinced of her sin and her faults seems to have been the cause of all her ills and deprivation of her goods.

He also convinces her of *justice* she is enlightened by this great truth, that true justice consists in letting *Jesus Christ return to his Father* and not trying to hold him here. That is to say, let everything go back to God that comes from him. In this way, as everything returns to its principle, justice is rendered, everything returns to everything. Nothing remains in nothing, which would be deprived of all good. Justice is done by this treatment. The soul rests in entire nudity and God takes away what is his, while she remains in conviction that God made her. In this conviction, she enters into the interests of God, and she has joy in this. But this light is not given until Jesus Christ returns to his Father.

The third effect is the exercise of *judgment against the prince of the world*. All that belongs to Adam's sin is condemned and judged. All of that will be destroyed without mercy. And all of these three things are truly operations of Jesus Christ within the soul.

> "I still have many things to say to you, but you cannot bear them now." (John 16:12)

Jesus Christ assures his disciples that the explanation of these three things is so great, that if he says this to them, the apostles *cannot bear them*. O, it is necessary to be strong to comprehend and support what this signifies! But also, souls who are happy enough to bear the divine justice, as it has just been explained, must be comforted because they hear this promise, that the prince of this world is already condemned! The demon has no more power over a soul in which restitution has been made and has been stripped of everything in pure annihilation and who sends back to God all that belonged to him. O in nothing, there is nothing to take. The soul that does not come of her nothing cannot fear the demon. The demon fears and flees her.

> "When the Spirit of truth comes, he will guide you into all the truth; for he will not speak on his own, but will speak whatever he hears, and he will declare to you the things that are to come." (John 16:13)

When the soul is placed in truth, and the *Spirit of Truth* is communicated to her, O it is then that she is enlightened with the purest light! He reveals to the soul the purest secrets she had ignored until then. *He will not speak on his own* because he proceeds from the Father and the Son. He may only *hear* through the Word because in the unity of God alone, and in the persons of the Trinity, God knows and hears through the Word, as he loves by the Spirit.

> "He will glorify me, because he will take what is mine and declare it to you. 15 All that the Father has is mine. For this reason I said that he will take what is mine and declare it to you." (John 16:14–15)

Jesus Christ speaks of the procession of the divine persons. As the Holy Spirit, proceeds from the Father and the Son, he can only give what is communicated to him by these divine persons. Then Jesus Christ says that he receives everything from the Father and he communicates everything to the Holy Spirit, but he receives nothing from the Holy Spirit.[6] As the principle of all communications, the Holy Spirit is the term of all divine communications outside of the Trinity. All communications to human beings are justly attributed to the Holy Spirit, because when the internal communications with God terminate, the Holy Spirit is the principle of all external communications. It is for this reason that the incarnation of the Word was done by the operation of the Holy Spirit. Mary received everything from the Word and the Father in the Holy Spirit who formed the Word in her body and blood.

For this reason, the prayer of the heart is necessary. For though the Holy Spirit has power over the entire soul, as well as the other divine Persons, his particular operation is in the will. In this way all the graces which are communicated to human beings, merited by Jesus Christ, are communicated to the will. All the other graces and illustrations which are not essential graces and are given only to dispose the will to receive the graces which must be communicated to her. It is necessary therefore to surrender the will and to carry out the principle exercise of the will. We must turn toward God with all the desires of the heart. God draws us toward him and fills our soul with himself.

This is also the reason why the descent of the Holy Spirit is necessary after Jesus Christ is taken into heaven. Without the coming of the Holy Spirit, the death and resurrection of Jesus Christ would have been useless, not because of lack of value or something missing. But because

---

6. Guyon's footnote: We know this as the constitution of his divine person and his divine operations. Otherwise it would be reflux. The Father and the Son would receive from the Spirit all that they have communicated to him.

the application of what was merited by Jesus Christ can only be done by the Holy Spirit, who came to the world and distributed to human beings the infinite merits that Jesus Christ took to heaven in triumph. He placed them in the hands of his Father to distribute to human beings all the same graces he had acquired.

Jesus Christ gave his Father all his merits, and the Father and the Son sent the Holy Spirit to apply these to human beings. O open our hearts to the divine Spirit, draw upon the God of love, and we will have with him all of the Trinity.

> "A little while, and you will no longer see me, and again a little while, and you will see me." 17 Then some of his disciples said to one another, "What does he mean by saying to us, 'A little while, and you will no longer see me, and again a little while, and you will see me'; and 'Because I am going to the Father'?" (John 16:16–17)

Few people understand the sense of these words until they extend themselves to him. This made difficulties for the apostles and compelled Jesus to say to them the following.

> Jesus knew that they wanted to ask him, so he said to them, "Are you discussing among yourselves what I meant when I said, 'A little while, and you will no longer see me, and again a little while, and you will see me'? 20 Very truly, I tell you, you will weep and mourn, but the world will rejoice; you will have pain, but your pain will turn into joy." (John 16:19–20)

Jesus Christ to enlighten them tells them about the loss of both his external and interior presence. He shows them the effects that his absence produces and the effects of the return of Jesus Christ in the soul produces. *For you*, he says, my disciples, when you lose the presence which is now your perceptible support, *you will cry* and *you will mourn* you will be disconsolate like poor orphans, like a sheep without a shepherd, like a person starving without food. *The world*, to the contrary, will have joy because they do not suffer from the loss of his presence. They have never tasted the sweetness of his presence. When the world rejoices during the deprivation of his good that they ignore, *you will have pain*, because although you possess this good, you do not know it, because the distinct perception of it is lost. But there will come a time when you know the truth of this state. O then *your pain will turn into joy* but an infinite and durable joy. Then you will know that what was believed to be deprivation is joy. Nothing explains the interior states more than when the soul passes through this passage. There are mortal pains, anxieties, and afflictions that pass all that can be said. But this pain is changed into joy and the measure of the pain is the measure of joy. To confirm and support what he has said, Jesus Christ uses the world's fairest comparison.

> "When a woman is in labor, she has pain, because her hour has come. But when her child is born, she no longer remembers the anguish because of the joy of having brought a human being into the world." (John 16:21)

It is true that the pains that the soul passes through are birthing pains. These are strange agonies, that the soul can only think of the present evil and cannot think of the good that must follow. When the fruits are hidden, we only feel the pain and often the danger of death. But when the child is born, we forget all the pains as we think of the pleasure of being a mother. In this way, Jesus Christ bore us all on the cross by bringing a new human out of our corrupt human. In the same way, we must pass through all these things. This is why Jesus Christ, after having spoken in general, applies these particular words to the apostles and said the following.

> "So you have pain now; but I will see you again, and your hearts will rejoice, and no one will take your joy from you." (John 16:22)

So you have pain now because you are going to enter into a total deprivation. I will separate from you in a perceptible manner, *but I will see you again*. I will give myself to you forever, so that you will never lose me again and *your joy* will be fulfilled. *No one will take your joy from you.* The joy that only exists in creation, no matter how noble it may be, is a joy that can always be lost. Because if the joy is supported by means, if the means are missing, the joy leaves also. But the joy which has its foundation in God alone, is immutable like God, and survives when everything is missing.

> "On that day you will ask nothing of me. Very truly, I tell you, if you ask anything of the Father in my name, he will give it to you." (John 16:23)

Then the soul can *ask nothing* and cannot desire any knowledge because she possess it fully. She is effectively placed in truth. She no longer feels ignorant because all she wants to know is given to her. What she desires to know is given to her. This is when all that is asked is given. The soul moves to ask and it is given to her.

> "Until now you have not asked for anything in my name. Ask and you will receive, so that your joy may be complete." (John 16:24)

To comprehend this passage, it must be known that it was not positively a reproach that Jesus Christ made to his apostles, *you have not asked for anything in my name*, as some people imagine that one must always ask, although sometimes it is impossible. What Jesus Christ says to his apostles is that the time of powerlessness to ask had previously been in them. But after we have lost all asking, and all facility to ask, he brings a time when we have the complete freedom to ask and with success. There is nothing that is not immediately granted. It is then that the joy of the soul *may be complete*.

> "I have said these things to you in figures of speech. The hour is coming when I will no longer speak to you in figures, but will tell you plainly of the Father." (John 16:25)

As long as the path of faith lasts, it is a way of parables and enigmas. The soul sees things only through shadows and lights. She has no assurance. For although faith is very certain in itself, it is full of uncertainty in regard to the soul which it leads. We do not speak here of theological faith, but of the faith that operates a prayer of this degree. I say that the soul who leads herself has uncertainty, doubts, fears, in continual blindness. And because this is so, she does not let faith support her in an imperceptible and hidden way, the soul always desires to give itself blindly to this conduct that it cannot distinguish and which becomes cruel to her. But after this time had passed, we see that the rigor was useful to the human being by making her die to her sentiments, O then he *will speak no longer in figures of speech* or parables. All is open and the full day that already has eternity.

> "On that day you will ask in my name. I do not say to you that I will ask the Father on your behalf; 27 for the Father himself loves you, because you have loved me and have believed that I came from God." (John 16:26–27)

O state, at what elevation do you put the soul! Jesus Christ assures that he will *ask on your behalf*, placing the soul in a great certainty about the goodness of God by the testimony that she receives every day, so that she may not doubt. Then faith will be rewarded by the infinite love of God, which will be all the greater for this poor creature because she had faith which she had less support and hope.

> "I came from the Father and have come into the world; again, I am leaving the world and am going to the Father." (John 16:28)

O child-God! What make you leave the bosom of your Father to come into the world? It is love. O man-God! what made you return to your Father? It is love. You came on earth to show humans the way to heaven. You returned to heaven to open the door and take us into heaven. You are telling us that having come out of you, we must return to you, as you *return to your Father, where you came from.* It is necessary that we leave ourselves for this, as you leave the world.

> His disciples said, "Yes, now you are speaking plainly, not in any figure of speech! 30 Now we know that you know all things, and do not need to have anyone question you; by this we believe that you came from God." (John 16:29–30)

It is a strange thing that happens in a soul not well-annihilated with testimonies and assurance. Faith does what it can to lead the soul by another way. That's why when the testimonies are passed, the certainty also passes away. But when a testimony returns, certainty awakens at the same time. How many times have the disciples had many more testimonies to the truth of Jesus Christ than these simple words he just told them? His miracles alone would have told them that he came from God. Faith supports the testimonies, but even when the loss of certainty happens with the loss of the testimony, it only awakens again the same testimony. It is not the same with the simple manifestation of the Word of God. It is a word all the more certain the more simple it is. As it puts things in perspective with evidence provided, it leaves no doubt after it. This Word is not heard in distinct words, but it is a simple word manifested and imprinted in the soul. This Word is manifested as verb. This is why the apostles say, *By this we believe that you came from God.*

> Jesus answered them, "Do you now believe? 32 The hour is coming, indeed it has come, when you will be scattered, each one to his home, and you will leave me alone. Yet I am not alone because the Father is with me." (John 16:31–32)

The first clear manifestation is ordinarily followed by an even grander way. O Lord, is it cruel to make known to the soul that she has a thousand weaknesses and she will be afflicted by them? Only weakness causes this and it is not that you offend your followers. You use it to annihilate their poor creature and make it die of pain. Still, the affliction of this soul would be little if the soul were supported in any place. But alas! Here is an entire dispersion. There is no one or nothing who remain. What to make this stranger, it is she who abandons her good Master. She sees that she is the one abandoning and that she *leaves him alone*. She does not look at her fault, but rather she wants to find him and run to him with all her strength. Alas, but in vain. He is not there. If she sees him, this afflicts her even more. When she envisions him, she sees him dying of pain and love. She understands that her unfaithfulness caused all his pain. O terrible blow! If she were less enlightened, the blow would be less rigorous. But alas! Having known him in such a special way and to lose him, and to lose him by our fault. This the strangest thing ever.

> "I have said this to you, so that in me you may have peace. In the world you face persecution. But take courage; I have conquered the world!" (John 16:33)

Jesus Christ says these things so that the soul does not put its peace in any created thing but finds *peace in him only*. The peace that depends on any created thing, however sublime and uplifted it may be, can always leave. But the peace that subsists in God alone, independent of all things, does not need anything to support it. This is why this peace is unalterable and the kind that the apostles and all abandoned souls have with him, which far from troubling them, pacifies them even more. Because their peace subsists *in God*, it is strengthened by the loss of all the rest. God alone can give this perfect peace.

But in what way do we acquire this peace? By crosses, afflictions, miseries, contempt, confusions, calumnies, all that appears to be a loss, is what actually establishes this soul. It is necessary to suffer and to *trust*. But in whom do we trust? In our virtue or courage? No. In the grand things done for God? No. Everything may perish and destroy our peace. We need to place our trust *in God* who has *conquered the world*. He must conquer and destroy the world that is within us and everything that depends on the world and any obstacles to this perfect peace. So we do not need sensible graces from creatures and ourselves, so that our peace is unshakeable because it is grounded in God alone. I say that the gifts, graces, and favors that God sends and which are received by creatures become part of creatures. Yet our peace does not subsist in these things but in the loss of things. But I call *the peace of God* that which has its foundation in God and has rapport only with him, without relation with us or any other creature. This is the peace that subsists in all things and can only be found in God by the merits of Jesus Christ who has *conquered the world*.

> After Jesus had spoken these words, he looked up to heaven and said, "Father, the hour has come; glorify your Son so that the Son may glorify you." (John 17:1)

O divine Savior! What glory do you ask from your Father? You say that *the hour has come*. It is true that the hour has come. But what hour? The hour of contempt, confusion, and the most extreme sadness as an infamous person. Is this the glory that you ask to glorify your Father? Yes, it is this glory, but glory that can only be understood by Jesus Christ and for those he unites to himself and changes into him. Jesus Christ was human and was God. He speaks as human and God. As human being, the greatest glory he will receive is shame, ignominy, infamy, and torture. As he was, or rather the nature in him by hypostatic union, received more shame than the rest of the human race together. Because as shame is the only true glory, Jesus Christ became infinitely more glorified in this way than all other humans. He is the shame and stigma of human beings, as said in Lamentations 3:30. His humiliation is so great, that in comparison with other humans, he passes other human beings. He is *a worm and not a human*, but the shame of all human beings. We say then that the greatest glory that human beings can have in rapport with God is to share in his shame, ignominies, and to be overwhelmed by his sufferings. This is the only glory Jesus Christ had. This is why he said to his Father in a way that the Evangelist noted, *He looked up to heaven* to show that humans must be elevated to understand in what consists true glory. In this elevation, I say, *He says to his Father, The hour has come*. Here is the blessed time when I suffer for you. *Glorify your Son* as human. Give him the most extreme suffering that is for his honor, *so that the Son may glorify you*. He speaks this to God, because the greatest glory that God may ever receive is to see a God below God, a God annihilated before God, a suffering God treated with contempt and abased in final infamy. He suffered these things only because he was a man. For if he were not a man and was not incarnate, he would have not been able to suffer or be humiliated because he was not a man. This could only happen by means of the incarnation, having taken a passing nature. This was the greatest glory that he could give to his Father and that his Father received from him, and that he himself could receive as a man.

> "Since you have given him authority over all people, to give eternal life to all whom you have given him." (John 17:2)

How, O divine Savior! *Your Father has given you authority over all people?* You have suffered and endured shame, the cross, and ignominies more than all other humans together. Here the authority of Jesus Christ has been established. And how is this established in this way? It is that he *gives eternal life to all whom you have given him.* But eternal life can only be achieved by suffering, following the testimony of Jesus Christ himself, *Was it not necessary that the Messiah should suffer these things and then enter into his glory?* (Luke 24:26). But if the Son of Man was to enter into his glory in this way, he only entered it to open the door for us; clearly, we may never go in by another way. We must see the necessity of his suffering and how it is an abuse to pretend to go to heaven without this.

> "And this is eternal life, that they may know you, the only true God, and Jesus Christ whom you have sent." (John 17:3)

The one true *eternal life* and the sovereign happiness of the soul, simultaneously the fruit and foundation of the purest love, is *to know God, the only true God*, only holy, only grand, only everything, and he must be alone in us. O God! When will you be *only God* in me? My God! It takes time to understand that God must be alone in the soul by Jesus Christ, and that all the rest must perish and be torn away. All creatures claim and wish to be something. We want to be something in God, or that God would do great things in us. But we do not aspire to God alone. O the soul is happy and truly in eternal life, when she knows *God alone and Jesus Christ whom he has sent*! All the rest is destroyed and torn away. O life, eternity rather than time, you are preferable to all other life! At what price do you not have to be bought! You may only be acquired through the loss of all the rest.

> "I glorified you on earth by finishing the work that you gave me to do." (John 17:4)

Jesus Christ has already *glorified his Father on the earth*, because he *has finished the work* of redemption for human beings and their instruction. He had taught them. He did the office of an apostle. But it was necessary to crown this work, which was more of heaven than earth.

The work of the cross was the work of the glory of God and the work of salvation for human beings. It was necessary to give them this means of salvation, so great, it is like a seal on all the rest. Jesus Christ took this way to serve as an example for us. Jesus Christ did not need salvation and the least of his actions were more than sufficient for the redemption of human beings, yet this was essential to show glory to God the Father as an example for humans, a way absolutely necessary for our salvation. But as Jesus Christ wanted to make a way for all humans, it was necessary that they walk in his steps, when the cross was the most essential glory that God could receive through Jesus Christ. He embraced this and served as an example to human beings. Is was as if he said, "Conform to the model that has been shown to you on the mountain." This model is Jesus Christ crucified.

This way of Jesus Christ is absolutely necessary for human beings. I say that all human beings who live and claim salvation, must suffer something. The greatest sign of salvation is suffering. The sign of a reprobate is not to suffer. As there are many little children and innocent souls who die without suffering, the cross of Jesus Christ and his merit is applied to them through baptism. In this way, Jesus Christ has suffered for those who die at an age of not being able to suffer. The cross therefore is the essential way of salvation. This is why we call Christians children of the cross. Jesus Christ bore us all on the cross, when his side was opened.

After this digression, I return to my subject and say that the cross was of the crown of the apostolic work and the greatest glory that God can receive from Jesus Christ. Once we see this as the consummation and crown of the apostolate, it is easy to see that the apostles crowned their apostolate by the death of their own life. Today it is the same. In truth we do not tear apostles away from their natural life. But alas! What cross, what persecutions do they suffer? What atrocious slanders are said to destroy the good? These persecutions bring the greatest glory to Jesus Christ; this has been proven. This work is the work from heaven for God alone and the crown of this on the earth. This is why Jesus Christ is crucified between heaven and earth because it shows the reconciliation that he has made.

> "So now, Father, glorify me in your own presence with the glory that I had in your presence before the world existed." (John 17:5)

But as the consummation of all work is the cross, also the consummation of the cross is the soul being lost in God. This is why Jesus Christ speaks of the glory he desires as human, which is the suffering, and then says he wants to return to his Father through this same suffering, adds: *So now, Father, glorify me* as human and God, but glorify me *in me* losing myself in you, *with the glory that I had in your presence before the world existed*. For then my glory was to go out from you and lose myself in you, reducing everything into unity. The glory I desire now is the same thing: to remain hidden in you and to be lost in you with other human beings. Jesus Christ is the end of all things when their life remains *hidden with Jesus Christ in God*, as St Paul says.

> "I have made your name known to those whom you gave me from the world. They were yours, and you gave them to me, and they have kept your word." (John 17:6)

Some souls are not common and general but belong to Jesus Christ in a totally particular manner. They truly know the name of God and Jesus Christ exercises his sovereign kingdom on their hearts. *They were yours*, O God! Jesus Christ says this, *You gave me them*. In giving these souls to Jesus Christ, God the Father has given the rights of the Creator to the Redeemer. Jesus Christ does not say that they have kept his word but *the word of the Father*. It is that they have obeyed him as Word. As they submit to him and have received the Spirit of the Word in them, they give the Spirit power to act and operate. This word is no other than the Word of the *Father* who spoke the Word, speaks the Word, and will speak it through eternity. Therefore, we must always listen.

> "Now they know that everything you have given me is from you." (John 17:7)

Jesus Christ speaks here of the knowledge and certainty that the apostles have in the truth of his divinity. But what is astonishing is that this knowledge of the apostles, so whole, as we see in the testimony of Jesus Christ himself, did not prevent them from falling, renouncing, and abandoning their good Master, even when they had the most knowledge of who he is. It was only when they received the Holy Spirit, and their charity was as perfect as their knowledge, that they stopped renouncing. Then they give their very lives for him. Truly all depends on charity. When Jesus Christ says, *Now they know that everything you have given me is from you*, he speaks of the generation of the Word and how he receives everything from the Father. Everything is derived from the Father and is united in this unity of principle. It is the ineffable commerce of the Trinity, where the Son received everything from the Father. The Father receives nothing and communicates only what is in the unity of principles. All he communicates is his because he may only communicate himself. He can receive nothing but himself in himself.

> "For the words that you gave to me I have given to them, and they have received them and know in truth that I came from you; and they have believed that you sent me." (John 17:8)

But where did this clear knowledge come from that the apostles had of Jesus Christ? It is *that I have given the words to them and they have received them*. The first step the knowledge of the faith and pure love is to receive the word. To receive we must listen and to be attentive. This word is received in both the interior and the exterior. In the interior it happens in a divine infusion spreading out in the soul. This is a word of life, a vivifying word. This is heard externally in the holy scripture. O if we knew the advantage of reading the holy scripture! I am astonished how we prevent the reading of the New Testament! What! Prevent the children from reading the testament of their Father, where all his will is written and explained? This prevents the children from practicing what their Father asks, because they will not know his will. His will is explained in the Gospels. This is why we should all know it by heart. Why do preachers preach anything but the gospel? The design of the church is always that her children read and understand the mass in liturgy. This is a sign that the church desires to explain this to children and we must not deprive them. I say that those who forbid the reading of scripture have good intentions and fear the misinterpretation of scripture. But we need to ask all the world to read scripture with respect and love. They are to receive all the lights that God gives them for their profit and never to depart from the beliefs of the church.

> "I am asking on their behalf; I am not asking on behalf of the world, but on behalf of those whom you gave me, because they are yours." (John 17:9)

All the persons who are with Jesus Christ in a particular way have this advantage, that he *prays* continually *on their behalf* and in them. This means that Jesus Christ prays for them in a particular way. *I am not asking on behalf of the world*, for the world is corrupt and wicked because it does not belong to God. The demon is the prince of the world. Far from praying for the world of sin of which Satan is the leader, Jesus Christ comes to overcome and conquer the world and to destroy Satan's empire. But Jesus Christ prays for his children, for those who are of God, and those who are fleeing the maxims of this world. Woe to those who are not of God for they are not in the prayer of Jesus Christ. Misfortune to those who are not in the prayer of Jesus Christ! We need to live in the world without being part of the world. Those who live in this way live as St Paul says: He is *crucified to the world* as the world is crucified to him (Galatians 6:14). The sign of knowing if it is of God is to be not of this world.

> "All mine are yours, and yours are mine; and I have been glorified in them." (John 17:10)

O infinite happiness of the prayer of Jesus Christ! How does this end? It is the reunion of all the souls to him and being *glorified in them*. O God! Glorify yourself in all souls and hearts. But how are you *glorified in them*? It is that you take them all to your Father. You give them to him by their redemption and reconciliation, tearing them out of the world to unite with them. Everything that belongs to the Father Creator also *belongs to the Son Redemptor*. Jesus Christ does not speak here about the commerce of the Holy Trinity in regard to himself, but in regard to human beings. It is easy to see this by the words that he adds, *I have been* glorified *in them* because my glory in them is yours. You will be glorified with me when I am glorified in them. As I have been glorified in myself by my sufferings, so they suffer also the reproaches, contempt, and torments. This is the glory that I desire to receive in them.

> "And now I am no longer in the world, but they are in the world, and I am coming to you. Holy Father, protect them in your name that you have given me, so that they may be one, as we are one." (John 17:11)

For me, says Jesus, *I am no longer in the world*, since I am ready to leave. But *they*, though they are not part of the world, do not leave the world. For me, *I am coming to you* to unite with you who are my principle. *Holy Father*, who alone are holy, I ask you to *protect them in your name*, that is to say, make them part of your holiness, that they are kept and preserved from all corruption and that you are holy in them. So that united in unity, we are all one, *so that they may be one*. This truth of the reunion of all the creatures is so clear that nothing more can be said however, we do not work at this reunion. To the contrary, we are always raised to this.

> "While I was with them, I protected them in your name that you have given me. I guarded them, and not one of them was lost except the one destined to be lost, so that the scripture might be fulfilled." (John 17:12)

It is you, O guardian of humans, who protects (Job 7:20). You only may do so. It is in vain that we work to guard the city, if the Lord does not guard this. As long as *Jesus Christ was on earth, he protected his apostles*, but how did he protect them? *In the name of God*, that is to say, in a way so pure, that he had only God in view as he protected them. He kept them only for the glory of God. He guards in the same way all the souls abandoned to him. O it is good to abandon ourselves to him without reservation and good that we are well-guarded! He keeps them until he loses them with him in divine unity. O then there is no other protection than this same unity, lost in the abyss and without foundation, where the soul is protected in being lost. When she is lost in the abyss, she discovers more there. O happy abandon to the divine Savior! O if he leads souls, even though he seems to lose them, why don't they trust him? He assures us that *not one of them was lost except the one destined to be lost*, the one who was lost according to his fault. But it had to be that way *so that scripture might be fulfilled*. Judas was a son of death and perdition, and his hidden malice led to his own death. He had built on his malice. Jesus says that whoever is with him will never rise up against him.

> "But now I am coming to you, and I speak these things in the world so that they may have my joy made complete in themselves." (John 17:13)

The apostles would have experienced desolation with the fall of Peter and the death of Judas, if Jesus Christ had not spoken these words of goodness to them. They had seen Judas' fate by perishing from his continual defiance. But this word that Jesus Christ says, no one who had been given to him would be lost, except the one, the son of perdition, who was destined to be lost. This must have filled the apostles with joy and trust that would prevent their fear that this would happen to them. Also, Jesus Christ says to them they will have his *joy complete* in them, a joy not corrupted with fear and defiance.

> "I have given them your word, and the world has hated them because they do not belong to the world, just as I do not belong to the world." (John 17:14)

When a person enters in the apostolic state, assuredly they will be persecuted and *hated* by all the world. We must notice the terminology Jesus Christ uses that makes you see that he speaks of the apostolic state. In all the other places he says, *They have received your word*, speaking of the interior word that is received, as he has already explained. But here speaking of the apostolic state, he says, *I have given them your word*, as he if he said, "I made them the depositories of your word to distribute to others." Once the apostolic word is given, we must expect many sorts of persecutions, because as we fight the maxims of the world, those in the world fight with all their power against the preachers of the gospel. *They do not belong to the world, just as Jesus Christ does not belong to the world*. This is why, being no partisan of the world, nothing prevents their condemnation. But where do we find preachers who have God's interest only?

> "I am not asking you to take them out of the world, but I ask you to protect them from the evil one." (John 17:15)

If these people were removed from the world after their consummation, who would help souls? Because a person to be fruitful and help souls must be both interior and consummated. If God took these souls out of the world, Alas! What would become of the world? He leaves them there, and *protects them from the evil one*, the evil of the world's corruption and the evil that human beings do. Yet the world's malice does not have all the success they claim. There are two types of people that God consummates. The ones he consummates for themselves and does not use for others. They are withdrawn from the world and consummated. There are others who God destines to serve other souls. He lets them live and Jesus Christ *does not take them out of the world, but he protects them from evil* and of the extreme dangers of the apostolic life.

> "They do not belong to the world, just as I do not belong to the world." (John 17:16)

But when these persons in the apostolic state are exposed in the world, *they do not belong to the world*. They are there, they converse with, but do not belong to the world, just as Jesus Christ *does not belong to the world*, although he was in the world.

> "Sanctify them in the truth; your word is truth." (John 17:17)

O God! The only sanctification is in your truth. What is this sanctification in your truth? The sanctification of the holy and innocent soul being placed in the all of God and the nothing of the creature. She sees in herself her annihilation and misery, and she knows that all holiness is in God. Content in her annihilation, she is delighted that God alone is holy. This is the true sanctification. All other sanctifications are usurpations of the holiness of God, where the soul claims things not of God so she appears holy, but she is not sanctified. God sanctifies by *the word* infused because this word *is the truth* and places the soul who listens in truth.

> "As you have sent me into the world, so I have sent them into the world." (John 17:18)

This verse refers to the apostolic state. In the same way Jesus Christ was *sent into the world* to preach and live the word, in the same way he *sends his apostles* to preach and live in the word in the same way.

> "And for their sakes I sanctify myself, so that they also may be sanctified in truth." (John 17:19)

My God, these beautiful words! And who can understand the power of their expression? The feather remains suspended in the force of what they contain. Jesus Christ says, *I sanctify myself so that they also may be sanctified*, because I will be their holiness and sanctification. O Jesus Christ! You are the holiness of abandoned souls, you are sanctified for us, you have holiness and merit for us. That's what gives us perfect joy in the middle of the hardest miseries because we know that you are holy in us and for us. Your sanctification for us is total sanctification, as your merit is total merit. The love we have for you is so grand and pure, that we are content even in their misery because we discover you in the middle of their holiness. O Jesus! Be my sanctification forever! But how does Jesus Christ sanctify himself for us? It is necessary that the holiness is in God alone, without which our holiness will only be a holy imagination and appearance, but not sanctification in truth. They will not be holy in God himself which is the true holiness.

> "I ask not only on behalf of these, but also on behalf of those who will believe in me through their word." (John 17:20)

This prayer is not only for the apostles but for those who *believe in him through the ministry of their word*. Jesus Christ explains this, so that there is no doubt that all Christians are called to such a sublime sanctification. But where does this come from? From the Spirit of Jesus Christ who gives the Spirit a place to flow within them. Yet some do not receive the sanctification that Jesus Christ makes for them based on his merits which are infinitely sufficient for them. His merits are present for all, but because of the indisposition of humans, they are not applied to all. Some suspect the sanctifying way of self-denial, renunciation, and the abandonment into the hands of God. This is the only way we can enter into the sanctification of truth which is Jesus Christ himself. Otherwise, there is only the appearance of holiness.

> "That they may all be one. As you, Father, are in me and I am in you, may they also be in us, so that the world may believe that you have sent me." (John 17:21)

These words alone convince us that God calls all human beings to *unite* and to *union* with God. It is extraordinary that we turn away from this path that leads to this. This path leads to human happiness and well-being, yet it is treated as if it leads to harm. This is a ruse of the demon, who under false pretexts stops souls from going this way. Those who are the most moderate agree that the way is good but still say that only the most extraordinary must walk on this. They cannot enter with a false humility, and so they stop others from entering. I believe that this happens because we ignore the dignity of being a Christian and we do not comprehend the grace of Christianity. If we understand this, we see that all the other graces are inferior and dependent on this grace. The grace of Christianity makes us *one with Jesus Christ*, makes us his member, and his merits are applied to us. The grace of Christianity gives thanks for the blood of God. The grace of Christianity *unites* us intimately with God. It is the grace of graces. This extraordinary grace moves for the end for which is it given, which is to *unite* us intimately with God.

Jesus Christ anticipates the malice of the demon. He covers us with humility and turns souls toward this great good of union with the Trinity. As he says, this prayer is not only for the apostles but for all Christians. What are you asking for in this prayer, O divine Savior? *That we all may be one* in an entire consummation of charity, that makes among Christians a unity of heart and one body. After he asks for unity among Christians, he asks for a perfect unity between God and the soul. He does not only ask this for a few individuals, but for everyone.

But what kind of union does he honor his poor creatures with, infinitely ennobled by the grace of Christianity? He wants the soul to participate in the *same union between Jesus Christ and his Father*. But how does it work? *As the Father is in the Son and the Son in the Father*, so must the soul be in God and God in the soul. In order for God to be in the soul, the soul must be empty. So that the soul is in God, the soul must leave herself and pass into God to become one.

> "The glory that you have given me I have given them, so that they may be one, as we are one." (John 17:22)

What is this glory that Jesus Christ gives to Christians to prepare them for this admirable unity? Jesus Christ gives the *glory that his Father has given him*. Jesus Christ has received two types of glory from his Father that he communicates to Christians so they participate in this union between the Father and the Son. The first glory is that of filiation, he honors Christians with this glory as St Paul says in Galatians 4:5. The second glory is that of suffering, ignominy, and the cross. These are the two glories that Jesus Christ has received from the Father and gives to Christians. These two glories carry Christians gradually into the consummation of unity. My God! This is a strange thing that almost all Christians live in ignorance of their grace. They ignore their nobility and what they are. They do not know what they owe to Jesus Christ and what he merited for them. Living in a baseness unworthy of their birth, they find their glory in what ought to be their shame. They look with contempt and take for base the things they should take as their noblest ambition.

> "I in them and you in me, that they may become completely one, so that the world may know that you have sent me and have loved them even as you have loved me." (John 17:23)

Jesus Christ is *in us as his Father is in him* and he in this way unites with us so we *become completely one*. But in what manner is he in us? By the flow of his Spirit and himself into us. All the advantage and perfection of the creature consists in giving a place to the Spirit of the Word to flow into our soul, as is seen in Mark 9. In the same way that the Father flows and produces continually in his Word, the same Word also flows and produces continually in the soul emptied of all the rest. This continual flow of the Father into the Word, and the Word into the soul makes a perfect and complete *unity* of the soul with God. The Word as it flows in this way empties, annihilates, destroys, and consummates the soul. When the soul is consummated, and there is nothing in her not consummated, she is then reduced into unity.

Jesus Christ after having spoken of this union, says again *So that the world may know that you have sent me*. It is as if he says, "My union with you is the greatest testimony of my mission and I want all the world to know that I call all souls to this union. I came to earth to consummate them in my unity. I also want everyone to know that the Father loves you, as you have loved me. That is to say, the same love that the Father loved me loves humans with the same love as he loves the Son. The love that the Father has for the Son is the door to give everything to him and to communicate everything to him. Through the Son, love is given to human beings."

> "Father, I desire that those also, whom you have given me, may be with me where I am, to see my glory, which you have given me because you loved me before the foundation of the world." (John 17:24)

The prayer of Jesus Christ is that he *desires that those who are given to him, may be with him* annihilated and lost *in God*. O it is good to belong to you, O divine Savior! You want for your children what you have yourself. They will *see my glory* that you had from all eternity in yourself and that they see and participate in the ineffable commerce of the august Trinity.

> "Righteous Father, the world does not know you, but I know you; and these know that you have sent me." (John 17:25)

Most assuredly, *the world does not know you, O just* Father or we would passionately love your justice. Yet the world hates your justice. O justice of my God, I want to be your advocate. Sinners hate you, because you hate sin and injustice, which is opposed to your justice. But the good person loves you, because he finds happiness in you. Only self-love quarrels with divine justice. Pure love has no fear and offers itself without self-interest. Because her only interest is God, she enters into the interests of divine justice, which gives to God what is due. *Righteous Father, the world does not know you!* If it knew you, it would act in a different way. Jesus says, *But I know you*. This is what brought me to give myself entirely to your divine justice. I want the divine justice to be fulfilled in me to the fullest extent and not let justice spare me. I want to live for justice entirely. Jesus Christ became a man, gave himself to death, so that justice would be satisfied. O justice, what will I say? You are cruel to me, but I love your cruelty better than all the sweetness of your mercy. Pardon me, O divine mercy, if I speak in this way. *O righteous Father*, be just to me. Do not look at human interests in me, but regard only your glory. Jesus Christ is the one who knew the justice of God and the world does not know this. But the apostles and faithful souls *know that God has sent Jesus Christ* to satisfy this divine justice, because all men were insolvent. Jesus Christ pays what all people owe.

> "I made your name known to them, and I will make it known,
> so that the love with which you have loved me may be in them,
> and I in them." (John 17:26)

Is there anything more positive than this passage to prove the advantage of being a Christian and what happens in the ineffable commerce between God and the soul? Jesus Christ *makes his father known* but in a pure way, that the soul distinguishes this knowledge only when in need. All that creatures say is like a beggar who destroys him. As scriptures say, the *mind of the Lord* infuses those worthy of him (1 Corinthians 2:16).

Jesus Christ always makes God known in the soul in whom he lives. But it must not be believed that this knowledge is distinguished by sudden knowledge and lights that mediate the grandeurs of God. Different from this, the soul is placed in knowledge which cannot be seen or distinguished, because it is infinitely greater than the soul. This *knowledge of God in the soul* rests in the substance of the soul, in a way appropriate to the soul. God is known in the soul and this knowledge produces the *same love* in which he loves himself. This is explained well in this verse. The Word comes in the soul by the special way of mystical incarnation. Necessarily God loves this soul *in the same love that* he loves the Son because he reveals in the soul the well-beloved Son who pleases him. Now there is nothing in the creature that displeases God because she no longer lives, but Jesus Christ lives in her.

> After Jesus had spoken these words, he went out with his disciples across the Kidron valley to a place where there was a garden, which he and his disciples entered. 2 Now Judas, who betrayed him, also knew the place, because Jesus often met there with his disciples. (John 18:1–2)

Jesus Christ having finished saying what was most perfect and the consummation of his love, having spoken to them in a language which he had not spoken before, goes out to deliver himself to others, so he merited the graces that he had promised. His exit was mysterious. It was not so much for Judas, who could have taken him easily in the place where he was, but to show his disciples that in a great good two things happen. First, the soul must come out of herself. Secondly, she *passes by the torrent of Kedron* and only drinks her waters in this way(Psalm 110:7) so that she is raised to such a great happiness.

> So Judas brought a detachment of soldiers together with police from the chief priests and the Pharisees, and they came there with lanterns and torches and weapons. (John 18:3)

Why do we think that the Evangelist has taken all the pain to describe all the circumstances that appear useless on their own? It is for us to think and understand these things. All that is written is written for our instruction. All these circumstances increase Jesus' pain, and symbolizes what happens in the persecution against the saints. First, it is always a friend, a person who appears affectionate and trustworthy, who betrays. This person is supported by magistrates and prelates, with others joining in. They are pushed to this and believe they have the light from the divine, represented by the *lantern and torches*. They are *armed* with the most specious reasoning from the world.

> Then Jesus, knowing all that was to happen to him, came forward and asked them, "Whom are you looking for?" 5 They answered, "Jesus of Nazareth." Jesus replied, "I am he." Judas, who betrayed him, was standing with them. 6 When Jesus said to them, "I am he," they stepped back and fell to the ground. (John 18:4–6)

Jesus Christ delivers himself to his death. Wanting and searching for his death, he goes to meet the one who betrays him and asks all of them, *Whom are you looking for*? He knew this well, but this is so that in the trouble of taking him, they do not do wrong. He says who he is. When Jesus Christ says his formidable name, so sweet to sinners, they fall to the ground.

> Again he asked them, "Whom are you looking for?" And they said, "Jesus of Nazareth." 8 Jesus answered, "I told you that I am he. So if you are looking for me, let these men go." 9 This was to fulfill the word that he had spoken, "I did not lose a single one of those whom you gave me." (John 18:7–9)

After they have fallen, he raises them from their fall and says again, *I am he*. But as he delivers himself to death, he cares for those who trust in him. *I am here*, he says, take me, I confess and want this. But *Let these men go.* And the Evangelist adds it was to fulfill these words that he had spoken, that *he did not lose a single one of those given to him.* O we receive good care when we are given to you, Lord!

> Then Simon Peter, who had a sword, drew it, struck the high priest's slave, and cut off his right ear. The slave's name was Malchus. (John 18:10)

Peter should not have been using literal weapons of a sword, but only bearing the word that sustains and fights for the interests of Jesus Christ. That is why Jesus Christ says to him:

> Jesus said to Peter, "Put your sword back into its sheath. Am I not to drink the cup that the Father has given me?" (John 18:11)

This is as if Jesus Christ said, Do not use your weapon. If you use the sword, it must not be to prevent me from suffering or not *drink the cup that the Father has given me*? The word: *Am I not to drink the cup?* Mark Jesus was indignant, as against a person who opposes the happiness of another person. This agrees with Matthew 16:23, when Jesus said to Peter, "*Get behind me, Satan! You are a stumbling block to me; for you are setting your mind not on divine things but on human things.*" He is transported with the same ardor and says, *Am I not to drink the cup that the Father has given me?* I sigh with longing for this, as if this will be the height of happiness. O, it will not be this way. These scriptures show the power of Jesus Christ's indignation and his extreme desire to suffer.

> So the soldiers, their officer, and the Jewish police arrested Jesus and bound him. (John 18:12)

He who came to deliver all human beings from being chained and held captive under the tyranny of sin, the one who frees us from servitude, is himself *bound* by those for whom he wants to be the liberator. How many are there who bind Jesus Christ, preventing from acting and operating according to his will? O Jesus, only in abandoned souls do you lead and command as their sovereign, while in the others you are bound and held captive yourself.

> First they took him to Annas, who was the father-in-law of Caiaphas, the high priest that year. 14 Caiaphas was the one who had advised the Jews that it was better to have one person die for the people. (John 18:13–14)

He who must judge the whole world must appear in front of a judge to be judged. Those who judge him are those who would condemn him to death and who advise others to kill him. This is a strange type of blindness. They know that a man must die to save the people and, therefore, this man must be their Savior. By casting out the one they recognized as such, they confess themselves to be ungrateful parricides who kill their liberator. Because he who dies to save all the people must be better than all people.

> Simon Peter and another disciple followed Jesus. Since that disciple was known to the high priest, he went with Jesus into the courtyard of the high priest, 16 but Peter was standing outside at the gate. So the other disciple, who was known to the high priest, went out, spoke to the woman who guarded the gate, and brought Peter in. 17 The woman said to Peter, "You are not also one of this man's disciples, are you?" He said, "I am not." (John 18:15–17)

Peter, who had wanted to die with Jesus Christ and who had first put his hand to the sword to defend Jesus Christ from the soldiers, appeared full of courage and ardor to sustain the interests of his Master. Now he renounces him with a word to a simple servant. Here is human weakness. After the manifestation of our Lord, the natural feelings of ardor must move into the effect of strength, or we fall at the first blow. Where do we find friends faithful enough not to abandon friends in persecution? Of those who do not abandon him altogether, how many will declare themselves for him with their words coming from their heart? Timidity and fear betray friendship.

> Then the high priest questioned Jesus about his disciples and about his teaching. 20 Jesus answered, "I have spoken openly to the world; I have always taught in synagogues and in the temple, where all the Jews come together. I have said nothing in secret. 21 Why do you ask me? Ask those who heard what I said to them; they know what I said." (John 18:19–21)

Jesus Christ had a doctrine from heaven and he *was questioned about his teaching and about his disciples.* He answered the questions of Caiaphas to show us what happens to those who preach or teach the purity of the gospel. In the beginning they applaud and the whole world follows; yet the same things will bring condemnation next. The same things that delight and charm at the beginning, are soon taken as bad, and are condemned, Then the outcry comes, *Crucify!* by those who previously said, *Blessed are those who come in the name of the Lord!*

> When he had said this, one of the police standing nearby struck Jesus on the face, saying, "Is that how you answer the high priest?" (John 18:22)

When Jesus Christ or his children are persecuted, those who do this believe it is righteous to violate all the ordinary rules and to treat them like the worst of the criminals. Even evil criminals receive compassion from the hands of justice who try to soften the taste of rigorous justice. But for Jesus and his servants, they *strike* and insult them as they would no other. Jesus receives this blow with gentleness. By his response, he instructs the apostles how to suffer insults. This is why:

> Jesus answered, "If I have spoken wrongly, testify to the wrong. But if I have spoken rightly, why do you strike me?" (John 18:23)

This shows us how to have patience and strength in support of the interests of God. We endure the offenses by the support of evangelical maxims say.

> Now Simon Peter was standing and warming himself. They asked him, "You are not also one of his disciples, are you?" He denied it and said, "I am not." 26 One of the slaves of the high priest, a relative of the man whose ear Peter had cut off, asked, "Did I not see you in the garden with him?" 27 Again Peter denied it, and at that moment the cock crowed. (John 18:24–27)

What an astonishing thing that Pater who was a foundation rock in the church, has such a great fall. He denies Jesus Christ three times in such an essential matter, yet Peter became the one to establish the truth of Jesus Christ and make this known to the world. Later he dies for the defense of Jesus Christ. Are we surprised at the weakness of even the most holy saints? It is a strange thing that when one falls, the demon makes a ruse and decries devotion itself. Yet God permits these faults in his servants for their annihilation and to make them see that God alone is holy. We recognize the weakness of creatures yet this is a call to trust and confide more in God. We support devotion because those who are not devoted fall infinitely more. Yet some use the fall of St Peter to criticize the church's foundation as weak and its edifice as nothing. This is impiety. Although Peter was weak in himself, when supported by and united to the living rock Jesus Christ, Peter becomes extremely strong.

> Then they took Jesus from Caiaphas to Pilate's headquarters. It was early in the morning. They themselves did not enter the headquarters, so as to avoid ritual defilement and to be able to eat the Passover. (John 18:28)

It is strange thing to be so attached to exterior ceremonies yet not enter into the spirit of the one who commanded them. They craved to do a simple external formality, yet they did not fear doing the greatest of crimes. They *fear entering into the headquarters*, but they do not fear giving over innocent blood to death by accusing him of crimes he did not commit. Hence, they killed justice itself. This is how justice is treated. We fear disturbing our social situation, but we do not fear ignoring the rights of our neighbor and committing the greatest injustice. We do not welcome a new day with faith; in a figure of speech, we do not drink the new day. Instead, we make plans to harm our neighbor.

> So Pilate went out to them and said, "What accusation do you bring against this man?" 30 They answered, "If this man were not a criminal, we would not have handed him over to you." (John 18:29–30)

Truth grounds a legitimate accusation. Instead, they said, *If this man were not a criminal, we would not have handed him over to you*. This accusation shows the malice of the accusers and the innocence of the accused. They should show what crimes were committed and how they were done.

> Pilate said to them, "Take him yourselves and judge him according to your law." The Jews replied, "We are not permitted to put anyone to death." 32 (This was to fulfill what Jesus had said when he indicated the kind of death he was to die.) (John 18:31–32)

The leaders said, *We are not permitted to put anyone to death*, but they believe that they can without scruple accuse him falsely and cause his death. People with only apparent piety use it in this way. Even they do not believe these accusations and so force others to accuse as well as arrange false witnesses.

> Then Pilate entered the headquarters again, summoned Jesus, and asked him, "Are you the King of the Jews?" 34 Jesus answered, "Do you ask this on your own, or did others tell you about me?" (John 18:33–34)

Why does Jesus say, *Do you ask this on your own, or did others tell you about me?* Jesus Christ knew well what happened, but this was to let

Pilate speak so that he may be instructed. It was as if Jesus Christ had said, "Is this a light given to you, or did someone tell you who I am?"

> Pilate replied, "I am not a Jew, am I? Your own nation and the chief priests have handed you over to me. What have you done?" (John 18:35)

They brought Jesus as an accused criminal before Pilate and asked for a conviction, yet the accused does not know the accusations. The judge says that he is guilty without knowing anything of the nature of the crime. These are the ordinary accusations made against the servants of God. The accusers impose on and accuse God's servants the darkest crimes as if they were the most evil of human beings.

> Jesus answered, "My kingdom is not from this world. If my kingdom were from this world, my followers would be fighting to keep me from being handed over to the Jews. But as it is, my kingdom is not from here." (John 18:36)

Jesus Christ has two types of kingdoms, one in heaven and one on the earth. But the one on the earth *is not from this world*. Jesus Christ does not reign in the world, because the world rejects his maxims and declares itself his enemy. But he reigns in the heart of the just. Only there does he command as sovereign, but this kingdom is known only to the one who experiences it.

> Pilate asked him, "So you are a king?" Jesus answered, "You say that I am a king. For this I was born, and for this I came into the world, to testify to the truth. Everyone who belongs to the truth listens to my voice." (John 18:37)

Pilate asked Jesus, *So you are a king?* Jesus take this occasion to say that he is truly a king in heaven, saying, *For this I was born,* he was made man, *for this I came into the world* to reign truly in the heart of humans. He *testifies to the truth* of who he is and what he does in souls. No one can be instructed in truth except through Jesus Christ. Those *who love the truth* and want to be taught, must *listen to Jesus Christ*.

> Pilate asked him, "What is truth?" After he had said this, he went out to the Jews again and told them, "I find no case against him." (John 18:38)

Pilate asks, *What is truth*? Then he leaves without hearing or learning it. If Pilate had listened to Jesus Christ in the least, Pilate's heart would have been completely taken, and he would have had the courage to not condemn Jesus Christ. We see the impression of that this word of *truth* had on him, for even without knowing what exactly it signifies, he goes to tell the people that he finds this man *innocent*. Yet the demon by forcing him to go out made a blow that stopped Pilate from converting. The sign that he was truly convinced of Jesus' innocence, though he was not touched or converted, was the proposition he made afterwards.

> "But you have a custom that I release someone for you at the Passover. Do you want me to release for you the King of the Jews?" 40 They shouted in reply, "Not this man, but Barabbas!" Now Barabbas was a bandit. (John 18:39–40)

The people envied Jesus and so did not accept Pilate's proposition. This proposition that came from Pilate's desire to save Jesus gave place (God using it in this way) to the bloodiest affront that Jesus Christ could receive, who saw a thief preferred to him. When God wants to afflict and crucify a soul, he makes use of the same things which seem to support and lift a soul from oppression only to bring him further down and increase his shame and humiliation.

> Then Pilate took Jesus and had him flogged. 2 And the soldiers wove a crown of thorns and put it on his head, and they dressed him in a purple robe. (John 19:1–2)

They should have believed an innocent man and declared him as such. Instead, they moved ahead with ignominies against Jesus Christ. They treated him as a criminal with an infamous and shameful *flogging* and treat the King of Glory as an infamous slave. Next they *wove a crown of thorns* to show that the royalty he would have over human beings was one of pain. O God! You are a King of glory and your diadem is a torrent of delights. You are a King on the earth, and your Diadem is a torrent of torment! The thorns serve as a crown to him who has deprived himself of all the celestial delights, while giving his delights to human beings. I am not surprised that putting on him a crown of thorns, they dressed him at the same time in a *purple robe*. Jesus Christ had dressed himself in extreme charity for human beings, which led to his crowning with a diadem of pain. O divine Savior! Your love led to your body now covered with blood. Did it have to be this way? This purple robe proves your love of having taken on a human body to redeem sinful human beings. You have the same charity for your executioners which you exercise in a most heroic manner, dying for those who are taking your life.

> They kept coming up to him, saying, "Hail, King of the Jews!" and striking him on the face. (John 19:3)

They attack Jesus Christ's kingdom over which he reigns with love. The demon at the beginning of the world opposed the kingdom of Jesus Christ. Because of the revolt in heaven, they did not want to submit to God made man. The demon inspired Adam with revolt in disobeying God and wanting to be like God. Today the demon still inspires many Christians to be led by him and not guided by Jesus Christ, so that Jesus Christ does not reign in him. This is why the demon is opposed to all the power of abandonment and cries out strangely against abandoned souls in whom Jesus Christ reigns.

> Pilate went out again and said to them, "Look, I am bringing him out to you to let you know that I find no case against him." 5 So Jesus came out, wearing the crown of thorns and the purple robe. Pilate said to them, "Here is the man!" (John 19:4–5)

O Pilate, you only care to find crimes in the one who came to banish crimes. Could the one, the essence of justice, have done injustice? He who had come to bring truth, and to end the infection of error and falsehood. Since Pilate recognized him as such, how did he find the audacity to condemn Jesus Christ as guilty? He appeared crowned with *pain* and *vested* with charity. Charity causes pain and pain increases charity. In this state, Pilate said, *Here is the man!* But what man? The man of pain and love. The man who came to reestablish humanity and make humans as they were in creation. The God-man is in pure perfection, yet human beings, losing the quality of being human, have become beasts. Here is the man, O human! You must imitate him, if you want to become a human being.

> When the chief priests and the police saw him, they shouted, "Crucify him! Crucify him!" Pilate said to them, "Take him yourselves and crucify him; I find no case against him." (John 19:6)

But the human enemies of human happiness, like ferocious beasts who have nothing of human being, *shouted, Crucify him!* This unique man dies, everything taken from him and suffering final torture. We see that Pilate makes him die while he says he is innocent of his death, yet Pilate perpetuated the crime by killing the just. As there is only goodness in

Jesus Christ, he himself is a living condemnation of crime and criminals. Sinners hate good people because they see in them their condemnation. They cannot suffer a life that reproaches the disorder of their life. They try to tarnish the good life with all their strength, so that by condemning virtue, they can elevate crime as a trophy. These guilty sinners pretend to pass as innocent. All sinners, or proud and imperfect devotees, conduct themselves like this. They condemn all the world as wicked, yet they believe themselves righteous and do not want to be condemned. If they are insulted, they are alarmed. They excuse inexcusable things because virtue can only be seen by charity. Because good, simple, and sincere people cannot believe the harm that others do, they do not think that others are doing evil. To the contrary, others judge the world based on themselves and find malice in the most innocent Christians. To condemn easily is ordinarily a sign of a guilty conscience, as charity is a sign of pure and innocent conscience.

> The Jews answered him, "We have a law, and according to that law he ought to die because he has claimed to be the Son of God." 8 Now when Pilate heard this, he was more afraid than ever. (John 19:7–8)

For a conviction, there is always some fundamental allegation about a point of the *law*. The Jews knowing they needed a Savior, far from condemning him, should examine his morals. If his life was without reproach, how would they not see him as holy, a doctrine supported by his miracles and extraordinary things? Their doubt is inconceivable. They are voluntarily blind and want to condemn his well-recognized holiness. Finally to judge goodness as evil, we seek in the source of goodness to make him guilty. *Pilate* feared because of this word: *the Son of God*; it was like a flash of light that enlightened him on this secret virtue.

> He entered his headquarters again and asked Jesus, "Where are you from?" But Jesus gave him no answer. (John 19:9)

The question that Pilate asked Jesus Christ showed that he believed and knew something. It was impossible not to see the divinity in this man because he had no corrupted nature. Without disorder, he had a wonderful order. His astonishing majesty earned respect. At this moment Pilate suffered the convulsions of death as he feared making this condemnation. My God! What makes us guilty is to refuse the offer of divine grace and its movements. Jesus *keeps* a profound *silence* when asked, *Where are you from?* It is as if Jesus said, "You have had enough testimonials to convince you of my divinity. What I would say would serve no purpose."

> Pilate therefore said to him, "Do you refuse to speak to me? Do you not know that I have power to release you, and power to crucify you?" 11 Jesus answered him, "You would have no power over me unless it had been given you from above." (John 19:10-11a)

O Pilate, you were wrong to believe that *you had some power over him* to whom all power was given in heaven and on earth! You only had the power Jesus Christ himself gave you. No one can rob him of life. It is he who leaves it voluntarily and freely. It is admirable to see the sweetness and patience of Jesus Christ's firmness and intrepidity. He did not appear to have any weakness and suffers without making any defense.

> "Therefore the one who handed me over to you is guilty of a greater sin." (John 19:11b)

Jesus Christ spoke about Judas who had been admitted into his company and received a thousand favors. He was infinitely more *guilty* than Pilate who did not know Jesus. Yet Pilate was still not justified because he had knowledge of Jesus Christ. The lights he received about Jesus Christ's innocence made him without excuse. When knowledge is stronger, the crimes are larger. This is why those who have received many favors from God and give them up are incomparably more criminal than those without knowledge of this. The outrages of a friend are more serious than those of an enemy. Also, the insults that Jesus Christ receives from the Christians are infinitely less supportable than those from pagans and will be punished more.

> From then on Pilate tried to release him, but the Jews cried out, "If you release this man, you are no friend of the emperor. Everyone who claims to be a king sets himself against the emperor." 13 When Pilate heard these words, he brought Jesus outside and sat on the judge's bench at a place called The Stone Pavement, or in Hebrew Gabbatha. (John 19:12-13)

Pilate condemns Jesus Christ to preserve his reputation. Pilate believes Jesus Christ innocent and said so multiple times. However, once they say he is no friend of the *Emperor*, Pilate changes from trying to free Jesus to condemning him. It is a frightful thing to do injustices and condemn an innocent person to force them to show their will. To put

Jesus Christ to death to please Caesar was not something that would have been approved of if Caesar had not known this. If we make a faithful report to kings, they will be very satisfied with justice. But out of fear of their displeasure to make unjust violence is something they will certainly not approve.

> Now it was the day of preparation for the Passover; and it was about noon. He said to the Jews, "Here is your King!" 15 They cried out, "Away with him! Away with him! Crucify him!" Pilate asked them, "Shall I crucify your King?" The chief priests answered, "We have no king but the emperor." (John 19:14-15)

God often draws the truth from the mouth of the father of lies and those who fight against truth are very often obliged to confess it. Jesus Christ was the legitimate *King of the Jews* but he was not received or known by them. This is why they say, *Away with him*, the King. We do not want his kingdom. Bad Christians are today the same. They want to shake off the sweet yoke of Jesus Christ. They love to be subjected to the tyranny of sin and receive this as their King. *Away with him* and *Crucify him*. He is truly crucified in them and they suffer a torment worse than the Jews.

> Then he handed him over to them to be crucified. So they took Jesus; 17 and carrying the cross by himself, he went out to what is called The Place of the Skull, which in Hebrew is called Golgotha. 18 There they crucified him, and with him two others, one on either side, with Jesus between them. (John 19:16-18)

The author of life is delivered to death. Jesus Christ who came to destroy the kingdom of death pays him the tribute. They hang and *crucify him with two* criminals. This is the end of the Savior of the world. O God! Is this the end of your preaching? To die as infamous. What a beautiful life, crowned by such a strange death! What was the need of so much brilliance at your birth, all the miracles and wonders to assure your doctrine, when your end came in this way? Is it not completely destroying what you came to establish? This is still the way that God leads his particular and chosen servants. There is much light at the beginning but it ends in opprobrium and ignominy at the end. In former centuries, the saints were distinguished by extraordinary things that God did for them and by them. Today they are distinguished by infamy, humiliation, calumny, and total destruction! O divine Savior! The other centuries served to express your strength, grandeur, miracles and to establish your doctrine. This century must serve to honor your humiliations, weakness, ignominy, and abjection. The martyrs gave an illustration for your sufferings. The saints of this century participate in your abjection and ignominy. The centuries will not pass away until all your words are fulfilled. So they will not be finished until all the features, even the slightest detail of the divine original, are encountered.

> Pilate also had an inscription written and put on the cross. It read, "Jesus of Nazareth, the King of the Jews." 20 Many of the Jews read this inscription, because the place where Jesus was crucified was near the city; and it was written in Hebrew, in Latin, and in Greek. 21 Then the chief priests of the Jews said to Pilate, "Do not write, 'The King of the Jews,' but, 'This man said, I am King of the Jews.'" 22 Pilate answered, "What I have written I have written." (John 19:19–22)

Where does it come from that Jesus wanted this inscription to be put in this way? What appears to be entirely natural and without thought is very wonderful providence. Jesus died to reign and to subjugate all hearts. The revolt of human beings caused his death. As he desired nothing except to give human beings proof of his love and to show what he wanted from them, he had put on the cross that he was King. He was dying as king, but a king ignored, unknown, and badly treated by his subjects. If we were even a little touched by his death, we have to give proof by letting him rule absolutely in our hearts. The leaders wanted to make his kingdom pass for a usurped kingdom and wanted to change the inscription, but Pilate possessed by the Spirit of God said, *What I have written I have written*. This was if he had said, "This was not written by me. A more powerful one has ordered this. The inscription must stay and let everybody know that he is legitimate King of the Jews." His people have not received this and he calls to his kingdom all those who will believe in him. What ends with the Jews extends over all humanity, as it is written, *But to all who received him, who believed in his name, he gave power to become children of God* (John 1:12). Consequently Jesus Christ has been given the right to reign in them. He calls them all, to participate in his kingdom that had been rejected.

> When the soldiers had crucified Jesus, they took his clothes and divided them into four parts, one for each soldier. They also took his tunic; now the tunic was seamless, woven in one piece from the top. 24 So they said to one another, "Let us not tear it, but cast lots for it to see who will get it." This was to fulfill what the scripture says, "They divided my clothes among themselves,

> and for my clothing they cast lots." And that is what the soldiers did. (John 19:23–25a)

It was quite right that those who crucified you shared your spoils because they held the place of all human beings who contributed to your death. All human beings were your executioner, because the sins of all human beings crucified you. Because all humans shared in your spoils, they have a part in your death and the redemption it brings. As this figure was whole, so the soldiers divided between them your clothes. It was noted *they divided them* into *four part*, as if to signify, the four parts of the world shared the spoils of Jesus Christ and were participating in the fruit of his redemption, which was extended to all humanity. *The tunic was seamless and woven in one piece from the top* and indivisible, to mark the unity of the church, composed of many Christians. These many indivisible points were led by the infallible fate of divine providence. This is done *to fulfill scripture* in the things regarding the things begun in Old Testament leading into the New Testament.

> Meanwhile, standing near the cross of Jesus were his mother, and his mother's sister, Mary the wife of Clopas, and Mary Magdalene. (John 19:25)

Standing while in extreme pain shows a very strong love and a consummated annihilation. Mary, full of pure love only found in a pure creature, first entered the interests of divine justice. She thought only of the glory that God received in the death of her Son. Her strong and perfect mother's love was given to the Creator's love and she carried the pain with as much force of her excessive love. We do not doubt that her nature's pain was very strong, following the words of Simeon: *A sword will pierce your own soul too* (Luke 2:35). But the generosity and nobility of her son's love gave her strength to support her in these blows. She was like pure brass that resonates and receives all the blows that her Son received. But as she received all of his blows, she maintained an interior harmony with him. This same love consummated and supported them. O Mary, it was necessary that you participate in the torture of your Son. As he delivered himself to death, you imposed on yourself this torture. Mothers or women stay with children in their punishment when they are some way complicit in the crimes. Mary assisted in the actions of her Son, as she participated in his love and provided the body that had to be immolated. It was necessary that she be present at his torture. Although there is one mediator between God and human beings, Mary is a mediator between sinners and her son. O Mary, full of pain and love! Who is the sinner who will not hope from your protection given by your Son? You accompany him to torture, finally to have the right to obtain the effusion of the infinite merits of this torture on human beings.

> When Jesus saw his mother and the disciple whom he loved standing beside her, he said to his mother, "Woman, here is your son." 27 Then he said to the disciple, "Here is your mother." And from that hour the disciple took her into his own home. (John 19:26–27)

O wonderful filiation! O strange change! It is no longer John, it is Jesus, because Jesus has passed into John and John has passed into Jesus. In this ineffable union made on the breast of Jesus from the heart was a wonderful transformation. John no longer lives, but it is Jesus living within John for John lived only in Jesus. But, O John, what greater witness of love could you hope for from your Master than this precious gift he gave you of his mother? Truly you know well that you are the disciple from the heart of Jesus, that you are the *disciple he loved*. All the other disciples are disciples of the doctrine and the Spirit of Jesus. But you, you are the only disciple from his heart. You reposed there to be taught by him. The other disciples are taught from words from his adorable heart. But you, O disciple of love, you are taught from the heart. Your heart listened and received without ceasing from the heart of Jesus who spread into your heart. What did his heart say? This is an ineffable secret, that is known only to you and his mother. O who will tell us what happened after having taken this precious treasure, that the Son gave you by his testimony! You were always with her. Without doubt Jesus' heart spoke frequently to you, as you had spoken frequently to your Master. Now you do no other function than obey this holy mother. She was your apostle and you are her interpreter. But if your happiness was without parallel, her pain was also without parallel because you were a continual memorial of what you were giving him. But this holy Mother was annihilated, she could not want things otherwise than they were. The will of God was as much and more for her than to be a mother of God.

> After this, when Jesus knew that all was now finished, he said (in order to fulfill the scripture), "I am thirsty." (John 19:28)

This thirst that Jesus has is the desire for the accomplishment or rather the consummation of salvation for humanity. He wants that all would be *fulfilled* according to the *scripture*. He desires to return to his Father, he wishes with ardor that all his merits were efficacious, and that human beings have no obstacle to receiving the application. He had fulfilled everything on his part for the redemption of humanity. He desires that human beings cooperate with all that he has done for them, so that the effect of redemption is consummated in them as he has consummated redemption for them.

> A jar full of sour wine was standing there. So they put a sponge full of the wine on a branch of hyssop and held it to his mouth. 30 When Jesus had received the wine, he said, "It is finished." Then he bowed his head and gave up his spirit. (John 19:29–30)

The man to quench the *thirst* of his master gives him only vinegar and bitterness, paying Jesus Christ's goodness with ingratitude. Far from satisfying his thirst, he increases Jesus' thirst by the beverage he has given.

When Jesus had received the wine, he said, "It is finished" on my part, I only have to go back where I came from. Having said that, he *gave up his spirit* and returned to his Father and his God, to his principle and to his final end. It was then that the greatest of all works, which carries into him all the others, was accomplished.

> Since it was the day of Preparation, the Jews did not want the bodies left on the cross during the sabbath, especially because that sabbath was a day of great solemnity. So they asked Pilate to have the legs of the crucified men broken and the bodies removed. 32 Then the soldiers came and broke the legs of the first and of the other who had been crucified with him. 33 But when they came to Jesus and saw that he was already dead, they did not break his legs. 34 Instead, one of the soldiers pierced his side with a spear, and at once blood and water came out. 35 (He who saw this has testified so that you also may believe. His testimony is true, and he knows that he tells the truth.) (John 19:31–35)

It was not necessary to *break the legs* of the one who died of love and by love. The legs of the holy body were not broken because his adorable flesh was pure and innocent and were to be without fracture. But for the heart, O it becomes opened, to show that his love was entirely pure. Through this opening Jesus Christ' crucifixion gave to his children with all that he suffered on the cross, the pains, and contradictions. This was a door to pass into him. This opening revealed to human beings the grandeur of his charity and to empty all that was left of his blood, as well as to empty his extreme love. Also, *at once blood and water came out* because there was no more blood to shed. This blood was a price to redeem human beings and the water cleansed them to purify them. After having emptied all the blood from the body and the veins, the blood of the heart is also exhausted and emptied. The blood is mixed with water from the heart and this is the one he prefers. Eyes saw this as well as the fact he poured out his pain and his love. We see the pain of having offended such an amiable God with the sweetness of his love. This makes the same effect in the heart. We must pour out our tears over the sadness of our sin and the love that Jesus has for us which made him spread the water of his heart. The divine Savior, with the power of his divinity signified by his blood, with the weakness of human nature represented by the water and this wonderful mixture operates the salvation of human beings. O violent love! O excessive charity of God! Will I say this? You give a fire so ardent to the heart, distilling the water from the blood. The disciple of love made the difference and lives it. Any other eyes could not distinguish this. He knows the ardent effect of his love. Because he himself has reposed on his heart, like a fiery furnace, he has already burned, melted, and liquefied. O ungrateful heart of human beings who have only little love for God so infinitely friendly and loving! Do you not die of pain, to see that such a beautiful fire has not yet been able to soften the icy heart, he who has distilled water from the heart of Jesus? O sinner, the ice of our heart is the nature of a diamond, that hardens in fire, far from melting.

> These things occurred so that the scripture might be fulfilled, "None of his bones shall be broken." 37 And again another passage of scripture says, "They will look on the one whom they have pierced." (John 19:36–37)

This confirms well what has been said, *None of his bones shall be broken*, but his side was opened to evaporate his love.

If Jesus Christ was careful that all the scriptures would be fulfilled in him, and if there a not a feature of Jesus Christ that was not in scripture, how would we believe that he had spiritual states that are not contained in the scriptures? What state did Jesus Christ not have? Jesus Christ has sanctified all the states. Therefore, if all the states of Jesus Christ are contained in holy scripture, is it not an absurdity to say that there are states so noted that they are not in scripture? Is it not better to admit that those who speak in this way do not discover them because they do not understand scripture?

> After these things, Joseph of Arimathea, who was a disciple of Jesus, though a secret one because of his fear of the Jews, asked Pilate to let him take away the body of Jesus. Pilate gave him permission; so he came and removed his body. 39 Nicodemus, who had at first come to Jesus by night, also came, bringing a mixture of myrrh and aloes, weighing about a hundred pounds. (John 19:38–39)

The disciples of Jesus Christ who declared themselves openly were poor people without knowledge, education and credit. There were few Pharisees or doctors who followed Jesus, as if they were blind. There are however *Joseph* and *Nicodemus* who were doctors because of their birth. But how did they relate to Jesus Christ? In a *secret* and hidden way. They had too much pride to declare themselves publicly, so they did so in secret. There are still many people in this way, who have too much pride to declare themselves for God, who are embarrassed of the gospel. Although Joseph and Nicodemus did this secretly, they do not fail to declare themselves generously when they could be apprehended for this and when many others renounced their faith. When a soul is well-born, he makes courageous efforts.

> They took the body of Jesus and wrapped it with the spices in linen cloths, according to the burial custom of the Jews. 41 Now there was a garden in the place where he was crucified, and in the garden there was a new tomb in which no one had ever been laid. 42 And so, because it was the Jewish day of Preparation, and the tomb was nearby, they laid Jesus there. (John 19:40–42)

He who gives to all humans the seed of incorruption, this continual Wisdom, who only preserves souls and bodies, is embalmed himself, as if he needed these things. Assuredly not. But the divine Savior let them do so after death. He had allowed them to harm him before death and embalm him afterwards. A dead soul is the same. It receives equally all the bad and the good that they want to do. She is in the hands of God and enemies, as a dead person cannot defend herself and can resist nothing.

Jesus Christ chooses *a new tomb in which no one had ever been laid* to show us how the first fruits of our affections are pleasant to him. Oh if hearts that have prostituted themselves and are miserable with their love of creatures, know the advantage of giving to God early on, and how those that give to God late, we would not want to do anything but give and consecrate ourselves to God. Because early we contract the good habit of virtue, that becomes for us easy and natural. For those who give later, they have all the pain of changing habits gained from the world and contrary to good. It is not just about doing good things, but losing bad ones and becoming completely different. Yet those who have not had the advantage of being with God at their birth, must console themselves in the sight of good divine pleasure, which has allowed these miseries for them to be humiliated and annihilated. They do not receive salvation in their works or purity, but in the pure goodness of God.

> Early on the first day of the week, while it was still dark, Mary Magdalene came to the tomb and saw that the stone had been removed from the tomb. 2 So she ran and went to Simon Peter and the other disciple, the one whom Jesus loved, and said to them, "They have taken the Lord out of the tomb, and we do not know where they have laid him." (John 20:1–2)

Magdalen loved too much to delay a moment and wait for the day to come seek Jesus. O Magdalen, the day of the Sabbath was for you a day of terrible travail when you could not search for your divine Master. The rest which you found in the will of God calmed you down and the law of the Sabbath stopped you going out. Therefore, Mary passed the day in peace, yet filled with sadness. As soon as it was passing, then her love seeing that the will of God had agreed to her duty, she runs but does not find what she is searching for. Her defiant and jealous love looks for her beloved. It is the characteristics of strong love to have similar defiance. What does she do in her double transport? She goes to find the prince of the apostles, as she may have no other remedy for her pain. But as her love and defiance are not satisfied by this, she goes to the disciple that Jesus loved, looking for this other lover. She believes he has the secret to this and will be able to tell her news of her God. Or at least, if he does not, he will be as impatient as she is to find him. As he was the disciple of love, as she was also, they agreed together. It seems to me, O beloved disciple, that you praise and admonish well. Could you say something grander and more advantageous, than what you said, *the disciple whom Jesus loved*. O this one word contains all the rest. Since he had made you the object of his love, he had put in you all the qualities to attract this love. But what am I saying? He had put himself in the beloved disciple. As he loves himself necessarily, he loved you. O favored disciple, disciple of the heart and love! Solomon had said that the greatest torment of the loving soul is to be ignored by the one she loves and the greatest pleasure is to be pleasing to one she loves. How you must be happy and content in the certainty of being the disciple whom Jesus loved! O favor that passes any other favor!

> Then Peter and the other disciple set out and went toward the tomb. 4 The two were running together, but the other disciple outran Peter and reached the tomb first. 5 He bent down to look in and saw the linen wrappings lying there, but he did not go in. (John 20:3–5)

Love gives wings. St John, who was entirely transformed in love and charity, *reached the tomb first*. He looked in and *saw linen wrappings* with the ardor of his love helping him precede St Peter. *But he did not go in* out of the deference he had for St Peter, who he regarded as his superior. I do not know what is the most admirable: the ardor of his love or the moderation of this same love. The charity of God has its character that it is discreet in its excess. Pure love cannot do anything against duty and is not contrary to obedience. It is true that there is this difference between the sentiment of love and the perfection of love. The sentiment and feeling are given in its excesses because the fire that evaporates has no restraint. But it is not the same in the perfection of love which does not cause an excess in the person. It was this double experience that the spouse had, where he had both the perfection of love increased by the sentiment of love. The bridegroom gave him the perfection of love, *He set in order charity in me* (Song 2:4). You gave this to me, O my love! A charity so pure and well-regulated that even as its ardor increases without ceasing, it does not make the soul go out of its bounds or of its duty. The reason for this is clear. The sentiment of love like a fire without a sphere makes lights, burns and flashes, making everything bright like the noon. Whoever who would like to stop this fire would do more harm. But the perfection of fire has no impetuosity. It is at rest in an admirable order in pure perfection.

Those who do not know this difference, seeing an impetuous love but imperfect, value this love highly. They are mistaken. Who would dispute the love of Mary? She had no imperfect failure but was in a strong tranquility because of the perfection of her love.

> Then Simon Peter came, following him, and went into the tomb. He saw the linen wrappings lying there, 7 and the cloth that had been on Jesus' head, not lying with the linen wrappings but rolled up in a place by itself. 8 Then the other disciple, who

> reached the tomb first, also went in, and he saw and believed. (John 20:6–8)

These fortunate disciples have the advantage of entering into the tomb of their Master. You enter into it dying and live in strength. The sepulcher of Jesus Christ served you as a tomb for your mystical death, you receive a new life in Jesus Christ. There is a difference between the entry of Peter and St John in the sepulcher, because John has found his death and life on the bosom of his Master, which served him like the phoenix who has a re-birth from the cinders of his death. But Peter, who do not have the same advantage as John, finds his life in the holy tomb. This is why the Evangelist does not say, as he said of himself, he *saw and believed* because then his experience was a faith beyond his faith. When St John said of himself that *he saw and believed*, he was not speaking of belief in the divinity of Jesus Christ, since he had understood more about it on Jesus' bosom and near the cross than he could express. But in the tomb, he was given new light again that had far-reaching ramifications for the future. He does not say he saw and believed to show a defect of faith that he had until then but only to show that he was given a testimony of faith to believe everything that was revealed. The difference between the faith of St John and St Thomas was that Thomas did not believe essential things that he saw. John believed without seeing but when he saw, his faith was strengthened and renewed. With great admiration, he went on believing all that as revealed to him.

> For as yet they did not understand the scripture, that he must rise from the dead. (John 20:9)

This passage confirms everything that has been said.

> Then the disciples returned to their homes. 11 But Mary stood weeping outside the tomb. As she wept, she bent over to look into the tomb. (John 20:10–11)

O John, was it not for you a strange cruelty? Magdalen, this faithful lover, warns you that she believes that someone has taken away her Lord. You know her love and you are witness to her pain. Even though you see her crying like that, you leave Magdalen desolate. But you, O Love! Do you know the pain of your lover, how do you now make her know the truth? O it is an admirable invention of love. He lets her pain increase to increase her pleasure. He pretends to hide himself, but it is for a greater advantage in revelation. O Love! These are your games! You reduce your lover to extremity, so that they will have more pleasure in the new life that they receive in you. The measure of sadness will be the measure of contentment.

> And she saw two angels in white, sitting where the body of Jesus had been lying, one at the head and the other at the feet. 13 They said to her, "Woman, why are you weeping?" She said to them, "They have taken away my Lord, and I do not know where they have laid him." (John 20:12–13)

O angels, you are capable of taking away the sadness of Magdalen, but they do not do it. I am crying, said this faithful lover, *because they have taken away my Lord*, the one I love uniquely, who reigns in me. It is he whom I search for with all the more pain and *I do not know where they have laid him*.

> When she had said this, she turned around and saw Jesus standing there, but she did not know that it was Jesus. (John 20:14)

Mary does not stop at the angels but continues seeking. She does not seek the angels and they cannot satisfy her love. This is why the Evangelists says without talking further, *she turned around* like a frightened lover looking for the one she seeks. But, Magdalen, why didn't you ask these angels where your well-beloved is? Alas! I do what I do. The love that possesses me excuses me. *She turned around and saw*. But, O faithful lover who does not stop at any other creature, not even at angels! She only passes them, like the spouse in the Song of Songs, to find her beloved. *She saw Jesus*, but she sees him first without knowing him. This is the conduct of love to be manifested only little-by-little. He does this because of the weakness of creatures, who could not bear such excessive joy after such extreme pain. O if all souls had the faithfulness to not stop until they are at Jesus alone! O they would have the advantage of Magdalen! It is not appropriate to stop at human beings or angel or visions or revelations and all the rest. But we continually reach beyond all things, as Magdalen did. We will not fail to find the beloved as soon as she.

> Jesus said to her, "Woman, why are you weeping? Whom are you looking for?" Supposing him to be the gardener, she said to him, "Sir, if you have carried him away, tell me where you have laid him, and I will take him away." (John 20:15)

What is the blindness of love? Mary asks Jesus if he is the gardener that has carried away her Savior, if he will tell her and *she will take him away*. Magdalen believes that all things are possible with love. And how, Magdalen, could you have carried this adorable body? She said, Oh, it would not be a burden for me. To the contrary, it would have been a relief for me. Alas! His body would be a dear treasure and I would be satisfied.

> Jesus said to her, "Mary!" She turned and said to him in Hebrew, "Rabbouni!" (which means Teacher). (John 20:16)

O sweet word! Mary had heard him too often not to recognize him. "*My teacher,*" responds this lover, "*Master!* Who taught and educated me, what do you want from me? *Mary* is a word of love and sweetness. *My Master, Rabbouni!* is an expression of a poor heart. My master who possesses me absolutely, what, I find you! What do you want me to do?" We note here that St John is the evangelist who writes a long history of Magdalen. Their hearts empathized together. They burn with the same fire. John knew the movements of Magdalen's heart. This is why he takes pleasure in describing the favorable adventure of Magdalen. He wants to make known that if we do not put limits to our love, Jesus Christ will not limit his favors to us.

> Jesus said to her, "Do not hold on to me, because I have not yet ascended to the Father. But go to my brothers and say to them, 'I am ascending to my Father and your Father, to my God and your God.'" (John 20:17)

Jesus Christ had previously allowed Mary to touch him to satisfy her love (for love makes all things equal). Now she eagerly wants to tell him that she knew him, and kiss him, and throw herself at his feet. *Jesus said to her, Do not hold on to me*. Yet this was not Jesus' refusal or rejection. But it was as if he had said: "It is not time to please the transports of your love. You must *go* preach *to my brothers*. I want to make you an apostle of the same apostles. But *I am ascending to my Father*. There we will have the leisure to see and be satisfied." Or, said in another way, Jesus Christ would like to teach Magdalen that, although she was deprived of his bodily presence, she would have the advantage that he had gone to his Father, she would possess him as truly as if we were on the earth. The true sense when he says, *Do not hold on to me, because I have not yet ascended to the Father* is a true promise that he made her to grant her these advantages again, when he gave his commission. *Go*, he said, *to my brothers*, those with whom I am associated with my filiation, who I have made my Father's adopted children. *Tell them, I am ascending to my*

Father and your Father. Because it is the right that I have acquired for you by my death to have God for Father. *To my God and to your God* because of the reconciliation that I have made with him, he has truly become your God as he is mine, my God full of clemency and goodness.

> Mary Magdalene went and announced to the disciples, "I have seen the Lord"; and she told them that he had said these things to her. 19 When it was evening on that day, the first day of the week, and the doors of the house where the disciples had met were locked for fear of the Jews, Jesus came and stood among them and said, "Peace be with you." (John 20:18–19)

Mary Magdalen was the apostle of the resurrection and her words were soon confirmed by an appearance of Jesus. He entered *into the room where the doors were locked*. This is the same way he comes into souls. What sign does be give of coming into the soul? None other than this one: *Peace be with you!* He brings with him peace. The soul tastes inconceivable and unalterable peace. This is the mark of his presence, as trouble is the sign of his distance.

> After he said this, he showed them his hands and his side. Then the disciples rejoiced when they saw the Lord. (John 20:20)

After Jesus filled the soul with peace, as he did his apostles, he manifests himself to them. He does in the interior by giving clearer knowledge of who he is and externally by showing them his sufferings. This favor *fills* the poor soul *with joy* and contentment with the revelation of his love.

> Jesus said to them again, "Peace be with you. As the Father has sent me, so I send you." 22 When he had said this, he breathed on them and said to them, "Receive the Holy Spirit. 23 If you forgive the sins of any, they are forgiven them; if you retain the sins of any, they are retained." (John 20:21–23)

Jesus Christ is not only content in giving them peace, he confirms this peace in them and then increases it. He gives them the Holy Spirit and the apostolic mission with the power to deliver *from sins*. This passage supports the priest hearing confession. We must note that he does not give the apostolic mission before giving peace and having confirmed them in peace, because we must have peace to be a true apostle.

> But Thomas (who was called the Twin), one of the twelve, was not with them when Jesus came. 25 So the other disciples told

> him, "We have seen the Lord." But he said to them, "Unless I see the mark of the nails in his hands, and put my finger in the mark of the nails and my hand in his side, I will not believe." (John 20:24–25)

Nothing is so much to be feared in communities as partiality. God gives his blessings in many communal ways. If St Thomas had not distanced himself from the apostles, and was not found with them, he would have a share in the advantage they enjoyed, which was to see Jesus rise again. He was deprived though of this good, because he voluntarily deprived himself of this holy company. The fault was his alone and it turned into incredulity. *If I do not touch and know*, if I do not have this experience, *I will not believe*. Here is a faith based on testimonies supported by his own thought and knowledge. This type of faith is not pure and subject to many deceptions. In place of being founded on God alone, and supported by his word, it is supported on testimonies that may be false or counterfeit. It is a faith based on vanity. Was it not more just to believe in the report of the church, which was united in the apostles and which assured the truth of the resurrection and supported by testimonies in scripture? Instead, this faith is supported by touch, the most misleading of senses. This is the fault of heretics, vain people, and spiritual misconducts, who stop at vain testimonies and do not proceed to infallible truth.

> A week later his disciples were again in the house, and Thomas was with them. Although the doors were shut, Jesus came and stood among them and said, "Peace be with you." (John 20:26)

Thomas was happier this time than the other because he was in the company of the other disciples and he part of their happiness. He received *peace*, which his unbelief had made him lose. God permitted this fault in his apostle to show us the weakness of the creature and how much trust is needed. We are only convinced of our weakness by the fatal experience we have of it. However, this is a very advantageous experience because it destroys our self-pride.

> Then he said to Thomas, "Put your finger here and see my hands. Reach out your hand and put it in my side. Do not doubt but believe." 28 Thomas answered him, "My Lord and my God!" (John 20:27–28)

Thomas' incredulity was useful to the church when he had the truth of the resurrection revealed to him for it is true that God brings good out of the most evil things. Not only does he bring good out of evil, but when the evil is done, we must be content that God derives some benefit from it for his honor or for the good of souls. Thomas takes occasion from his infidelity to increase his faith with a transport of faith as elevated, as the depth of his infidelity. Then he cries, *My Lord and My God!* My faith, he says, does not stop at the testimonies based on touch, which I have asked for out of weakness. But surpassing all these things, I believe in God when I see a man. I believe in immortal God, when I see a resurrected man who still bears the marks of his suffering and death but without separating God from man or man from God. *My Lord and my God*, you are God and man, and entirely powerful and suffering, immortal and dead, immutable and resurrected!

> Jesus said to him, "Have you believed because you have seen me? Blessed are those who have not seen and yet have come to believe." (John 20:29)

By these two words, Jesus Christ shows the difference between a luminous, supported, and sustained faith by testimony and a naked, bare faith, stripped of all testimony.

The first ones believe what *they see* and their faith even surpasses their light. But those who are led by a nude faith, without support and testimony, *believe* infinitely. Although their obscurity increases every day, O truly *they* are *blessed* and all the happier that their faith so pure and nude has God as its foundation and support. Although the soul that is led by this way does not know it, she sometimes thinks she is without faith because it is pure and nude.

> Now Jesus did many other signs in the presence of his disciples, which are not written in this book. 31 But these are written so that you may come to believe that Jesus is the Messiah, the Son of God, and that through believing you may have life in his name. (John 20:30–31)

What was *written* about Jesus Christ was absolutely necessary to sustain our faith and instruct us. It is not to be doubted that Jesus Christ did and said a lot of things that are known only to the apostles who have witnessed them or have been revealed to some good souls. But there is an infinity of things that even the apostles have ignored which will only be known in eternity. If we pay even a little attention to what we know, who will not die of love, gratitude, and desire to confess with all his might to this adorable original and to obey him in all things?

> After these things Jesus showed himself again to the disciples by the Sea of Tiberias; and he showed himself in this way. 2 Gathered there together were Simon Peter, Thomas called the Twin, Nathaniel of Cana in Galilee, the sons of Zebedee, and two others of his disciples. 3 Simon Peter said to them, "I am going fishing." They said to him, "We will go with you." They went out and got into the boat, but that night they caught nothing. (John 21:1–3)

To *fish by night* and to fish without Jesus is fruitless work. There is a difference between work that we do for ourselves and work that we do for others. Work for one's self is better at night because Jesus, who is present, works all the more the less we know him. He hides his work from us, so that we cannot rob his glory away from him, and do not prevent his activity. But it is not the same with those who work for others in the apostolic state, represented by fishing. There it is necessary to work in the day, in the light of truth. God ordinarily heals them in order to help others efficaciously by putting them in the light of truth. He gives them the mission and they are not concerned about themselves. Because they take nothing, it was for his instruction that God allowed this useless fishing.

> Just after daybreak, Jesus stood on the beach; but the disciples did not know that it was Jesus. 5 Jesus said to them, "Children, you have no fish, have you?" They answered him, "No." 6 He said to them, "Cast the net to the right side of the boat, and you will find some." So they cast it, and now they were not able to haul it in because there were so many fish. (John 21:4–6)

Jesus Christ appears at the *break of day* in the light, which is the apostolic state, he gives the mission and commands them to *cast the net*, where the fish are even more abundant. O God! It is only you that make these catches! The creature is only your base instrument and you want her to know this. You want her to know from her experience that she is nothing with you. If she does something when you order it, she owes you all the glory and regards herself as a useless subject. You are pleased to use her, but she has no virtue of herself, except that which is borrowed from the hand which makes it act.

> That disciple whom Jesus loved said to Peter, "It is the Lord!" When Simon Peter heard that it was the Lord, he put on some clothes, for he was naked, and jumped into the sea. (John 21:7)

The disciple whom Jesus loved knows his Master, not so much by sight as to the taste of the heart. This heart felt that he was the one he loved, and whom he loved tenderly. This is why he gave the knowledge to Peter. Jesus Christ did not make himself known and sight could not discover him. It was the heart of John who felt the heart of his Master, like a magnet attracting him. O St John, you have done well to have Communion by lying on the chest of your Master! This private love was familiar. You have been attracted by his magnetic heart, yet this was done for the good of others and to attract many more. Once Peter heard that it was his Master, all burning with the desire to see him, Peter *threw himself into the sea*, unable to wait for the boat to arrive. O God! We would lie in any abyss and precipice, if we were sure to find you!

> But the other disciples came in the boat, dragging the net full of fish, for they were not far from the land, only about a hundred yards off. (John 21:8)

Peter was so eager to see his dear Master and give him proofs of his love, that he abandoned his fishing that he had worked so hard on. In this action, he shown the strength and detachment of his heart that valued God above everything in the world. He was ready to serve souls. This is the disposition that all apostolic humans must have: to be ready to serve or not to serve, not to trouble about success. However, the other disciples brought in the fish that Peter had caught.

> When they had gone ashore, they saw a charcoal fire there, with fish on it, and bread. 10 Jesus said to them, "Bring some of the fish that you have just caught." (John 21:9–10)

This *fire* was miraculous. While they worked, Jesus Christ took care of everything that was needed. When one is in the apostolic state and thinks only of doing the will of God in the service of souls, we forget our own interests and only have time to work on charity. Jesus Christ is careful to light, burn, and increase the fire. When we think of only his glory, he works only to gain our advantage.

> So Simon Peter went aboard and hauled the net ashore, full of large fish, 153 of them; and though there were so many, the net was not torn. (John 21:11)

It was just that Peter should complete the capture he had just made by the command of his good Master. Although the other disciples serve him as help, they do not pull fish from the sea but St Peter came to pull them out. The fish symbolize what Pete would soon do in favor of the church as he became the foundation rock of the church and made the first conversions.

> Jesus said to them, "Come and have breakfast." Now none of the disciples dared to ask him, "Who are you?" because they knew it was the Lord. 13 Jesus came and took the bread and gave it to them, and did the same with the fish. 14 This was now the third time that Jesus appeared to the disciples after he was raised from the dead. (John 21:12–14)

Is there anything more admirable than Jesus' disciples becoming familiar with the goodness of God, even after his resurrection? He makes them eat. He regales and encourages them. He shares with them sweetly to prepare them for the cross which they must suffer. He has all the living functions of a human being after his resurrection to show that the soul is truly resurrected and has no difficulty doing anything. If a person has problems doing things, they are still in death and not resurrection.

> When they had finished breakfast, Jesus said to Simon Peter, "Simon son of John, do you love me more than these?" He said to him, "Yes, Lord; you know that I love you." Jesus said to him, "Feed my lambs." (John 21:15)

O Lord, how do you ask Simon a question that you know better than he? Can he judge of his love after the weakness he has shown? Alas! He had shown a strange defiance. Yet all the words Jesus says to him predict that something else must happen to him. It is not the same with love and present love. It is an admirable thing, that a human being who has truly experienced his misery and weakness, can no longer promise faithfulness, gratitude, or perseverance, none of this. If Jesus asks Peter, Will you be faithful? He would respond, Alas, Lord, I have nothing in my foundation that supports faithfulness! I will be if you give this to me. But when God asks, *Do you love me?* The heart cannot stand it and in from the most extreme misery, he cannot stop himself from saying that he loves. O God! It is the only testimony that testifies to a soul who is in a state of death and of abjection, to find that when he has hit bottom, it seems to him that he loves God. But alas! He ignores that he loves. It is as if he says, If I do not love you, I do not love anything in this world, because then the soul is stripped of all created love. St Peter responds to Jesus as other hearts like him would respond, *Yes, Lord, you know that I love you.* Jesus says to him, *Feed my lambs.* So you ask only for love and pure love for a pastor to be able to feed your flock. The only disposition needed is pure love, this perfect charity contains all the true dispositions of a pastor. Because loving only his God and not loving himself, he thinks only of satisfying this love and gives his life for the care of the flock entrusted to him.

> A second time he said to him, "Simon son of John, do you love me?" He said to him, "Yes, Lord; you know that I love you." Jesus said to him, "Tend my sheep." 17 He said to him the third time, "Simon son of John, do you love me?" Peter felt hurt because he said to him the third time, "Do you love me?" And he said to him, "Lord, you know everything; you know that I love you." Jesus said to him, "Feed my sheep. (John 21:16–17)

O love! Is not this cruelty to press a poor heart like this? It is to make him die of pain. I am not surprised that *Peter felt hurt*. Who would not be? It seems, O God, that you defy this heart, and the heart sees that you doubt his love. Peter doubts himself and fears, despite the testimony that he gives, that he loves you. He feels this after answering two times, *Yes, Lord, you know that I love you* that his own heart was suspected and that his tongue was criminal. He says, Alas! *Lord, you know everything, you know* the truth of my love, *you know that I love you*. I cannot say anything else, except that I love you. To this triple testimony of love, Jesus Christ gives a triple quality of pastor. This merits explanation.

The first love is an acting love that makes the pastor act and watch closely to keep the flock of Jesus Christ. He is always in action to teach, guide, and govern. The second love is a suffering love, that makes the pastor ready to suffer for the flock of Jesus Christ. The third love is a uniting love that unites the soul to his God in intimacy, that makes him participate in the quality of a pastor, by the charity given to this soul. These are the three loves that Jesus Christ asks of Peter and then were given to him so he is a faithful and vigilant Pastor.

We must pay attention to what Jesus Christ says two times *Feed my lambs* and the third time, *Feed my sheep*. This follows the three loves. The acting and suffering love is for the lambs who signify the common souls who are the general church. But the uniting love is for the sheep who are chosen, espoused, interior souls who produce lambs and who bear souls to Jesus Christ. When he says, *Feed my lambs*, is for a simple pastor. But when he says, *Feed my sheep* it is for a pastor of pastors.

> "Very truly, I tell you, when you were younger, you used to fasten your own belt and to go wherever you wished. But when you

> grow old, you will stretch out your hands, and someone else will fasten a belt around you and take you where you do not wish to go." 19 (He said this to indicate the kind of death by which he would glorify God.) After this he said to him, "Follow me." (John 21:18–19)

The literal sense of this passage according to the Evangelist is describing the death of Peter as he is crucified like his good Master. However, this words also explain the interior state that souls pass though whom God destines for a perfect imitation of his Son.

St. Peter as the rock foundation of the church participates much in the interior state. Because the church is only composed of living members and these members are truly living, they must be filled with the living Holy Spirit, the Spirit of life, inspired by the Father. This Spirit is that of the Word. That being, the souls who are destined in a particular way to *follow Jesus Christ* in all his states and to receive plentifully of his Spirit can really experience these words that our Lord said to Peter: *When you were younger*, when you were a an infant in piety and in the interior, *you used to fasten your own belt and go wherever you wished*, that is to say, you served God according to your inclination and practiced what virtues that you wanted. You did what you proposed. O God! It is easy to walk in this way! We have a good will and we carry his will the way we want to, properly fastened like a *belt*. But when the soul has *grown old* by the long habit of things and by great progress in the interior life, O then *another*, who is a strong and secret virtue of the All-Powerful, *binds* this will which as a proper girdle. Then this soul no longer wants anything from the world, however good it appears; she is in perfect indifference. And even more, when she does not want things from the world, she finds herself without power and in a kind of helplessness in all things. And that's when you are *taken to where you do not wish to go*. But to the measure you are guided to a place you do not want to go without a natural inclination, which is, *you will stretch out your hands*, then the soul is placed in liberty and an admirable extension. People who have experienced this will see how clear this passage is in expressing this.

This passage depicts well the two types of saints who are in the church of God. The first are living saints and the last are the dead and annihilated saints. The first are sanctified in an admirable way by doing all the penances and practices they have done, they are rich in gifts, graces, and favors. They have a light-filled illustrious life. They are where they want to be because God gives them all they desire. God does their will and these grand saints are the lights of the centuries in which they are found. They shine and their brilliance never goes out.

The second type of saints are different. God is pleased to glorify himself in their annihilation. You only see what is wrong, the misery, confusion without success. If God gives success, he then destroys it then by great confusion and large reversals. These people never have what they want. But God takes pleasure in making them do *what they do not wish* with all their fears and apprehensions. These are the saints of God.

> Peter turned and saw the disciple whom Jesus loved following them; he was the one who had reclined next to Jesus at the supper and had said, "Lord, who is it that is going to betray you?" 21 When Peter saw him, he said to Jesus, "Lord, what about him?" 22 Jesus said to him, "If it is my will that he remain until I come, what is that to you? Follow me!" (John 21:20-22)

St. John, who had suffered the mystical death and who was in a state of resurrected life in God, would not suffer the state that St Peter would bear. Yet Peter, not unaware of how much he loved Jesus Christ, wished to know whether the disciple Jesus loved would have any part in this. This is why he asks Jesus, *Lord, what about him?* Jesus said to him, "For him in whom I died and resurrected, I want him to remain that way until I come because the soul that is resurrected has nothing to do but live from this life which is communicated to him always in abundance until Jesus Christ comes to take him from the world."

> So the rumor spread in the community that this disciple would not die. Yet Jesus did not say to him that he would not die, but, "If it is my will that he remain until I come, what is that to you?" 24 This is the disciple who is testifying to these things and has written them, and we know that his testimony is true. (John 21:23-24)

The apostles took these words of Jesus Christ literally and misinterpreted this. They did not penetrate to the mystical meaning. The disciple about whom the words were said understood well what was meant but his humility prevented him from saying this. He contented himself with saying that Jesus Christ was not talking about *corporal death*. Instead, he was speaking of a permanent state that the disciple would be in until he died.

> But there are also many other things that Jesus did; if every one of them were written down, I suppose that the world itself could not contain the books that would be written. (John 21:25)

This verse cannot be understood by the letter, but as to mean that *if every one of them were written down* that Jesus Christ *did*, and to give them the meaning that *world would not contain the books*. This only means that Jesus Christ had a great quantity of words, actions, and miracles. But besides this, it is certain that there is not a word or an action of Jesus Christ was not admirable. A single action of Jesus Christ with all that it expresses and contains is capable of many volumes. All of the world can only express a part of it. It is impossible to discover in the infinity of God himself what Jesus Christ's words and actions are and what they contain. This is why meditation cannot reveal Jesus Christ. It is necessary to be in God by death with the loss of the rest to have the true revelation of Jesus Christ. Also, the soul that has this revealed to her is charmed and sees the infinite within infinity itself. It is necessary to be there, so that Jesus Christ is revealed. But to whom is Jesus Christ revealed? *Those little ones.*

The world itself could not contain the books that would be written. This can be understood from the fact that humans are too weak to understand and conceive of the ways of God and of Jesus Christ's operations in souls.

Bibliography

Anonymous. "Supplement to the Life of Madame Guyon." Translated by Nancy Carol James. In *The Pure Love of Madame Guyon*, 85–104. New York: University Press of America, 2014.

Bedoyere, Michael de la. *The Archbishop and the Lady*. New York: Pantheon, 1956.

Bergsma, John. "John: Signs and Sacraments. An Advanced Study." Recorded lectures. Boutte, LA: Catholic Productions.

Bossuet, Jacques Benigne. *Quakerism a-la-mode, or A History of Quietism: Particularly that of the Lord Archbishop of Cambray and Madam Guyone*. London: Printed for J. Harris and A. Bell, 1698.

Bremond, Henri. *Apologie pour Fenelon*. Paris: Perrin, 1910.

Caussade, Jean Pierre de. *Abandonment to Divine Providence*. New York: Image, 1975.

———. *On Prayer: Spiritual Instructions on the Various States of Prayer according to the Doctrine of Bossuet, Bishop of Meaux*. Translated by Algar Thorold. London: Burns, Oates & Washbourne, 1931.

Conzemius, Viktor. "Quietism" In *Sacramentum Mundi*, Vol. 5, 169–172. New York: Herder & Herder, 1970.

Fénelon, Francois de Salignac de La Mothe. *The Archbishop of Cambray's Dissertation on Pure Love, with an Account of the Life and Writings of the Lady, for Whose Sake the Archbishop Was Banished from Court*. London: G. Thomson, 1750.

———. *The Complete Fénelon*. Brewster, MA: Paraclete, 2008.

———. *The Maxims of the Saints Explained, concerning the Interior Life*. Bordeaux: n.p., 1913.

Gondal, Marie-Louise. *Madame Guyon: un noveau visage*. Paris: Beauchesne 1989.

Gough, James. "Comparative View of the Lives of St. Teresa and M. Guion." In *Life of Lady Guion*, 237–39, Bristol, UK: S. Farley, 1772.

———. "Life of Michael de Molinos and Progress of Quietism." In *The Life of Lady Guion*, 308–24. Bristol, UK: S. Farley, 1772.

Green, Joel B: *Conversion in Luke-Acts: Divine Action, Human Cognition, and the People of God*. Grand Rapids: Baker Academic, 2015,

Guyon, Jeanne de la Mothe. *Autobiography of Madame Guyon*. Vols. 1 and 2. Translated by Thomas Taylor Allen. London: Kegan Paul, Trench, Trubner, 1897.

———. *Divine Love: The Emblems of Madame Jeanne Guyon and Otto van Veen, Volume 1*. Illustrations by Otto van Veen. Translated by Nancy Carol James. Eugene, OR: Pickwick, 2019.

———. *Jeanne Guyon's Apocalyptic Universe: Her Biblical Commentary on Revelation with Reflections on the Interior Life*. Translated by Nancy Carol James. Eugene, OR: Pickwick, 2019.

———. *Jeanne Guyon's Christian Worldview: Her Biblical Commentaries on Galatians, Ephesians, and Colossians with Explanations and Reflections on the Interior Life*. Translated by Nancy Carol James. Eugene, OR: Pickwick, 2018.

———. *Jeanne Guyon's Interior Faith: Her Biblical Commentary on the Gospel of Luke with Reflections on the Interior Life*. Translated by Nancy Carol James. Eugene, OR: Pickwick, 2019.

———. *Les justifications de Mme J.-M.B. de La Mothe-Guyon, ecrites par elle-meme, avec un examen de la IXe et Xe conferences de Cassien touchant l'etat fixe d'oraison continuelle, par M. De Fénelon*. 3 parites, Cologne: n.p., 1720.

———. *Les livres du Nouveau Testament avec des explications et reflexions qui regardent la vie interieure*. Pierre Poiret, 1713.

———. *Le Nouveau Testament de Notre-Seigneur Jésus-Christ avec des explications et réflexions qui regardent la vie intérieure*. 12 vols. Cologne: Poiret. 1714–15.

———. *Les livres de l'Ancien Testament de Notre-Seigneur Jésus-Christ avec des explications et réflexions qui regardent la vie intérieure*. 12 vols. Cologne: n.p., 1714–15.

———. *The Soul, Lover of God*. Translated by Nancy Carol James. New York: University Press of America, 2014.

———. *The Way of the Child Jesus: Our Model of Perfection*. Translated by Nancy Carol James. Arlington, VA: European Emblems, 2015.

Holcombe, William H. *Aphorisms of the New Life: With Illustrations and Confirmations from the New Testament, Fénelon, Madame Guyon, and Swedenborg*. Philadelphia: E. Claxton, 1883.

James, Nancy C. *The Apophatic Mysticism of Madame Guyon*. Ann Arbor, MI: UMI Dissertation Services, 1998.

———. *The Complete Madame Guyon*. Brewster, MA: Paraclete, 2011.

———. *I, Jeanne Guyon*. Jacksonville, FL: Christian Books, 2014.

———. *The Pure Love of Madame Guyon*. New York: University Press of America, 2007.

———. *Standing in the Whirlwind*. Cleveland: Pilgrim, 2005.

James, Nancy C., and Sharon D. Voros. *Bastille Witness: The Prison Autobiography of Madame Guyon*. New York: University Press of America, 2012.

James, William. *Varieties of Religious Experience*. New York: Collier, 1961.

Johnson, Luke Timothy. *The Gospel of Luke*. Collegeville, MN: Liturgical, 1991.

Kuffel, Thomas P. *St. Thomas' Method of Biblical Exegesis*. Roman Theological Forum, No. 38, 1991.

La Combe, Francois. *A Short Letter of Instruction, Shewing the Surest Way to Christian Perfection*. Translated by J. Gough. In *Life of Lady Guion*, 295–307. Bristol, UK: S. Farley, 1772.

Mudge, James. *Fénelon the Mystic*. Cincinnati: Jennings and Graham, 1906.

Poiret, Pierre. "The Theology of Emblems: Preface to the Emblems of Father Hugo and Madame Guyon." Translated by Nancy Carol James. In *The Soul, Lover of God*, xxxiii–xl. New York: University Press of America, 2014.

Ramsay, Chevalier. "Life of Francis de Salignac de la Mothe Fénelon, Archbishop and Duke of Cambray." In *Life of Lady Guion*, Vol. 2, 325–72. Bristol: S. Farley, 1772.

Saint-Simon, Duc de. *Historical Memoirs of the Duc de Saint-Simon.* Vols 1 and 2. Edited and translated by Lucy Norton. New York: McGraw-Hill, 1967.

Underhill, Evelyn. *Mysticism: A Study in the Nature and Development of Man's Spiritual Consciousness.* 12th ed., Cleveland: World, 1965.

Upham, Thomas C. *Life and Religions Opinions and Experience of Madame de la Mothe Guyon.* 2 vols. New York: Harper & Brothers, 1847.

Wesley, John. *An Extract of the Life of Madame Guion.* London: R. Hawes, 1776.

www.ingramcontent.com/pod-product-compliance
Lightning Source LLC
Chambersburg PA
CBHW071239230426
43668CB00011B/1506